D1229958

# THE POLITICS OF ENGLISH DISSENT

# *The Politics of English Dissent*

The Religious Aspects of Liberal and Humanitarian Reform Movements from 1815 to 1848

*by Raymond G. Cowherd*

Associate Professor of History
Lehigh University

*New York University Press* · *Washington Square* · *New York · 1956*

Library of Congress Catalogue Card Number: 56-9977



Manufactured in the United States of America

TO MY WIFE

whose criticism and encouragement have
greatly aided the writing of this book

# *Preface*

That the three decades and more from the end of the Napoleonic Wars to the European revolutions of 1848 comprised a remarkable age of English social and political reform has generally been conceded. The expansion of religious liberty, the beginning of elementary education, the abolition of colonial slavery, the broadening of the Parliamentary franchise, the shortening of the factory working day, and the removal of restrictions on trade were movements that carried England along the road from aristocracy to democracy and improved the social conditions of both the middle and the working classes.

The reform movements were both liberal and humanitarian. The liberal reforms, such as the repeal of the Corporation and Test Acts, the Catholic Emancipation Act, the Reform Bill of 1832, and the repeal of the Corn Laws, consummated the religious and political traditions of the seventeenth century and, in the main, enabled the lower and middle classes to participate more freely in local and national government. The humanitarian reforms, such as the emancipation of slaves, factory legislation, and elementary education, ameliorated the harsh conditions of the working classes and provided underprivileged groups with larger opportunities to improve their social status and living standards.

Humanitarianism, the leaven of the age of reform, was a revulsion from suffering and a compassion for the miserable. As people were increasingly able to heal their diseases through medical science and supply their wants through the technologies of machine production, they confidently hoped to unloose all those burdens that hindered them in running a good race. Having glimpses of the promised land, they sanguinely hastened to enter in.

Humanitarianism was inseparable from the Evangelical revival. The resurgence of Protestantism during the eighteenth century, chiefly as a result of John Wesley's preaching, convinced many that all those obstacles to individual salvation, whether ignorance, slavery, or poverty, should be removed. Motivated by strong convictions and animated by a lively hope, the Evangelicals within the Church of England and among the several Dissenting groups, especially among the Quakers and the Methodists, led the humanitarian crusades for social uplift.

If humanitarianism may be understood in terms of the beliefs and aspirations of the Wesleyan revival, liberalism must be pushed beyond Wesley to the revolutionary Protestantism of the seventeenth century. The religious faith of the Independents in Cromwell's army is the source of the ideas and the aspiration that produced the liberal reforms of the early nineteenth century. The Protestant doctrine of the competence of the individual to comprehend moral and religious truth, unaided by higher authority, whether political or ecclesiastical, was the starting point of both political and religious liberalism. Since the individual possessed such competence, the state, the Dissenters believed, should not interfere with his search for truth or with the expression thereof. During the late eighteenth century the Rational Dissenters, such as the Unitarians, expanded the doctrine of religious liberty to include civil liberty. This meant especially the reform of Parliament.

Liberal and humanitarian reforms, however, cannot be understood alone in terms of religious traditions. The great reforms eventually came because the middle classes, having acquired great wealth and influence from the new manufacturing industries, demanded a larger part in the social and political life of the nation. Manufacturers, lawyers, and bankers, in the rising cities of Leeds, Manchester, and Birmingham, generally supported both liberal and humanitarian reforms. Under changing economic conditions, the country gentlemen and the aristocrats, whose wealth and social privileges derived largely from the ownership of land, found it increasingly difficult to maintain their political monopoly and their exclusive social privileges.

The impact of economic and social change ultimately disrupted the Whigs and the Tories, the traditional political parties. In the midst of great confusion during the 1830's the political leaders sought new alignments. Gradual and complex in formation, these new alignments were eventually known as the Liberal and Conservative parties. By giving careful attention to the several religious groups who enunciated the aspirations and resentments of the middle classes, I have attempted to identify the moral and social ingredients of the Whig and the Liberal parties. Without desiring to extol one religious sect above another, I have primarily emphasized the Dissenting groups as the leaders of liberal reform and the Evangelicals of the Church of England as the principal exponents of humanitarian reform.

My interest in the social movements of the early nineteenth century I owe to Professors Edward P. Cheyney and William E. Lingelbach, of the University of Pennsylvania, who shared with me their knowledge on this subject. I am also grateful to Professors Conyers Read and Leonidas Dodson, of that university, who have read portions of the manuscript and have made valuable suggestions. Since becoming a member of the faculty of Lehigh University I have had the constant encouragement of Professors George D. Harmon and Lawrence H. Gipson. I wish to thank the members of the staffs of the University of Pennsylvania Library and the Lehigh University Library for their untiring assistance. Without the financial grants from the Lehigh Institute of Research and from the American Council of Learned Societies I could not have completed this research.

CONTENTS

# THE POLITICS OF ENGLISH DISSENT

# *1. Social and Political Alignments*

At the beginning of the nineteenth century the Dissenters were primarily middle class. Aristocrats having long since passed from the rough benches of the chapels to the more comfortable pews of the Church of England, the Dissenters identified themselves with the interest of commerce and industry and looked to the merchants and the manufacturers for money to build their flourishing chapels and to promote their thriving missionary work. They consciously advocated free trade to benefit commerce and bestowed their blessings upon expanding industrial enterprises. The morals proclaimed from their pulpits—thrift, honesty, and diligence—belonged to the market place. Far from being ashamed of such moralizing, the Dissenting preachers extolled the increasing respectability of the middle classes. Their ablest contemporary historian proudly acknowledged that the Dissenters "occupy precisely that middle station in society which is most affected by the stagnation of trade and the increase of taxation." [1]

Despite the growing wealth and respectability of the middle classes, the several Dissenting denominations had social rank below that of the leading families of the Established Church. The Quakers and Unitarians had the highest social standing among the dissenting groups. Somewhat below them in rank stood the Congregationalists, Baptists, and Methodists. More than other Dissenting denominations, the Methodists recruited their ministers and members from the lower classes. But notwithstanding their aggressive evangelism many working-class people remained unchurched.[2]

By the beginning of the nineteenth century the major Dissenting denominations had adopted John Wesley's evangelistic message and techniques.[3] Owing to this common faith and practice they

Notes to this chapter begin on page 169.

united to form Bible, tract, and missionary societies with the primary purpose of saving souls. Though they preached salvation in the theological terms of eternal damnation and everlasting life, the preachers saved the people from the sins of sloth, frivolity, improvidence, and drunkenness and converted them to industry, seriousness, serious thrift, and sobriety.[4]

When the evangelists went into the northern counties they found the fields white, ready for harvest. The increase in population and its concentration in the new factory towns gave them the opportunity to make thousands of converts. Consequently, when a survey of these populous areas was made in 1811, the Dissenters' chapels outnumbered the Anglican churches by 3,454 to 2,535.[5] In precisely those industrial areas where Dissent flourished most the Established Church, save for the Evangelicals, suffered its worst weakness.[6]

Dissent included all the religious groups refusing to conform to the Established Church. Roman Catholics and Jews as well as Protestants suffered many social and legal disabilities because of their religion; consequently, on several occasions these bodies, notwithstanding their inherent antagonism, united in a common course of action to extend the area of religious liberty. The Wesleyan Methodists, though Dissenters by circumstance rather than by choice, united with Dissenters to obtain the freedom to propagate their faith.[7] The traditional Dissenting bodies were the Presbyterians, Congregationalists, and Baptists. Associated with these older denominations and sharing their views on civil and religious liberty were the Quakers or Society of Friends. These four bodies, which possessed a common legal status after the Toleration Act of 1689, existed as second-class citizens, a distinct religious and social minority.[8]

The Unitarians, however, did not gain toleration until 1813.[9] Abetted by eighteenth-century rationalism, Unitarians flourished among the Dissenters and took possession of some of the most important Congregational, Baptist, and Presbyterian pulpits. Better educated than their Evangelical brethren, the Unitarian preachers were called to serve the oldest and wealthiest congregations in London, Manchester, and Birmingham. During the last half of the eighteenth century the Unitarian preachers Richard Price and Joseph Priestley rationally defined the doctrines of civil and religious liberty; and during the early nineteenth century their ablest preachers, Lant Carpenter, Thomas Belsham, Robert Aspland, and William J. Fox, perpetuated the rationalist tradition and successfully guided the less philosophical Dissenters in extending the area of religious liberty. Unencumbered with dogma and lacking Evangelical enthusiasm, the Unitarians devoted themselves to the pursuit of those temporal rewards which the Evangelicals presumed to disdain. Although the Evangelicals grew increasingly restless under the political leadership of the Unitarians, they did not overthrow them until after the repeal of the Corporation and Test Acts.

While the Unitarians formed the most liberal branch of Dissent, the Wesleyan Methodists, standing at the opposite pole, formed the most conservative branch. The Methodists seldom manifested hostility toward the Establishment and rarely espoused religious freedom as an abstract right.[10] Though they were generally found on the Tory side of most political questions, they emphatically denied that they had political interests.[11] Their preachers frequently admonished their congregations against the dangers of political reform; and their most eminent ministers, Jabez Bunting and Robert Newton, eschewed democracy as much as sin. The Wesleyans, nevertheless, considered it their religious duty to support righteous causes. While they were piously renouncing political action, they were agitating for temperance, the abolition of the slave trade, the emancipation of the slaves, and laws to protect the Lord's day. These righteous causes brought the Wesleyan Methodists and other Evangelicals, contrary to their professed desires, into the midst of politics.

A religious movement as virile and comprehensive as the Wesleyan revival could not long be confined by a narrow clerical authority. While Wesley lived, his pre-eminence united the Methodists; but soon after his death several groups, rejecting the authority of the Conference, seceded from it and formed separate denominations.[12] The Methodist New Connection, the Unitarian Methodists, the Protestant Methodists, and the Bible Christians, who left the Conference, took their position with the militant Dissenters.[13] Along with the repudiation of clerical authority they rejected the Toryism of the Conference. These new Methodist groups, Whig and sometimes Radical in politics, loyally supported John Wilks and the Protestant Society for the Protection of Religious Liberty and readily entered into the struggle to enlarge the boundaries of civil and religious liberty.

Not all the Evangelicals who had been influenced by the Wesleyan revival abandoned the Church of England. Those remaining formed the Low Church party; and although only a small minority, even a despised sect, they became the leaders of humanitarian reform.[14] They also endeavored to mediate between Churchmen and Dissenters and to conciliate the hostilities of the lower classes toward the aristocracy.[15] The Clapham Sect of London provided leadership for the Evangelicals of both Church and Dissent. William Wilberforce, the leader of the Clapham Parliamentary "Saints," was honored by all varieties of religious enthusiasts.[16]

The Wesleyan revival fulfilled Wesley's dream of a common Christian fellowship of Churchmen and Dissenters. By the year 1800 the Dissenting denominations, except the Unitarians, had become predominantly Evangelical. Their ministers preached with the same passion on the same themes selected from the same texts. They readily exchanged pulpits. Their congregations sang similar hymns, often Wesleyan hymns, of repentance and forgiveness. Possessing a common theology, they preached almost exclusively the doctrines pertaining to personal salvation.

As a consequence of the Wesleyan revival, the Dissenters, in cooperation with Evangelical Churchmen, formed missionary, tract, and Bible societies to spread their hopeful message of salvation at home and abroad. A sermon preached by William Carey in 1793 led directly to the formation of the Baptist Missionary Society.[17] Two years later the Dissenters jointly established the London Missionary Society. At first Evangelical Churchmen supported it but soon they organized and promoted their own Church Missionary Society. The Religious Tract Society, established in 1799, grew out of the London Missionary Society. A Congregationalist, George Burder, and a Baptist, Joseph Hughes, were its founders.[18] The most famous of the societies, the British and Foreign Bible Society, which originated in 1804, was managed jointly by Dissenters and Churchmen. Animated by a truly ecumenical spirit, the Evangelical denominations labored side by side until the creedal tests of the 1830's disrupted their fellowship.

Though primarily religious and propagandistic, the Evangelical societies had considerable political influence. They not only provided a common meeting place for the Evangelical leaders of both Church and Dissent, but they also brought together those Whigs and Tories who put philanthropy above partisan politics. Similar in organization, the societies usually enlisted some pious aristocrat or benevolent Member of Parliament to preside at their annual meetings. They usually appointed some wealthy merchant or banker to serve as their treasurer. The Bible Society, for example, elected Lord Teignmouth as president, William Wilberforce as vice-president, Henry Thornton as treasurer, and Joseph Hughes as permanent secretary. If financially the greatest and religiously the most influential, the Bible Society was not unique otherwise. A score or more of such societies, with an income of several hundred thousand pounds, met annually in May and shared the same meeting places.[19]

In the beginning the Evangelical societies were not dominated by clergymen to serve denominational ends or clerical ambitions; on the contrary, they were controlled by laymen, judicious men of affairs, and managed as agencies of their philanthropy. By means of these organizations William Wilberforce exercised a popular leadership that equaled, and perhaps surpassed, that of any other contemporary statesman.

The party of Evangelical "Saints" in London, the Clapham Sect, published the *Christian Observer*. Edited by Zachary Macaulay from 1802 to 1816, it was the chief advocate of humanitarian reform.[20] Though managed by the members of the Church of England, the *Christian Observer* advocated those causes dear to all Evangelicals. In addition to it, the Dissenters published the *Evangelical Magazine* and the *Eclectic Review*, which differed from the *Christian Observer* only on the question of religious establishments. Even the strictly denominational magazines, such as the *Methodist Magazine*, *Baptist Magazine*, and *Congregational Magazine*, agreed at first to minimize their differences and to emphasize their common beliefs. Thus able to speak with a united voice, the "Saints" in Parliament decisively influenced legislation on such questions as colonial slavery, factory conditions, the reform of prisons, and amelioration of penal laws.[21]

The Dissenters exercised political influence through several organizations which advanced the cause of religious liberty. The British and Foreign School Society promoted elementary education. Guided by the doctrine of religious liberty, this Society sought to educate children so broadly as to include all Protestant denominations. In pursuit of this objective the Society brought the Dissenters into association with leading Whigs. Its chairman for many years was the Duke of Bedford; and later his son, Lord John Russell, filled the same office. Its treasurer, William Allen, was looked upon by the Whigs as the national spokesman for Dissent on matters of education.

The Dissenters also possessed two distinctly political organizations, powerful pressure groups, with the functions of protecting and expanding religious liberty. The older and more important of these was the Dissenting Deputies. The congregations of the Three Denominations (Baptist, Presbyterian, and Congregational), within London and the adjacent area of ten miles, appointed annually two Deputies to defend their civil rights.[22] At an annual meeting the Dissenting Deputies elected a permanent committee of twenty-one members, which included some of the ablest lawyers of London, to serve as a Parliamentary lobby and to provide legal counsel for those who had been deprived of their civil rights.[23] Supplementing and guiding the work of the Dissenting Deputies, the Ministers of the Three Denominations met in annual and extraordinary meetings to make pronouncements on public policies and to arouse public opinion on questions of civil and religious liberty. The Dissenting Deputies as well as the Dissenting Ministers made the repeal of the Test and Corporation Acts their primary object for more than a century.

As chairman of the Dissenting Deputies from 1805 to 1832, William Smith was the national leader of Dissent on questions of civil and religious liberty. He entered Parliament in 1784 and retired in 1830 after the longest tenure in office of any living member. A Unitarian, he took a rational view of religion and placed common political action above theological differences. He was both liberal and humanitarian. He cooperated with Charles J. Fox and Lord John Russell to extend the areas of civil and religious liberty, and he was so closely associated with William Wilberforce that he was counted one of the "Saints." [24] During his long and distinguished career William Smith advocated factory legislation, the abolition of slavery, the repeal of the Test Acts, Catholic Emancipation, and the reform of Parliament.

When William Smith retired from Parliament in 1830, John Wilks succeeded him as the Parliamentary spokesman for Dissent. A Radical member of Parliament for Boston, Wilks owed his prominence to the Protestant Society, which he had founded in 1811 and which he served as secretary for twenty-five years. The Protestant Society held its annual meeting in London during May and selected Whig members of Parliament as its presiding officers. Soon after its inception, it acquired such political importance that it could command the leading Whigs to take its pledge of religious freedom.[25]

The Dissenters, because of their doctrines and organizations, had an important voice in effecting liberal and humanitarian reform. Like the Evangelicals of the Church, they desired to save people from ignorance, sloth, and drunkenness. They desired to remove all obstacles to salvation. Their tradition of religious liberty, which they did not forsake when they came under the influence of the Wesleyan revival, made them Whig in politics and put them at odds with the Wesleyan Methodists and the Church of England on questions of religious establishments. Moreover, because they were closely identified with the middle classes, the Dissenting preachers advocated freedom—freedom in trade, freedom in government, freedom in religion. These slogans were their political weapons against the monopolies and exclusive privileges of the aristocracy in church and state.

# 2. *The Growth of Religious Liberty*

By the end of the eighteenth century the Dissenters had acquired the solidarity of a religious minority. Although they were not persecuted so severely as they sometimes thought, nevertheless the badges of their inferiority were everywhere obvious. They suffered disabilities at the most delicate occasions of life, at birth, marriage, and death. They could not register the birth of their children unless they baptized them according to the rites of the Established Church. The conscientious would not submit; and the Baptists, who rejected infant baptism, could not. Moreover, to be married the Dissenters had to bow to the authority of the Church and to submit to rites which they rejected on principle. Even in death they did not escape the consciousness of their social inferiority. To find a resting place for their dead in the village graveyard they must again comply with the rites of the Church.[1]

Only those Dissenters who conformed to the Church and subscribed to the Thirty-nine Articles could enter Oxford University; and although they might matriculate at Cambridge without religious tests, they had to subscribe before taking degrees. The lack of a university degree, furthermore, handicapped them in professional life. The College of Physicians and Surgeons admitted only university graduates, and the Inns of Court admitted persons with degrees to the bar after three years of study, whereas those lacking degrees had to spend five years. Since the Dissenters were excluded from the English universities, they sent their children to Scotland where there were no religious tests.

The Dissenters objected even more strongly to those civil disabilities which excluded them from public life. The Toleration Act of 1689, which had granted them freedom of worship, did not repeal the Corporation and Test Acts. The Corporation Act of 1662 com-

Notes to this chapter begin on page 171.

pelled them to conform to the Anglican Church to hold municipal office.[2] The Test Act of 1673, although directed primarily against Roman Catholics, effectively disqualified the Dissenters from holding civil and military offices under the Crown.[3] The Indemnity Acts, which were passed annually after 1727 to remove the penalties of occasional conformity, benefited only nominal Dissenters who did not conscientiously reject the Church sacraments. The Corporation and Test Acts, therefore, for a century remained the badge of social inferiority and a barrier to political office.

Humiliated by social inequality and civil disabilities, the Dissenters increasingly demanded full religious freedom. No longer content with the right to exist, they sprang to the offensive, boldly demanding civil equality and attacking all religious establishments as contrary to Christian truth. By the end of the eighteenth century their greatest preachers, Joseph Priestley and Richard Price, had so clearly defined and widely propagated the doctrine of religious liberty, that the Dissenters' slogan of "religious freedom" began to rival the Anglican cry of "Church in danger."

During the first quarter of the nineteenth century the Unitarian, Baptist, and Congregationalist polemicists perpetuated the doctrine of religious freedom. Thomas Belsham was the leading Unitarian preacher of his time.[4] The son of a Congregational minister, he was educated at Daventry Academy to follow in his father's career. But in 1789 he abandoned orthodoxy for Unitarianism. He became a teacher at the Unitarian Academy at Hackney and succeeded Priestley there as the minister of the Gravel Hill Chapel. A few years later he moved to the more famous Essex Street Chapel in London, where he continued to win popularity as a preacher of civil and religious liberty.[5]

On the question of civil and religious liberty there was little difference of opinion between the Unitarians and the orthodox Dissenters. Robert Hall, the greatest Baptist preacher of the time, recognized that religious liberty was the unifying and guiding principle of all Dissenters:

> The religious opinions of Dissenters are so various that there is perhaps no point in which they are agreed except in asserting the rights of conscience against all human authority. From the time of Elizabeth, under whom they began to make their appearance, their views of religious liberty have gradually extended. . . . Their total separation from the church did not take place for more than a century after; till despairing of seeing it erected on a comprehensive plan, and being moreover

> persecuted for their difference of opinion, they were compelled at last reluctantly to withdraw. Having thus been directed by a train of events into the right path, they pushed their principles to their legitimate consequences, and began to discern the impropriety of all religious establishments whatever; a sentiment in which they are now nearly united.[6]

During the first quarter of the nineteenth century the doctrine of religious liberty was clear and precise. It meant that every individual ought to have the right to read the Bible and to act upon its teaching unhindered by either religious or civil authority. It meant that the freedom of conscience was "a natural and an inalienable right," and that religion was a no-man's land where the state must not intrude to help or to hinder.[7]

United and guided by the principle of religious liberty, the Dissenters first demanded the repeal of the Corporation and Test Acts. In 1787 Henry Beaufoy, their spokesman in the House of Commons, introduced a motion to repeal the laws that barred them from political office. Although Charles James Fox spoke in favor of the motion, it failed by a vote of 178 to 100.[8] The House of Commons later rejected a similar motion less decisively by 124 votes to 104.[9] In 1789 the Dissenters felt that their day of deliverance had come when Fox himself introduced a motion for the repeal of the Test Acts.[10] But Edmund Burke and William Pitt, who had already turned their backs on liberty, refused any concession to the Dissenters, and Fox's motion was lost.[11]

As the tide of liberalism ebbed, the reaction against the French Revolution became a flood. During the ensuing period of reaction the Dissenters, after enduring harsh repression, sadly relinquished their crusade for religious liberty. Their United Committee "found the times too unfortuitous to continue." [12]

Tory Churchmen organized and guided this reaction against the Dissenters. They formed associations to protect "liberty and property against the attempts of republicans and levellers." [13] At Birmingham the reaction against the Dissenters caused the riots of 1791, from which the Unitarians suffered most. Joseph Priestley, a Unitarian minister and the foremost apostle of Dissent, had previously carried on a long theological controversy with the Anglicans, and his praise of the French Revolution aggravated the already inveterate religious hostilities. When Priestley's friends met at a public dinner in his honor to extol the ideas of 1789, a hostile crowd gathered outside and protested by smashing the windows of the hotel. Fomenting ferocity, the mob moved on to sack the Unitarians' Old Meeting House, to burn their New Meeting House, and to destroy Priestley's house and scientific laboratory.[14] Other prominent Dissenters also lost their property; altogether twenty houses and chapels were destroyed or damaged. The rioters continued their havoc until the Government sent in troops to quell them; and the troops had to remain for a decade to prevent further violence.

During the period of reaction religious and political strife also disturbed the peace of Manchester.[15] While the Dissenters of Manchester were agitating for the repeal of the Test Acts, the High Church party was petitioning in favor of those laws.[16] When the Dissenters formed the Constitution Society to agitate for Parliamentary reform, the High Church party countered by organizing the Church and King Club. At a celebration of the King's birthday in 1792, patriotic fervor of the Church and King Club so excited the populace that mobs rioted and attacked the Dissenters' chapels. As long as the war with France lasted, the Church and King Club dominated Manchester politics and compelled the innkeepers to ban all meetings of the reform societies. "To be a Dissenter and a reformer was bad enough," a contemporary observer wrote of this period; "to be a friend of peace was worse."[17]

In London the Dissenters also suffered from the Tory reaction to the French Revolution.[18] After suspending the Habeas Corpus Act in 1794, the Tory Government suppressed the agitation for religious liberty. As a result, the Dissenters had to close the doors of Hackney Academy; and Priestley, who had come there to teach after losing his property in Birmingham, fled to Philadelphia for refuge.[19] During the war years the Dissenters struggled desperately to defend their legal rights. From 1800 to 1811 the Dissenting Deputies handled no fewer than sixty-five cases involving the disturbance of worship, refusal to grant licenses to preach, refusal to bury the dead, and the illegal assessment of church rates.[20]

Although the Dissenters failed to extend the area of civil and religious liberty, they experienced a religious revival that expanded their membership at a rapid rate. They increased greatly in the rising factory towns and in the northern industrial counties. Adopting the theology and the propaganda techniques of Wesley, the Dissenting preachers moved into fields already ripe for harvest. Preaching emotional messages of salvation, they gained converts wherever they set up their pulpits. Nearly every convert in this age of jubilant evangelism became a Bible teacher to edify and indoctrinate others in the Christian faith. In this manner the Dissenting denominations were able to keep pace with the unparalleled expansion of an industrial age.

The High Church Tories, however, did not look with equanimity upon this rapid growth of the Dissenters. Especially alarmed by their advance, Lord Sidmouth introduced a motion in the House of Lords in 1809 demanding that an accounting be made of the number of licenses granted to Dissenting preachers and to new meetinghouses.[21] When seconding Sidmouth's motion, the Archbishop of Canterbury declared that the "growth of sectaries and Dissenters . . . was so great that none could doubt it."[22] Subsequently the survey of the number of preachers and places licensed since 1760, which had been made at Sidmouth's demand, revealed what everyone knew already: that the numbers of Dissenting preachers and chapels were increasing rapidly.[23] Lord Sidmouth, consequently, introduced a bill in the House of Lords to restrict the licensing of itinerant and untrained preachers.

The opponents of Lord Sidmouth's illiberal measure quickly mustered their opposition to resist the Tory interference with the preaching of religious doctrines.[24] Before long the rumbling of the Dissenters' wrath could be heard like distant thunder, and then they descended on London in such numbers that for several days there were no vacant seats in the stagecoaches. On the day fixed for the debate of Sidmouth's bill in the House of Lords, "the Peers could hardly get to the doors," Lord Holland recalled, "because the avenues were so crowded with men of grave deportment and puritanical aspect."[25]

This overwhelming opposition compelled the Tories to abandon Lord Sidmouth's bill. Retreating as gracefully as possible, Lord Liverpool declared that while he favored the bill he thought it unwise to stir up religious trouble.[26] The Whigs, who rarely had an occasion to celebrate, rejoiced in the defeat of Sidmouth, Eldon, and the High Church Tories. Lord Stanhope, the faithful exponent of religious liberty, said he "never felt more pleasure in his whole Parliamentary career. . . ." He rejoiced because of the "immense heap of petitions that was strewed upon the floor. . . . There had been a kind of silly talk going about that there was no public, but he saw today that there was a public, and a public opinion, and a public spirit."[27]

Disregarding popular opinion, Sidmouth and Eldon, with the backing of the High Church, got a favorable decision from the

Court of the King's Bench which granted local magistrates a wide discretion in licensing preachers. The decision aroused as much popular opposition as Lord Sidmouth's bill. In response to the Dissenters' renewed agitation, Lord Holland pressed the Tory Government for legislation to protect them.[28] But the Tories, divided by the High Church and Evangelical factions, preferred to postpone action on so controversial a measure.[29]

While waiting for the Tory Government to act, Lord Stanhope introduced a bill based upon the principle "of the most complete religious freedom."[30] The Whig bill, too extreme for most of the Lords, compelled the Tories to enact their own measure based upon religious toleration. The Toleration Act of 1812 legalized itinerant preaching and allowed the Evangelicals of different sects to pursue evangelistic work. The new law also raised from five to twenty the number of persons who might gather for worship in unregistered meetinghouses.[31] Although the law did little more than legalize what the Dissenters had long practiced, they considered it a major triumph. In the House of Commons William Smith praised it as "the most liberal which had hitherto been passed."[32]

Once aroused to defeat Lord Sidmouth's bill, the Dissenters moved forward to extend the area of toleration. In 1813 William Smith carried through Parliament a bill granting toleration to the Unitarians.[33] In the same year they united with the Anglican Evangelicals to amend the East India Company's charter admitting missionaries to India. For twenty years William Wilberforce, Charles Grant, Henry Thornton, Zachary Macaulay, and other members of the Clapham Sect had struggled to send missionaries to India.[34] During these two decades Protestant missions expanded at such a rapid rate that all the denominations, even the sedate Unitarians and the quiet Quakers, had caught the fever of "saving the world." The Baptists first organized a society in 1793 to send William Carey to India.[35] The Evangelicals of several denominations formed the London Missionary Society, and the Evangelicals within the Church established the Church Missionary Society.[36] All of these groups united in 1813 to compel the government to modify the charter of the East India Company.

The Dissenting Deputies of London also waged a campaign for freedom to send missionaries to India. They first published Robert Hall's *Address to the Public on the Renewal of the East India Charter*. They then prepared and circulated petitions. Their agitation grew so hot that Wilberforce feared lest Churchmen might oppose him because the Dissenters were so much for him. To slow down their agitation he wrote as follows to Joseph Butterworth:

> Now if I mistake not, the organization of the Dissenters, and still more of the Methodist body, is so complete that any impulse may be speedily conveyed throughout the whole frame. It appears, therefore, expedient for the Dissenters and Methodists not to show themselves till the members of the Church have actually committed themselves (according to our parliamentary phrase) or till it be seen that they cannot be prevailed on to come forward.[37]

When Parliament met in 1813, the Tory Government, despite the agitation, refused to modify the charter to admit missionaries. Wilberforce, therefore, delayed action on the charter until he had aroused public opinion. Dissenting and Evangelical pulpits were his sounding boards. As a result of his exhortation petitions were sent to Parliament in "a greater number than ever known. . . ."[38] The popular demonstration compelled the Government to modify the charter and to open the doors of India to Christian missionaries.

With the revival of a liberal spirit toward Dissenters, the Irish Catholics renewed their demands for relief from the penal laws. Their flood of petitions in 1813 encouraged Parliament to consider the explosive question of Catholic relief. The Protestant Dissenters supported the Catholic agitation for religious liberty. The Dissenting Ministers of the Three Denominations, petitioning for Catholic relief, declared that "the right of worshiping God according to dictates of their own consciences to be derived from the Author of their being . . . and therefore not to be subject to the control of human authority. . . ."[39] When presenting their petition in the House of Commons, William Smith pledged himself "never to stand up in that House to exclusively obtain the removal of laws operating against the Dissenters, without coupling with it a motion for the restoration of their rights to the Roman Catholics who were equally entitled to relief."[40] Though supported by the Dissenters and the Clapham Sect, the Catholic relief bill was rejected in the House of Commons by a vote of 251 to 247.[41]

The winds of religious liberty, having risen in the night, were quickly spent. With the end of the Napoleonic Wars there came a new wave of reaction against liberal reformers. When economic depression came with the postwar deflation and filled the streets with people demanding jobs and bread, the Tory Government answered them with legislation depriving them of their civil liberties.

During these years of reaction the Dissenters struggled to protect their civil rights. John Wilks, as secretary of the Protestant Society, handled scores of cases involving the violation of Dissenters' rights.[42] In 1816 he fought against the assessment of chapels for the poor rate. In 1819 he resisted successfully the Poor Rates Misapplication Bill which would have taken the children away from parents receiving poor relief in order to give them moral and religious training in public institutions.[43] In the following year the Dissenters waged a national campaign to defeat Lord Brougham's bill which would have given the Church control of elementary education.[44]

After the Peterloo Massacre of 1819, the reaction subsided, and the Dissenters resumed their campaigns for religious liberty. The Dissenting Deputies again took up the task for which they had been organized in 1735 and which they had laid aside, as a garment out of date, at the beginning of the French Revolution. Led by William Smith, the Dissenting Deputies presented a petition bearing 100,000 signatures for the repeal of the Corporation and Test Acts.[45] The petition of 1820 added nothing to the arguments of thirty years before. Restating the doctrine of religious liberty, the Deputies declared that conscience should not be subject to law or penalized for the sincere expression of faith. They advocated private judgment as a natural and an inalienable right. The Dissenting Deputies, moreover, insisted that the Indemnity Act, granting amnesty to those refusing to take the sacramental test, benefited nominal Dissenters but barred the conscientious from political office.

During the 1820's the Dissenting polemicists published a vast quantity of literature against the Test Acts. The Baptists, Congregationalists, and Unitarians issued monthly magazines to promote religious liberty as well as their separate denominational interests. The Evangelical Dissenters supported the *Eclectic Review* which was devoted to civil and religious liberty. Founded in 1805, it gained importance when Josiah Conder became its editor and enlisted such able writers as Robert Hall, John Foster, James Mill, and Thomas Chalmers. For twenty years and more the *Eclectic Review* was a steady advocate of religious liberty.

The first fruit of the Dissenters' renewed campaign for religious liberty was relief from paying turnpike tolls on Sunday.[46] The greatest evidence of a more liberal spirit came in 1825 when the House of Commons passed a Catholic relief bill, only to have it rejected by the House of Lords.

In spite of the Lords' rejection of the Catholic claims, the Protestant Society laid plans at its annual meeting in 1826 for a campaign against the Test Acts. At this meeting Lord Lansdowne, who presided, promised to sponsor a relief bill in the next session of Parliament.[47]

In the following year the Dissenters came to London for the opening of Parliament, confidently expecting to repeal the Test Acts. Delegates representing the Board of Congregational Ministers, the Baptist Ministers, and the Unitarian Association formed a United Committee. The Dissenting Deputies, who led the agitation against the Test Acts, invited other religious groups to join the United Committee. The Society of Friends, however, refused the invitation to join the Committee, not because they lacked a tradition of religious freedom, but because they wished to keep alive their separate testimony. The Wesleyan Methodist Conference, still clinging to their Tory traditions, rejected the invitation. Other Methodist groups, however, who had left the Conference, were represented in the United Committee by John Wilks and the Protestant Society.[48] Although the Established Church of Scotland did not support the United Committee, the Associated Presbytery of Seceders readily joined the movement for the repeal of the Test Acts.[49]

The United Committee, under the guidance of the Dissenting Deputies, directed the campaign for the repeal of the Test Acts. It published the *Test Act Reporter* as the official organ of repeal. It authorized its secretary, Robert Winter, to draw up *A Statement of the Case of the Protestant Dissenters under the Corporation and Test Acts* and to circulate it among the Members of Parliament. It communicated with 1,500 ministers and instructed them how to petition against the Test Acts. It obtained a favorable petition from the Corporation of London. Finally, it promoted a joint meeting with the Whigs and obtained pledges favoring repeal from thirty Members of Parliament.[50]

Lord John Russell, who had proposed the Whig motion for repeal in 1827, decided not to proceed with a bill because time was short and because the Whigs did not want to upset Canning's unstable Government. Upon Russell's advice, therefore, the United Committee postponed its demands until the next session of Parliament.

During the closing months of 1827 the several religious bodies composing the United Committee carried on separate campaigns for the repeal of the Test Acts. The Protestant Society circularized its followers, particularly the Calvinist and other independent Methodist groups, urging them to send their petitions to the "less liberal members who supported the Government." [51] In preparation for the opening of Parliament in 1828, the United Committee circulated thousands of petitions and sent to Parliament another paper barrage against the Test Acts.[52] The House of Commons received 1,700 petitions and the Upper House received 861 petitions in favor of repeal.[53]

In the Upper House Lord Eldon, the defender of the Test Acts, strongly censured the Dissenters for their political activities:

> From the petitions presented in favor of the bill, it was easy to discover the intentions of the petitioners, and to perceive that the measure was founded upon revolutionary principles. He knew well how these numerous petitions were got up; nothing more was necessary than to establish a committee in London, and to open communications with the various Dissenters throughout the country. The plan was to send three forms of petitions to the Dissenting minister in each parish; one was to be presented to the Dissenters for their signatures; the next was intended to be shown to such of the Established Clergy as they might reckon upon joining with them; and the third form of petition was for the liberal-minded persons whose enlightened views of things far exceeded those which he or any simple Church-of-England man entertained.[54]

In addition to presenting petitions, the Dissenters exacted pledges from the Members of Parliament who represented their towns. The effectiveness of this political action Lord Brougham acknowledged:

> Of this I am quite satisfied, that the representatives of every town will hear from the places they represent, the voice of their constituents, in approval of the vote which they shall give in support of my noble friend's motion; for everywhere there has arisen a body of constituents, intelligent, wealthy, and if I may use the expression, intelligent to a degree of which those who have not well considered the subject can form no adequate notion—I mean the Dissenters. . . .[55]

The United Committee, moreover, supplied Parliament with statistical and legal information. Benjamin Hanbury, the dispenser of statistics, claimed that the United Committee represented 2,324 congregations of nearly 1,000,000 Dissenters; and, in addition, the Wesleyan Conference and the Society of Friends, who were not cooperating with the Committee, possessed 2,597 congregations embracing another 1,000,000 persons. Besides supplying statistics, the United Committee appointed a subcommittee of lawyers, headed by Christopher Richmond, to draft the bill repealing the Corporation and Test Acts.[56]

On February 26, 1828, Lord John Russell introduced the Dissenters' bill in the House of Commons "to repeal so much of the laws which require persons, before they are admitted to office or place in corporations or having accepted any office, civil or military, or any place of trust under the Crown to receive the sacrament of the Lord's Supper according to the rites of the Church of England." [57] In defense of the bill Russell attempted to refute the Tory contention that the Test Acts were of no practical grievance. He cited many cases to show how severely they were penalized. "The consequence is," he said, "that not one tenth part of the Dissenters who ought, in proportion to their numbers, at present hold office." [58] Following Russell, Lord Brougham pointed out the social consequences of the Test Acts. ". . . The Dissenter under such circumstances," he said, "will not seek office. He will go to his country home or his library—he will withdraw himself from public life, and seek in private that occupation which in public is denied to him. . . ." [59]

At first Sir Robert Peel and the Tories opposed the bill to repeal the Test Acts; on the only division which occurred they lined up against it.[60] But when they saw they were badly beaten, they lamely offered to compromise by substituting for the sacramental test a declaration that Dissenters pledge themselves not to subvert the Established Church. The Dissenters, of course, objected to this Tory compromise. Daniel W. Harvey resentfully said that the *Declaration* was required only to "gratify the affected pride of the Church." [61] William Smith thought "the Dissenters had a right to ask for repeal without any condition whatever." However, the Dissenters gave way when Sir Robert Peel promised to make repeal "a perfectly open question" if they would accept his *Declaration.*[62]

In the Upper House, the Duke of Wellington followed the line of compromise already laid down by Sir Robert Peel. "It is certainly true," he said, "that my right honorable friends in the other House did oppose the bill when it was first introduced to their notice. . . . Afterward, however, on finding the House of Commons agreed to the bill, they accepted it." Wellington also adopted Peel's *Declaration* but sought to strengthen the security of the Church by adding the words, "I recognize the Books of the Old and New Testament as truly expressing the revealed will of God." [63] The Archbishop of York endorsed the amendment which obviously intended to exclude the Jews. Eventually a majority of Lords adopted Lord Grey's softer but no less exclusive amendment to the *Declaration*, "on the true faith of a Christian." Notwithstanding the *Declaration*, the Ultra-Tories refused to make the slightest concession to the Dissenters; Lord Eldon, in particular, regarded the bill "as bad, as mischievous, as revolutionary as the most captious Dissenter would wish it to be." [64]

After the bill had passed Parliament, the Dissenters celebrated their victory. On May 26 the Ministers of the Three Denominations held an extraordinary meeting to express their gratitude to Lord John Russell and Lord Holland for carrying the bill through Parliament. They also thanked the Tory Government for "yielding so candidly." [65] Evangelical Churchmen also joined in this celebration of victory because they believed "a profane prostitution of a sacred ordinance" had been cast out of the temple.[66] Unlike High Churchmen, they felt no anxiety for the security of the Establishment, for they confidently believed that "our reverend Church . . . can afford to depend upon her own zeal and excellence. . . ." [67]

The United Committee honored the Whigs with a victory banquet to which they invited 420 guests including 43 Members of Parliament. They chose the Duke of Sussex, a friendly member of the royal family, to preside over their celebration.[68] They selected representatives from several denominations to propose toasts; and these pious men profusely praised the Parliamentary friends of Dissenters, most important among whom were Lord John Russell, Lord Holland, and William Smith. The Duke of Sussex, when making the principal address, reminded the Dissenters that they must continue to work for religious liberty by relieving the Roman Catholics. In response to his plea, the United Committee adopted as their last will and testament a resolution in favor of Catholic Emancipation.[69]

Relief for the Catholics had long been associated with the repeal of the Corporation and Test Acts. Since the days of Priestley many Dissenters had been convinced that they could win freedom for themselves only in conjunction with the Jews and Catholics.[70] Robert Hall, who was honored by all Dissenters, taught them to defend the Catholic claims.[71] Though many Dissenters regarded

Catholicism as "a harmful superstition," they could not consistently refuse Catholics the benefits of religious liberty.[72]

Shortly after the repeal of the Test Acts, the Unitarians began a campaign to emancipate the Roman Catholics. Under the leadership of Richard Potter, the Dissenters of Manchester met to demonstrate that they were "of one heart and one soul" on the Catholic question. After this success the Unitarians promoted a similar meeting in London "to strike a final blow at bigotry and intolerance." [73] As soon as Parliament had convened in a new session, the London Ministers of the Three Denominations petitioned in favor of Catholic relief.[74]

In addition to petitioning Parliament, the Dissenters had a hand in formulating the Catholic relief bill along the lines of religious liberty. Fearing that the Tories had proposed Catholic relief merely as a means of pacifying Ireland, the Dissenters intervened to prevent the subsidizing of the Irish priests. "To give them civil rights," they insisted, "is not the same thing as to actively support a corrupt Church, denounced by God, and proved most baneful to man." [75]

While Dissenting ministers were agitating for Catholic relief, the Anglican clergy were whipping up petitions against it. Churchmen sent in hundreds of petitions against the relief bill. When the Catholic relief bill reached the House of Lords, the bishops spoke emphatically against it. The Archbishop of Canterbury argued that civil rights could not be granted to Catholics because the British constitution was Protestant. On an important division 10 bishops voted for Catholic relief, while 19 voted against it.[76]

The passage of the Catholic relief bill, a major turning point in politics, disrupted the old Ultra-Tory, High-Church party.[77] It divided families and broke the warmest friendships. During the debates on the question, "the three royal dukes, Clarence, Cumberland, and Sussex, got up one after another and attacked each other . . . very vehemently," Greville reported, "and they used toward each other language that nobody else could have ventured to employ, so it was a very droll scene." [78]

After the passing of the Catholic relief bill, the Dissenters celebrated a second victory for religious liberty. Gathering at the London Tavern, they drank their toasts to John Wood and William Smith, Dissenters who had fought for the measure in the House of Commons. As a tribute to the occasion the Protestant Society invited Daniel O'Connell, the Irish leader, as principal speaker, and "he addressed the assembly in a strain of fervid congratulation and of gratitude for the aid rendered by Protestants to Catholics in this great struggle." [79]

The proponents of religious liberty had still other battles to fight. The following year Robert Grant, a member of the Clapham Sect, introduced a bill in the House of Commons to emancipate the Jews. The Dissenting bodies again petitioned Parliament for the removal of religious penalties. But now the Churchmen were fully aroused against further concessions. Contending that freedom for the Jews would destroy the Christian constitution, the Tories defeated the Jewish relief bill on its second reading.[80] Thus the virulent opposition which had been aroused by the contest over Catholic relief made it necessary for the Jews to wait many years to obtain the removal of their disabilities.

The granting of relief to Catholics and the repeal of the Corporation and Test Acts did not end the struggle for religious liberty. Many grievances remained to be redressed. But inasmuch as the Dissenters were equally desirous of promoting civil liberty, that is, the reform of Parliament, they postponed their agitation for religious liberty until after the passing of the Reform Bill.

# 3. *The Rise of Popular Education*

Popular elementary education arose during the last quarter of the eighteenth century as a consequence of the Wesleyan revival. John Wesley inspired his disciples with an earnest desire to read the Bible and to study sermons on salvation. He also trained his followers to distribute tracts and place the Bible in the hands of all who could read. Their task did not end there. Those who could not read must be taught to read.

Deeply affected by the ignorance and low morals of the working people, Wesley labored among them to enlighten their minds and to raise their morals. He established a society at Oxford with the object of teaching the poor to read. In numerous tracts and sermons he expressed his concern for education. Other Evangelicals expanded the work which he had begun. Robert Raikes, Hannah More, and William Wilberforce, to name only the most famous leaders, founded schools to teach the Bible and to encourage better morals and manners.[1]

The Sunday school, which was first organized by Robert Raikes in 1780, became a powerful agency for popular education. Although its means were narrowly limited and its methods inadequate, it enabled many persons among the lower classes to read and write. In 1785 the Sunday School Union, one of the earliest Evangelical societies, was founded to promote the work of the schools. At about the same time Hannah More began her religious career, working with a Sunday school at Cheddar in Somerset. Within ten years she had established schools in twelve parishes for 3,000 children; within twenty-five years she could number 20,000 children, chiefly from miners' families, who had been taught in her schools. As a consequence of Evangelical zeal the Sunday schools spread rapidly to all parts of the country. When the first

Notes to this chapter begin on page 176.

religious census was taken in 1851, it counted 318,000 teachers and 2,400,000 scholars enrolled in the Sunday schools.

The Sunday schools laid the foundation for national education. "The establishment of the Sunday schools," Sir James Kay-Shuttleworth wrote, "prepared public opinion for the more general efforts to form voluntary associations for the promotion of elementary education by means of the day schools." [2] Such schools had their greatest importance in the new industrial towns. "The fact that on Sunday many thousands of the middle class devote three hours of their rest from business life to the pious office of instructing the children of the humblest ranks shows how powerful the cohesive influence of Christian charity has been. . . ." [3]

At the beginning of the century two voluntary societies, representing the two principal religious divisions, church and chapel, began the education of poorer children. Dissenters of various denominations cooperated with the British and Foreign School Society; and the Anglicans, not to be outdone by their rivals, established and maintained the National School Society. Born of religious controversy, the two societies were often hindered by their own warfare from doing the main job at hand; nevertheless, their zeal and benevolence eventually aroused the nation to the responsibility of educating the children of the poorer classes.

Joseph Lancaster, a man of great but erratic ability, laid the foundations of the British and Foreign School Society. Lancaster, born in 1778, was a member of a large Calvinistic family. Though lacking formal education, he became an avid reader and early in life began to prepare for the career of a Dissenting minister. He was a zealous youth. After reading Clarkson's *Essay on the Slave Trade,* he left home at the age of fourteen with the mission of teaching the slaves of Jamaica to read. Friends fortunately intervened to prevent the fulfillment of his precocious plan and returned him to his preparation for the ministry. This career came to an end when he accepted the principles of the Society of Friends.[4]

His newly acquired religious convictions directed his enthusiasm into teaching. He began his first school in a shed attached to his father's property. Soon outgrowing its limits, his school won the financial aid of some sympathetic Quakers and in 1798 they helped him establish a free school at Borough Road.[5] Two years later he published a tract, *Improvements in Education,* which described the work of his school and set forth the principles on which it was founded. In this tract he rejected the teaching of all sectarian dogmas and proposed the founding of schools on a broad and inclusive principle, open to children of all religious denominations. He also explained the monitorial system, which had made it possible for him, unaided, to teach 500 children.

Lancaster, however, did not originate the monitorial system. Several years before this Andrew Bell, a clergyman of the Church of England, had devised the system while he was the superintendent of an orphans' school in Madras. In 1797 Bell published a book, *An Experiment in Education,* describing the monitorial system. After reading this account, Lancaster reorganized his school at Southwark and demonstrated—to his own satisfaction—that he could educate hundreds of children by employing older pupils to train the younger. He divided the children into eight classes, each under a monitor, and placed the monitors under the supervision of a monitor general. The economy of the system at once attracted the attention of the frugal and humane Quakers, who wished to help the thousands of children on poor relief. William Allen, a Quaker, testified before a Parliamentary committee in 1816: "I saw that it was a system pregnant with the greatest benefits not only to the country but to the whole world . . . capable of educating children at the expense of five to fifteen shillings each *per annum.*" [6]

With the abilities of a good promoter, Lancaster quickly won the patronage of aristocrats, statesmen, and wealthy merchants. He early solicited the financial support of the leading Whigs including Lord Brougham and Samuel Whitbread. In 1805 he gained national prominence by obtaining the patronage of King George III.[7]

Romantic in temperament, Lancaster lacked the prudence to confine himself to the limits of a financial budget. To carry the burden of his increasing debt, several friends in 1808 organized a society to obtain more aid. William Corston, a hatmaker, and Joseph Fox, a dentist, meeting with the esteemed educator, formed the Lancastrian Society. They were devout men—Fox, a Baptist; Corston, a Moravian; and Lancaster, a Quaker—with humanitarian zeal for those projects which they considered practical Christianity. The founders of the Society soon enlarged their Committee to include Joseph Forster and William Allen, two benevolent London Quakers. Allen as secretary and Fox as treasurer soon became the principal men of the Society. As their influence increased, Lancaster's influence decreased, and by 1810 control had passed into their hands.

The Lancastrian Society was organized like other Evangelical societies. Following the pattern of the British and Foreign Bible Society, it held annual meetings in May and selected its presiding officers from benevolent aristocrats and its permanent officers from frugal businessmen. Its motives were missionary and international, not denominational or national. William Allen, for instance, wished to extend its work beyond England to all the "vast regions opening up before commerce and Evangelical zeal." [8] The British West Indies became an area of concern because several of the Society's supporters, including Clarkson and Wilberforce, were engrossed in the struggle against slavery.

In 1814 the Society, because of Lancaster's mismanagement, changed its name to the British and Foreign School Society. Thereafter, under the financial management of the London Quakers, it obtained additional aid from several great Whig families. Lord Holland and the Marquis of Lansdowne were among its generous patrons.[9] The sixth Duke of Bedford associated himself with its work until his death in 1839; thereafter the seventh Duke of Bedford continued the family support.[10] Lord John Russell, the greatest of Whig reformers, was an early exponent of the Society's principles.[11]

The Dissenters who supported the British and Foreign School Society did not at first object to state aid for education. In 1807 they endorsed Samuel Whitbread's bill reforming the Poor Law and establishing schools supported by local rates.[12] When proposing this measure, Whitbread sanguinely expected that Lancaster's system of education would make the Poor Laws obsolete. "The principles upon which he [Lancaster] proceeds at the free school in the Borough," he said, "are . . . so obviously founded in utility and economy they must prevail and will finally . . . furnish a mode of instruction not only for this country, but for all the nations advanced in any degree of civilization." [13] The Tory opponents of Whitbread's bill, fearing that education would make the poor insolent and rebellious, allowed the bill to pass the House of Commons knowing that it would be thrown out by the House of Lords.[14]

Lord Holland introduced Whitbread's Parochial Schools Bill into the Upper House where it was received with the expected hostility. Lords Redesdale and Eldon firmly resisted it. The Archbishop of Canterbury objected to it because it did not safeguard the Church's traditional right to educate the people. "This would go far to subvert the first principle of education in this country," the Archbishop said, "which had hitherto been under the control and auspices of the Establishment." [15] In defense of the measure, Lord Stanhope declared that the Dissenters and Catholics should have the right to educate their children. It was an "abominable principle," he thought, "that no part of the population ought to receive education unless in the tenets of the Church." [16] In spite of the able Whig leadership, the Lords decisively defeated Whitbread's bill. After the Tories returned to office in 1807, they disregarded urgent pleas for state aid to education.

The contest between Whigs and Tories in Parliament echoed the larger controversy between Dissenters and Churchmen throughout the country. Claiming a monopoly of education, Anglicans were alarmed when the King patronized the Lancastrian schools. In several places opposition arose against the schools and their founder. Sarah Trimmer, a stout foe of Dissent, assailed Lancaster as the "Goliath of schismatics" whose schools usurped the prerogative of the Established Church.[17] Not to be outdone by Dissenters, she encouraged Andrew Bell, already prominent as an educator, to open schools at Whitechapel. With the generous help of the Anglican clergy his schools achieved immediate success.

The Society for Bettering the Condition of the Poor was the chief agency awakening Churchmen to their duties. In its *Reports* the Society expressed alarm that "the Dissenters of every sect are at present actively and honorably employed in the works of education. Their labors are extended to other societies of Christians, not excluding the poor of the Established Church." [18] At great length the *Reports* burdened Churchmen with the dread of what might happen if they did not supply their own children "with the inestimable benefit of education." [19]

The Society for Bettering the Condition of the Poor, in its requests for more funds, directed its appeal to aristocratic conservatism as well as to religious zeal. Fearful that the children of the poor might become "defenseless prey to the sophistry and delusion of the teachers of infidelity," the Society recommended the adoption of "a system of moral and religious instruction connecting the rising generation with our civil and ecclesiastical establishments. . . ." The Society further recommended that kind of instruction "which fits and prepares the individual to thrive and to be useful in his appropriate station." [20]

The *Reports* of the Society and Sarah Trimmer's cries of "Church in danger" awakened Churchmen to the need of elementary education. The Anglican clergy, who were supporting Bell's schools, resolved to establish an educational society to promote Anglican schools. In June 1811 Herbert Marsh preached a charity sermon in which he urged the formation of a national school society. A distinguished group in his audience, including Archbishop Manners Sutton, responded to his challenge and decided to form a national society to educate the poor in the principles of the Church. In October of the same year a larger group of Churchmen, under the presidency of the Archbishop of Canterbury, officially launched the National Society for the Promotion of the Education of the Poor in the Principles of the Established Church.[21]

In the beginning the National Society was organized on an exclusively Church of England basis. Its constitution, published in its first *Annual Report,* required "that all children received into these schools be instructed in the liturgy and catechism and that . . . the children of each school shall constantly attend divine service in the parish church."[22] Jews and Dissenters, if admitted to the schools, were obliged to attend worship in the parish church. Moreover, the National Society was closely controlled by the Anglican clergy. The local committees were associated with the parishes and the dioceses. The bishops were *ex officio* members of the permanent committee which directed the National Society. Dominated by the clergy, the National Society was a powerful agency in extending not merely parochial education but also the Church's influence.[23]

For two decades the National Society and the British and Foreign School Society undertook the enormous task of educating the nation without government aid. During this time prominent people in politics and literature used their influence to aid one society or the other. Before long persons of nearly every shade of political opinion, from conservative to radical, conceded the necessity of educating the poor. But they could not agree on what kind of religious instruction should be given or who should do the teaching.

In the financial struggles of the two societies the National Society soon emerged superior. Royal letters, which permitted parochial collections from time to time, brought into its treasury annually £10,000. During the first four years of existence the National Society obtained £60,000 from its donors; whereas, in a similar period, the British and Foreign School Society received only £9,000.[24] From 1808 to 1815 the British School Society received only £16,127, an amount less than its expenditures. Owing to its hard-pressed condition, Samuel Whitbread approached Lord Liverpool in 1815 seeking a government grant of £20,000. But the Tory Prime Minister refused to recommend such a grant when Lord Sidmouth, who was always hostile to Dissenters, opposed it.[25]

In order to bring the needs of education before the House of Commons, Lord Brougham obtained a Select Committee in 1816 to investigate "the education of the lower orders in the Metropolis." The Select Committee, which included earnest reformers such as Sir James Mackintosh, Sir Samuel Romilly, William Wilberforce, Francis Horner, and Sir Francis Burdett, extended its investigation beyond London to the whole of England, Wales, and Scotland. The Committee uncovered abuses in the administration of the endowments of the public schools; and its *Report,* consequently, was assailed vehemently by the Church Tories in *The Quarterly Review.*[26] Inasmuch as the endowments were administered by the Anglican clergy for the benefit of Established Church, the Dissenters demanded that the funds be applied, as originally intended, to the education of the poor.[27]

Lord Brougham's Committee, appalled by prevalent ignorance and superstition, lamented the dearth of education. It reported that only one person in sixteen had an opportunity for education and that many persons depended on Sunday schools and dame's school, where the facilities were inadequate if not notorious.[28] The Committee reported at the same time that conditions in Scotland, where one person in nine had an opportunity for education, were superior to those in England and Wales.

Convinced that voluntary efforts would never supply the needs of the people, Brougham's Committee recommended a national system of education supported by a Parliamentary grant and managed by the parish vestry and Anglican clergy. These recommendations, however, immediately alarmed the Dissenters, who feared encroachment upon their religious liberty and, therefore, preferred voluntary education to a national system dominated by the Church. When asked if a Parliamentary grant would hinder voluntary efforts, William Allen, who spoke for the Dissenters, replied: "Certainly I do; for we universally find that those things which the public enter into with spirit, from a consciousness of their importance to the community, are best supported by that zeal when left to itself."[29] Allen also objected to the Committee's recommendation that the choice of schoolmaster be placed in the parish vestry subject to the approval of the parson and the bishop. He believed, on the contrary, that the person best able to teach ought to be chosen regardless of his religion.[30]

Many Dissenters had accepted the voluntary principle in education long before Lord Brougham undertook his investigation. As early as 1768 Joseph Priestley had written against state-controlled education; and though a friend of France in 1789, he never accepted the French principle of secular education.[31]

Although the Benthamite Radicals believed in national secular education, they preferred the comprehensive system of Dissent to the exclusive system of the Established Church. Religion hindered, but did not prevent, James Mill, a freethinker, from collaboration with the Dissenters in the British and Foreign School Society.[32] When the Anglicans formed the National Society in 1811, Mill wrote a tract against it, *Schools for All, Not Schools for Churchmen Only,* which allied the Radicals with the Dissenters.[33] Dependent upon the Dissenters for political support at the polls, the political-minded Radicals, James Mill and Sir John Bowring, tried to counteract the anticlerical influence of Jeremy Bentham.[34] The Radicals learned in 1820, if they had not known before, the political power of the Dissenters, for in this year they arose to defeat Lord Brougham's education bill.

On June 28, 1820, after having presented the report of his Select Committee, Henry Brougham introduced a bill providing for the building, supervision, and maintenance of parochial schools. The debates on the measure did not concern whether or not the state should educate the people.[35] The big questions were: What should be taught, and who should do the teaching?

Henry Brougham was clear on the main issues. He invited "the House to observe how he had united and knitted the system with the Protestant Establishment." [36] To qualify for teaching, the master "must be a member of the Established Church, and take the sacrament in testimony of that fact one month previous to the election." After gaining certification from the Church, the master might then be elected by housekeepers paying the school rates. Lord Brougham made a concession to the Dissenters by recommending that only the Bible be used as reading lessons. Churchmen, of course, regretted the exclusion of the Prayer Book from weekday instruction. The bill, however, did require the attendance of all children, except Dissenters, at catechetical classes on Sunday, a requirement which would have enabled the Church to indoctrinate the children of indifferent parents among the lower classes.

The Dissenters at once set up their cry for religious liberty and unanimously opposed Brougham's bill. The Ministers of the Three Denominations as well as the Protestant Society hurriedly enacted resolutions against it, and then formed a United Committee to serve as a pressure group. On behalf of the Dissenters William Allen testified that Brougham's bill was the worst attack on religious liberty since Lord Sidmouth's bill of 1811.

The Dissenters' vociferous opposition bore its fruit. When the bill came to its first reading on July 11, Brougham hurriedly retreated. "He wished to notice and allay an alarm which . . . his bill had excited amongst two very numerous and highly respectable classes . . . the Protestant Dissenters and the Roman Catholics. The House could hardly believe the extent to which the alarm had gone." [37] Moreover, he tried to placate the Dissenters by omitting the sacramental test as a qualification for teaching. But this slight concession did not quiet their opposition. Rather than place themselves in the invidious position of petitioning against education, they renewed their drive for religious liberty. When William Smith and Lord Nugent presented the Dissenters' petitions for religious liberty on July 13, they kept Lord Brougham's bill from a second reading.

The Whigs, nevertheless, hoped to save part of their scheme. In August they addressed the principal article of the *Edinburgh Review* to the Dissenters, reminding them "that we have uniformly taken the side of Dissenters and fought their battles with equal zeal and constancy." [38] They recognized, further, that the real block in the progress of education was "the mutual jealousy of the Established Church and Dissenters." If the Dissenters, therefore, would keep in view the common object of educating the people, "they must concur in adopting that plan which most easily and permanently secures the object by means of existing institutions. . . ." [39] This argument of expediency, however, failed to persuade the Dissenters to accept national education from the hands of their Whig friends. Looking back on this defeat, several years after the hostilities had subsided, Lord Brougham explained it as follows: "The Church wished for education but they wished to keep down the sects a little more. The Dissenters wished for education, they wished to pull down the Church a little more."[40]

For a decade following the defeat of Lord Brougham's bill, national education rarely gained the attention of Parliament. Many

Tories continued to look upon education as an aristocratic privilege; and even the more liberal Lord Canning preferred the voluntary patronage to state support.[41]

While the Tories were neglecting national education, the two voluntary societies increased their activities. They built hundreds of schools and enrolled thousands of pupils. The rapid progress of education converted even Henry Brougham to the voluntary principle. To assure himself on this point he made a personal inquiry in 1828 into the conditions of education. He sent more than 700 letters of inquiry to representative parishes and received 487 replies. These indicated that the number of children receiving education had doubled during the preceding decade.[42] Lord Kerry's more complete returns of 1835 showed that the number of schools had increased from 14,000 in 1818 to 31,000 in 1834; and that the number of scholars enrolled had grown from 478,000 to 1,144,000.[43] The voluntary system, despite its remarkable progress, inadequately supplied the need for education. After the passing of the Reform Bill in 1832, the Whigs made the first Parliamentary grant which marked the beginning of a national system of education. The story of the formation of national education will be told in a subsequent chapter.

# 4. *The Abolition of Colonial Slavery*

The mass movements against slavery and the slave trade arose during the last quarter of the eighteenth century and accumulated strength to abolish the slave trade in 1807, to abolish colonial slavery in 1833, and finally to emancipate the colonial slave apprentices in 1838. These three movements, spanning more than a half century, were religious crusades. Those who participated in them, both leaders and followers, felt a religious compunction to do so. Moreover, they were sustained for a long period of time to continue in the cause when there was no prospect of fulfillment. The antislavery movement did much to transform the morals and opinions of great numbers of people and gave to them a sense of responsibility for the welfare of the people at home and overseas. It even spread beyond England to inspire the Abolitionists in America, and it raised up leaders in other countries who were profoundly committed to the welfare of the Negroes.

The crusade against slavery had a doctrinal basis. In the first place, it rested on the Dissenters' doctrine of the individual's competence to know and please God without the aid of sacraments or episcopal authority. According to this belief all individuals, whether rich or poor, white or black, possessed immortal souls precious in the sight of God. The movement also rested on the Wesleyan doctrine of salvation. John Wesley had taught that the individual could, by reading the Holy Scriptures or hearing them preached, discern his own guilt and turn to Jesus Christ as his Saviour. This faith, which was held by the Evangelicals of both Church and Dissent, as well as by the Wesleyan Methodists, gave birth to a host of religious tract, Bible, missionary, and educational societies. It gave to all Evangelical groups a common language, sentiment, purpose, and practice. It brought a unity rare in the history of Protestantism.

Notes to this chapter begin on page 178.

The doctrine also effected many social reforms touching daily life. For whatever hindered salvation, whether ignorance, penal laws, factory conditions, or slavery, had to be remedied or removed.

Because of these religious foundations, the antislavery crusades cannot be separated from the missionary movement. This great endeavor began during the 1790's with the formation of the Baptist Missionary Society and the London Missionary Society. These societies, and later the Wesleyan Missionary Society, sent missionaries to the British West Indian colonies to convert and educate the Negro slaves. Once the missionaries had begun their work—a work, it should be remembered, far more fervent than mere church extension—they found slavery an insurmountable obstacle to Christianizing the Negro. They found the British planters hostile to their work. Their letters to the English churches and chapels and the countless sermons by the preachers at home supplied the congregations with detailed information concerning the wretched conditions of the slaves and the hostility of the planters. Their sympathy for the Negro and their resentment of the planters were the emotions that sustained the antislavery crusades.

The Quakers were foremost among the religious groups seeking to liberate the Negro. They not only helped to finance, but they also wisely guided, both the Abolition Committee and the Anti-Slavery Society. As early as 1671 the founder of the Quakers, George Fox, had recommended that his followers Christianize their slaves and eventually set them free. The Society of Friends ultimately acted upon his admonitions. In the year 1727 the Friends prohibited the importation of slaves, and in 1758 they forbade participation in the slave trade.[1] Finally, in 1787, the Quakers formed the Abolition Committee to work for the complete abolition of the slave trade. Of this original Committee nine members were Quakers and three, including its agent, Thomas Clarkson, and its chairman, Granville Sharp, were Evangelical members of the Established Church.[2]

Although the Quakers possessed wealth and prudent leadership, they lacked the numerical strength and the propaganda techniques to transform their opposition to slavery into a national movement. Fortunately, John Wesley and his aggressive preachers supplied what the Quakers lacked. In 1774 Wesley aligned his followers against slavery in his tract, *Thoughts upon Slavery.* During the rest of his life he labored and preached against what he called "the execrable sum of all villainies." In 1780 he commanded the Methodist ministers overseas to free their slaves.[3] Finally, in 1791, only a week before his death, he wrote to William Wilberforce, who had just introduced a bill in Parliament against the slave trade, encouraging him to be steadfast in what surely appeared to be a long struggle and to "go on in the name of God and in the power of His might." [4]

John Wesley had a genius for organization and propaganda. He converted thousands of persons during his long preaching ministry, which touched most of the towns and cities of England, and he organized the new converts in classes taught by his disciples. By 1800 other Evangelical preachers had adopted Wesley's message of salvation and his mode of preaching. They demanded of their congregations repentance from sin and a public profession of faith. Repentance and profession together constituted religious conversion. The two greatest leaders against the slave trade, Clarkson and Wilberforce, undertook the abolition of slavery as a direct consequence of a religious conversion.

Thomas Clarkson first became interested in the question of slavery while a student at Cambridge University preparing to become a clergyman in the Church of England. To meet an academic requirement he selected as the theme of his essay the question: "Is it right to make slaves of others against their will?" When seeking information for his essay, he chanced upon Anthony Benezet's *Historical Account of Guinea,* which supplied him with ample factual knowledge. The writing of the essay, however, became more than an academic exercise, for he found it a gloomy subject from morning to night. He later recorded his reaction to it: "In the daytime I was uneasy. In the night I had little rest. I sometimes never closed my eyelids for grief. It became now not so much a trial for academical reputation, as for the production of a work which might be useful to injured Africa." [5]

An essay written in the heat of passion easily won first prize, and Clarkson at once turned to the Quakers to get financial help to publish it. The Quakers readily assisted him in publishing the essay and also challenged him to devote his full time to the abolition of slavery. This challenge brought an emotional crisis which caused his religious conversion, an experience he later described in his *History of the Abolition of the African Slave Trade:*

> . . . and the question was whether I was prepared to make the sacrifice. In favour of the undertaking I urged to myself that never was

> any cause, which had been taken up by man in any country or in any age, so great and important. . . . Against these sentiments, on the other hand, I had to urge that I had been designed to the Church, that I had already advanced as far as deacon's orders in it, that my prospects there on account of my connections were then brilliant. . . . I had ambition. I had a thirst after worldly interest and honours, and I could not extinguish it at once. I was more than two hours in solitude under this painful conflict. At length I yielded, not because I saw any reasonable prospect of success in my new undertaking . . . but in obedience, I believe, to a higher Power. And this I can say, that both on the moment of this resolution, and for sometime afterwards I had more sublime and happy feelings than at any former period of my life.[6]

A similar religious experience induced William Wilberforce to abandon a brilliant political career and to break an intimate friendship with the younger William Pitt, who was already Prime Minister, in order to assume the onerous duty of advocating the abolition of the slave trade.

William Wilberforce was born at Hull in 1759, the son of a successful merchant. After his elementary schooling at Hull, he went to Cambridge, where he enjoyed social life too much to distinguish himself as a student. Upon leaving the university he decided against a career in business and entered Parliament. In 1780, when only twenty-one, he was elected for Hull; and four years later he represented the great constituency of Yorkshire. During his first years in Parliament he stoutly supported Pitt, a man of his own age to whom he was bound by the most intimate ties of friendship. However, in 1785 a drastic change came in Wilberforce's political career —a change "abrupt and profound." [7]

Wilberforce was converted to Evangelical Christianity by Thomas Milner and the Rev. John Newton. On two occasions he toured the Continent with Milner as his companion. On their first tour they read together Doddridge's *Rise and Progress of Christianity;* and on the other, the New Testament in Greek. This was the beginning of a new life. Under John Newton's tutelage, Wilberforce began a long period of serious self-introspection that brought fits of depression. After days of self-censure and distrust, he resolved to turn his back on his previous carefree social life and to accept the solemn responsibilities of the Evangelical faith. This conversion experience prepared him to accept the abolition of the slave trade as his Christian duty.[8]

In 1788 Wilberforce began his long Parliamentary struggle against the slave trade. William Pitt, in order to keep his able ally active in Parliament, carried a motion binding the House of Commons to consider the question of the slave trade in the next session. This gave Wilberforce his opportunity, and on May 12, 1789, he introduced his first bill to abolish the slave trade. Though Pitt supported the bill, it was not made a government measure because the Tories were badly divided on the question. The Whigs at this time were also divided; consequently, the House of Commons delayed action on the bill.[9]

The next year Wilberforce obtained a committee of inquiry and began collecting additional information in preparation for a second bill. While making this inquiry, he gathered about himself a group of devout Evangelicals who were soon known as the "Saints."[10]

Upon being defeated again by the House of Commons in 1791, Wilberforce decided to start a public campaign against the slave trade in order to put public pressure on the Government. Thomas Clarkson led this campaign. He toured the country making scores of speeches against slavery and urging the people to petition Parliament against the slave trade. He urged them also to boycott slave-grown sugar. As a result of his campaign he reported that 300,000 persons, "both rich and poor, churchmen and dissenters," had stopped using sugar.[11] When Wilberforce introduced another abolition bill early in 1792, he was able to present 517 petitions to support his measure. After this demonstration of popular sentiment the House of Commons passed the bill but amended it with the word *gradual,* which enabled the House of Lords to delay action on the bill and finally to nullify it altogether.

The popular antislavery campaign, which had been conducted by Thomas Clarkson, was suddenly halted in 1792 by the "September Massacres" of the French Revolution. Following this outbreak of violence, the English reaction to the Revolution suffocated the antislavery sentiment along with other liberal reform movements. The defenders of the slave trade began to accuse the Abolitionists of being Jacobins. From this curse there was no escape. Popular meetings could no longer be held, corresponding societies had to disband, and mass petitions could not be sent to Parliament. Even the Tory "Saints" of the Clapham Sect were regarded with suspicion. Thus for a decade, while England was waging war against the French republic, the antislavery crusade was silenced.

Meanwhile, the Quakers and the Evangelicals, without abandoning hope for the ultimate suppression of the slave trade, turned their attention to enterprises less political in character. They enthusiastically promoted tract, Bible, and missionary societies. They sent missionaries to Africa and the West Indies. This great revival of Christianity, which continued during the first decade of the nineteenth century, transformed the old Dissenting sects, increased their numbers, and brought them new zeal. These Dissenters met with the Evangelicals of the Church of England annually in May to promote their religious and benevolent enterprises; and the unity thus achieved enabled the London Quakers and the Evangelicals of the Church of England to exercise a national leadership.

Wilberforce was foremost among the London leaders. He contributed generously to many of these philanthropic organizations and sat on the governing boards of several.[12] The publication of his *Practical View,* which went through twenty-five editions and sold thousands of copies, made Wilberforce the counterpart of Wesley in the realm of Christian social reform. At the beginning of the century, therefore, he commanded such a national following that, when the opportunity arrived, he was able to turn all the Evangelicals against the slave trade.

In the year 1804 Wilberforce and his friends decided that the time had come to renew the agitation against the slave trade. In this year they reorganized the Abolition Committee and added several new members, including William Allen, the famous Quaker philanthropist, and the Evangelicals Robert Grant, Zachary Maccaulay, and Lord Teignmouth.[13] The next year the Committee called Clarkson from his retirement and persuaded him to undertake another national agitation against the slave trade. He was again able to arouse a national enthusiasm against slavery, for he "found the old friends of the cause still faithful to it." [14]

Another campaign, however, was hardly necessary. The formation of a new Ministry, at the death of Pitt in 1806, virtually assured the passage of an abolition bill. The Whig leaders of this coalition Ministry, Lord Grenville and Charles James Fox, were strong foes of the slave trade. On January 2, 1807, Lord Grenville, therefore, introduced a bill to abolish the slave trade and quickly pushed it through the House of Lords.[15] Lord Howick (later Earl Grey of the Reform Bill), who became the leader of the Whigs when Fox died, assumed responsibility for the bill in the House of Commons and made the principal speech in its behalf. Thus, with the help of the Whigs, Wilberforce and his Tory friends were able to carry the abolition bill on its third reading by a vote of 283 to 16.[16]

The abolition of the slave trade was, to a large extent, the achievement of the Evangelicals of the Church of England, the Methodists, the Quakers, and other Dissenting groups. In particular, it was a triumph of the religious faith of Wilberforce and Clarkson, both of whom had forsaken their intended careers, one in politics, the other in the Church, to satisfy the extortionate demands of their consciences. They had begun the work on faith when there were no rational grounds for its success; and they continued it on faith during the years of reaction, believing that God had ordained its ultimate victory.

Shortly after the passing of "An Act for the Abolition of the Slave Trade" Lord Grenville's government ran aground on the question of liberal concessions to the Dissenters and the Irish Catholics. After only a brief term in office, the Whigs were not to return again for twenty-three years. During the desperate years of the Napoleonic Wars there was little opportunity to arouse and organize popular sentiment against slavery; and when peace finally came, in 1815, the Tories, still imbued with anti-Jacobinism, effectively resisted modification of old institutions and any encroachment upon property rights. Eventually the reaction spent itself as the fears of France disappeared. Consequently, various liberal groups, including the Dissenters, the Parliamentary reformers, and the Abolitionists, took up those causes which suspicion had so long held in abeyance.

William Wilberforce and the Evangelicals sensed the rebirth of liberalism. After years of patient negotiation with foreign governments to abolish the slave trade, they had become convinced that the trade would never be abolished so long as slavery existed.[17] In 1821, a year marked by the introduction of several liberal reform measures in the House of Commons, Wilberforce initiated an agitation against slavery itself. No longer able to assume the full responsibility for the movement, owing to illness and failing eyesight, he chose as his successor Thomas Fowell Buxton, a man whose Evangelical piety was as intense as his own.

Thomas Fowell Buxton was born in 1786, the son of a large landowner in Essex and the high sheriff of his county. Thomas' father baptized him in the Church of England, but when he was only six years old, his father died, leaving to his mother the responsibility for his early education. A member of the Society of

Friends, his mother was eager to give her son "a deep regard for the Holy Scriptures and a lofty moral standard." [18] Since she shared the ethical views of the Quakers, she instilled in her son an abhorrence of slavery that remained with him throughout his life.

Owing to his mother's Quaker connections, Thomas early became acquainted with the Gurney family of Earlham Hall, the most influential Quaker family of Norwich. From his first visit at Earlham, when he was only sixteen, he was associated with this devout and benevolent family. He formed an intimate friendship with Joseph John Gurney, who became a distinguished minister among the Evangelical Quakers.[19] He was also greatly influenced by Elizabeth Gurney Fry. His ties with the Gurney family were drawn tighter when, in his twenty-first year, he married Hannah Gurney.

Upon moving to London, Buxton joined a Quaker firm of brewers and rapidly succeeded in the brewery business—which was to cause him much embarrassment after the temperance movement arose. From 1808 to 1811 he attended the Friends' Meeting and supported the benevolent enterprises of William Allen and other London Quakers. While working for the Bible Society, he met an Evangelical clergyman, the Rev. Josiah Pratt, who deeply influenced his religious life. Under Pratt's guidance he experienced a religious conversion which changed the course of his career. This experience he has related in his *Memoirs* as follows:

> I was seized with a bilious fever in January. When I first felt myself unwell, I prayed that I might have a dangerous illness, provided that illness might bring me nearer God. I gradually grew worse; and when disorder had assumed an appearance very alarming to those about me, I spent an hour in most fervent prayer. I had for some years been perplexed with doubts; I do not know if they did not arise more from the fear of doubting, than from any other cause. The object of my prayer was that this perplexity might be removed; and the day, when I set about examining my mind, I found that it was entirely removed, and that it was replaced by a degree of certain conviction, totally different from anything I had before experienced. It would be difficult to express the satisfaction and joy which I derived from this alteration. "Now I know that my Redeemer liveth" was the sentiment uppermost in my mind, and in the merits of that Redeemer I felt a confidence that made me look on the prospect of death with perfect indifference. No action of my life presented itself with any sort of consolation. I knew that by myself I stood justly condemned; but I felt released from the penalties of sin, by the blood of our sacrifice.[20]

After this conversion Buxton devoted more of his time to religious and benevolent pursuits. In 1817 he toured the Continent to promote the work of the Bible Society. The following year he entered Parliament from Weymouth to assist Elizabeth Fry in reforming prison discipline and the penal code. As Elizabeth had persuaded him to enter into this work, so Priscilla Gurney persuaded him to undertake the abolition of slavery.[21] In the last stage of a long illness, from which she died in March 1821, she appealed to Buxton to commit himself to the work she was unable to finish. Hence, when Wilberforce proposed to him on May 24, 1821, that he become the Parliamentary leader of the Abolitionists, Buxton was prepared to do so as his religious duty.[22]

Shortly after the appointment of Buxton as his successor, Wilberforce began the second crusade against slavery by writing *An Appeal to the Religion, Justice, and Humanity of the Inhabitants of the British Empire in Behalf of the Negro Slaves in the West Indies.* At about the same time the venerable Thomas Clarkson also prepared an antislavery tract, *Thoughts on the Necessity of Improving the Condition of the Slaves in the British Colonies with a View to Their Ultimate Emancipation.* To finance the circulation of these and other tracts their Quaker and Evangelical friends in January 1823 formed the Society for the Mitigation and Gradual Abolition of Slavery Throughout the British Dominions.[23]

The Anti-Slavery Society was composed chiefly of Quakers and the Evangelicals of the Church of England.[24] The new Society, however, was broadly representative of all Christian groups. William Smith, the chairman of the Dissenting Deputies, was one of its vice-presidents. On its central committee the Rev. Robert Aspland represented the Unitarians, the Rev. Jabez Bunting represented the Methodists, and Henry Waymouth, as vice-president of the Dissenting Deputies, represented the Dissenters. The Society took its place among the May Meetings at Freemason's Hall, and later at Exeter Hall, so that the delegates attending the Bible, tract, and missionary societies might also attend the Anti-Slavery Society. The Abolitionists had gained by this time such prestige that the Duke of Gloucester loaned his name to the new society as patron and president, and five other members of the nobility accepted the title of vice-president.

The first fruit of the new campaign against slavery was a petition from the Society of Friends. When Wilberforce presented it to the House of Commons on March 18, 1823, he acknowledged that he had been disappointed in his expectation of improving the condition of the slaves by the abolition of the slave trade. He therefore thought it necessary to attack the institution of slavery directly. He also took the occasion to introduce Buxton as the new Parliamentary leader of the Abolitionists.[25]

On May 18, 1823, Buxton proposed his first resolution against slavery, recommending abolition "with as much expedition as may be found consistent with a due regard for the well-being of the parties concerned."[26] Immediately George Canning, on behalf of the Tory Government, amended his resolution by proposing that the Privy Council undertake the amelioration of the conditions of the slaves and the gradual abolition of slavery. This policy of gradualism had been resorted to by the Tories in 1792 to prevent the abolition of the slave trade, and now Canning adopted it as a conservative strategy to prevent the abolition of slavery. Recognizing it as a method of delaying abolition, Buxton and Wilberforce demanded that a date be set, after which the children of slaves would be born free. But this request Canning refused. In debating Canning's amendment some Whigs demanded the immediate abolition of slavery; for example, William Smith, the chairman of the Dissenting Deputies and the leading advocate of religious liberty in the House of Commons, wanted the principle recognized that property in people was contrary to Christianity.[27]

Sir George Rose, himself a West Indian planter, took this occasion to pay tribute to the Christian missionaries who had been working among the Negroes. He praised especially the London Missionary Society for its work on Demerara, and the Baptist Society for its work on Jamaica. The Wesleyan Methodists, he thought, had done the most extensive work, for they had been admitted to nearly all the islands. Since this voluntary work had already Christianized one eighth of the population, he recommended that the landholders be compelled "to procure teachers of the Gospel for the Negroes."[28]

After the adoption of Canning's resolution, Lord Bathurst, the Colonial Secretary, sent letters to the West Indian governors instructing them to abolish the driving system—the use of the whip in the field—to end all flogging of females, and to make Sunday a day of rest, recreation, and religious worship.[29] When this good news spread through the West Indian plantations, the slaves, understanding it to mean they were free, rioted against their masters in several places. Such an insurrection occurred in Demerara in August and spread to the estate where John Smith, an Independent of the London Missionary Society, had a chapel for the Negroes. Although Smith had attempted to keep the peace, he was arrested, court-martialed, and found guilty of starting the insurrection. His exhausting trial had lasted six weeks, and while in prison awaiting the execution of his sentence, he died of an illness from which he had previously suffered.[30]

John Smith was now a Christian martyr, and his martyrdom greatly excited indignation against slavery.[31] When the London Missionary Society petitioned Parliament on his behalf, Brougham saw his opportunity to make political capital of the incident. He discussed the incident at length in the House of Commons and demanded that the minutes of the case be laid before Parliament. On June 1, 1824, he reviewed the case in great detail, declaring the proceedings illegal and proving Smith innocent of the charges against him.[32] The information of the trial was widely circulated through the Dissenters' magazines. It became the subject matter for countless sermons. At the first anniversary meeting of the Anti-Slavery Society, its orators, including the young Thomas Macaulay, gave additional publicity to the Smith case.[33]

Scarcely had the furor subsided when the country was excited again by the Parliamentary investigation of an incident involving Shrewsbury, a missionary of the Methodist Society.[34] The white population at Bridgetown, in the Barbadoes, resenting Shrewsbury's work with the slaves, attacked his chapel, and since the colonial government would not protect him, forced him to flee from the island. Whereupon the Methodists appealed to Buxton for help. Buxton then brought their petition to the House of Commons and carried a motion, after a long debate, requesting the British Government to provide ample protection for the missionaries.[35] This and other incidents of religious persecution turned the Baptists, Methodists, and Independents against the Tory policy of gradualism.[36]

The Anti-Slavery Society kept up a steady and noisy campaign against slavery from its beginning in 1823 until the final emancipation of the slaves in 1833. The Society's receipts increased from £1,093 in its first year to £3,321 in 1830. This income enabled the Society to distribute thousands of tracts in addition to its magazines, *Negro Slavery* and the *Anti-Slavery Monthly Reporter;* in 1830, for example, it distributed 97,500 copies of the *Reporter.*[37] The Society also used its income to organize antislavery associations in the major towns of England and Scotland, and in most of these towns it formed separate organizations for women. The Abolitionists in Manchester, Liverpool, Birmingham, and Edinburgh became sufficiently aggressive to encourage the London Society, which was inclined to cooperate with the Government's policy of gradualism, to take a bolder stand against slavery.

At the annual meeting on May 15, 1830, the Anti-Slavery Society abandoned the policy of "amelioration and gradualism" and adopted, instead, a policy of total abolition. By taking this stand, which the Quakers had preferred from the beginning, the Abolitionists clearly aligned themselves with the Whig advocates of civil and religious liberty. By 1830 the Society had already become virtually a Whig organization. The orators at its annual meetings and its honored vice-presidents, except for a few Evangelicals, were also the leading advocates of Parliamentary reform. Under the influence of its Whig leaders, the Society petitioned Parliament for the abolition of slavery just before the general election of 1830.[38]

On July 1, 1830, Brougham presented its petition in the House of Commons with a full knowledge of its political import; and a few days later he spoke again against slavery, in what was to be his most important campaign speech.[39] Though unable to match Brougham's eloquence or to command similar attention throughout the country, Buxton's speech in the House of Commons favoring abolition was likewise a plea for the election of liberal Whig candidates.

The Anti-Slavery Society met on July 7, 1830, at the beginning of electioneering, and adopted an *Address to the Electors and People of the United Kingdom*. The *Address* instructed the Abolitionists to question each candidate publicly and to demand of him a solemn pledge to vote for the termination of slavery.[40] The Society sent out 36,000 copies of these instructions advising that election committees should be formed, that public meetings should be held, and that "exhortations of the Press should be employed." Although the candidates of both parties were to be interviewed and pledged, the appeal for total abolition showed a clear preference for the Whigs over the Tories.

The Anti-Slavery Society's *Address to the Electors* in 1830 won a quick response from the Dissenters and the Wesleyan Methodists. The Dissenting Deputies "pledged every assistance in its power." [41] Although the Wesleyan Conference had forbidden antislavery agitation in 1825, it now reversed itself and permitted the Methodists to join the hue and cry against slavery. With the endorsement of both the Dissenters and the Methodists, the Society's campaign was undoubtedly decisive in several constituencies. As a result of the elections, during which the question of Parliamentary reform caused the greatest excitement, the Whigs were able to form a government for the first time in twenty-three years.

While Parliament was occupied during 1831 with the Reform Bill, the Anti-Slavery Society strengthened its public campaign by organizing the Agency Committee. This new Committee, financed largely by the Quakers, had the primary function of hiring lecturers to tour the country.[42] In 1831 the Agency Committee received for this purpose £1,189 in addition to the £3,500 spent on publicity by the parent society. During the fall and winter months its six lecturers toured England and delivered scores of public addresses against slavery.

In preparation for the general election, which came because the Reform Bill had been defeated in the House of Commons, the Anti-Slavery Society convened at Exeter Hall on April 23, 1831, and adopted another *Address to the People of Great Britain and Ireland.* As in the previous year, the speakers at this meeting advocated Parliamentary reform as well as the abolition of slavery. Its honored vice-presidents, T. Spring Rice, Thomas Denman, Daniel Sykes, and W. W. Whitmore, were Whig reformers. The devout Evangelicals, Lord Suffield and Charles Grant, were likewise supporters of both reform and emancipation. Because of the close cooperation between the Abolitionists and the Whig reformers, the passage of the Reform Bill in 1832 assured a favorable consideration of the antislavery question.

In the midst of the struggle over the Reform Bill, Buxton, though friendly to the measure, attempted to keep the question of emancipation alive in Parliament. On May 24, 1832, he introduced a resolution for "the extinction of slavery throughout the British dominions." [43] The Whig Ministers, however, refused to consider the question at such a crisis, and Buxton had to be content with the appointment of a committee of inquiry.

In the summer of 1832 reports of rioting and religious persecutions in Jamaica added new fuel to the flames of antislavery sentiment. When an insurrection occurred among the Negroes, the Colonial Church Union, which had taken the lead in suppressing it, accused the Dissenting missionaries of stirring up the revolt and resolved to drive them from the island. One regiment of local militia at Falmouth destroyed thirteen Baptist and six Wesleyan chapels. William Knibb, one of those whose chapel had been destroyed, returned to England in June 1832 to tell this story of religious persecution. The Dissenting Deputies of London, who took up his cause, contributed £200 to the Baptist Missionary Society in order to publish Knibb's report, *Facts and Documents Connected with the Late Insurrections in Jamaica.* The Dissenting Ministers of London also sent a deputation to Colonial Secretary Goderich to demand additional protection for the missionaries.[44]

William Knibb's tour of England during the summer of 1832 prepared the way for the Anti-Slavery Society's campaign in the general election which came at the end of the year. The Society again sent an address to the electors instructing them to vote only for candidates pledged to "total and immediate abolition."[45] The Agency Committee again placarded the walls of London against slavery.[46] The emotionalism of this mass agitation greatly dismayed the old-line politicians, many of whom must have shared the sentiment of Charles Greville's observations:

> Of all political feelings and passions—and such this rage for emancipation is, rather than a consideration of interest—it has struck me as most extraordinary and remarkable. There can be no doubt that a great many of the abolitionists are actuated by very pure motives; they are horrified at the cruelties which have been and still are very often practiced towards the slaves. Their minds are imbued with horrors they have read and heard of, and they have an invincible conviction that the state of slavery under any form is repugnant to the spirit of the English constitution and the Christian religion, and that it is a stain upon the national character which ought to be wiped away.[47]

Since many Members of the first reformed Parliament had pledged themselves to abolish slavery, the Anti-Slavery Society carefully scrutinized their conduct. The Anti-Slavery Associations sent hundreds of petitions to Parliament bearing thousands of signatures.[48] Early in the session Lord Suffield presented several petitions requesting "total and immediate abolition"; among those presented, one from Edinburgh was signed by 21,291 persons, one from Sheffield by 11,000, and one from Glasgow by 31,000.[49] When Buxton presented similar petitions in the House of Commons on March 19, Lord Althorp announced the Government's intention to sponsor an abolition bill.

Meanwhile, outside Parliament the Anti-Slavery Society excited more indignation against slavery by printing and circulating 200,000 copies of Henry Whiteley's *Three Months in Jamaica.* A business-man and a Methodist lay preacher, Whiteley had gone to Jamaica in September 1832 to preach the gospel, but religious persecutions compelled him to leave the island after only three months. When he returned to England, he wrote an account of what he had seen, case after case of flogging, in appalling details.[50]

Because religious liberty had again been violated in Jamaica, the Dissenters increased their demands for the abolition of slavery. Their most distinguished leaders attended the meetings of the Anti-Slavery Society. To unify the action of all the denominational bodies, the Dissenting Ministers of London, in an extraordinary meeting on April 25, agreed to postpone petitioning for the redress of religious grievances until slavery had been abolished.[51]

In addition to the public pressure put on Parliament by the London Society, the Anti-Slavery Associations elected 339 delegates and sent them to London to watch the procedure of the bill. On April 19 these delegates interviewed the Whig Ministers and urged them to proceed at once with abolition. Lord Althorp promised them prompt action, but again there was delay while Lord Stanley replaced Goderich as Colonial Secretary.[52]

Finally, on May 12, 1833, Lord Stanley introduced the Government's resolutions to abolish slavery.[53] He proposed to free all children under six; and for other slaves he recommended an apprenticeship for a period to be fixed by Parliament. He further recommended compensation to the slaveholders for their loss of property. When these resolutions were embodied in a bill on July 5, Buxton and his friends amended it to reduce the period of apprenticeship to seven years for those who worked in the fields and to five years for all others.[54] When the bill finally became law, it abolished property in people, provided an apprenticeship as a period of transition to freedom, and compensated the slaveholders £20,000,000 for their loss of property.[55]

The abolition of colonial slavery occasioned great rejoicing among most religious groups. The Dissenters celebrated it as a victory for religious liberty, for they had been able to defeat the amendments limiting the Negro's freedom to worship. The Evangelicals regarded abolition as a new opportunity to convert the Negro to Christianity. The Wesleyan Methodist Conference in its next annual letter appealed for £48,800 to send additional missionaries to the West Indies. At a meeting of the London Missionary Society in 1834,

Buxton, the honored speaker of the occasion, requested the Independents and other Evangelicals present to send more missionaries that they might make emancipation truly effective. Through the missionary societies and through political organizations, such as the London Deputies and the Protestant Society, the Dissenters had clearly taken their stand against slavery. Only the Church of England—except the Evangelicals who were still an unhappy minority—refrained from joining the crusade. Its bishops were still too hostile to Methodist enthusiasm and too much a part of an aristocratic tradition to participate in the mass demonstrations against slavery.[56]

There were Abolitionists, however, who celebrated the victory of 1833 with misgivings. Many Quakers deeply felt that their testimony against slavery had been compromised; for they could not tolerate a little bit of slavery more than they could join in fighting a small war. While Buxton and the London Evangelicals were waiting to see how the Colonial Office would enforce the law, the Quakers of Birmingham, who had formed the aggressive Agency Committee, appointed themselves guardians of the Negro apprentices. Before long this small group began a third, and perhaps the loudest, campaign against slavery.

Joseph Sturge, a Quaker and a Radical in politics, was the leader of this movement.[57] In Scotland, where the hostility to apprenticeship was very great, Sturge was ably assisted by George Thompson. Together they revived the *Anti-Slavery Reporter* to publish news of the apprentices. In the summer of 1835 the *Report from the Select Committee of the House of Commons on Negro Apprenticeship* convinced them that the Whig Ministers were only half-heartedly enforcing the law and providing inadequate protection for the Negroes.[58] Sturge and three companions, therefore, went to the West Indies late in 1836 to collect information against the system. For six weeks he and Thomas Harvey toured Antigua and Jamaica, while Lloyd and Scoble were touring other islands. Upon their return home in May 1837 they brought with them a Negro, James Williams, whose freedom they had purchased, and proceeded to publish an account of his experience as an apprentice. *The Narrative of James Williams* was assured a wide circulation when Thomas Price, the editor of the *Eclectic Review,* agreed to write a preface recommending it to the Dissenters.

In July 1837 Sturge, having decided to begin an agitation on behalf of the Negro, appealed to the Central Committee of the Anti-Slavery Society to undertake a national campaign against apprenticeship. When the Central Committee refused to comply with his request, Sturge formed a provisional committee in Birmingham which initiated the campaign. On November 14, 1837, 140 delegates, who had been elected at Sturge's request by the Anti-Slavery Associations, met in London and organized the Central Negro Emancipation Committee. The first operation of the new Committee was the hiring of lecturers to tour the country against Negro apprenticeship.[59] The lecturers received ample information about the apprentices when Sturge and Harvey published early in 1838 *The West Indies in 1837: Being a Visit to Antigua, Montserrat, Dominica, Barbadoes, and Jamaica. . . .*

During the early months of 1838 the Central Negro Emancipation Committee intensified its agitation. It held five demonstrations in London and public meetings in every part of the country, which sent up hundreds of petitions seeking the abolition of apprenticeship.[60] As soon as Parliament had convened, the black-coated delegates met at Exeter Hall to present petitions and press their demands on the Government.

Lord Brougham responded to the Abolitionists' petitions by introducing a resolution on February 20 that apprenticeship should end on August 1, 1838. The House of Lords, however, decisively defeated his resolution by 31 votes to 7.[61] But in the Commons, where a similar motion was proposed by Sir George Strickland, the Whig Ministers, with the aid of the Tories, were able to defeat it by only a slim majority in a full House; and when they were defeated on May 22 on a similar motion, they decided to abolish the system of apprenticeship.[62] The Colonial Office then made such a recommendation to the West Indian governments. Some of the colonial legislatures had already taken such action, and now the others did so. On August 1, 1838, therefore, the slaves were at last free and the struggle of a half century against slavery and the slave trade was at an end.

Thomas Fowell Buxton, who had been defeated at the last election, was in the gallery of the House of Commons with his Quaker friends on the memorable night of May 22 when the Abolitionists won their last great victory. On the following day he conveyed the good news to a friend: "I must write to tell you that Joseph Sturge and that party, whom we thought all in the wrong, are proved to be all in the right." [63]

Thus the Quakers who had formed the first Abolition Committee in 1787 remained steadfast to the end. The flame of their conscience had lighted the long, long way, and Quaker merchants and bankers had paid out of their pockets much of the cost. But this Quaker cause might never have gained national attention without the aid of the Evangelical preachers and missionaries who gave to it their religious enthusiasm. Although the Abolitionists were often ignorant men carried along by their emotions, they were saved from fanaticism and bigotry by the wise leadership of Buxton, Wilberforce, and the other pious men of the Clapham Sect.

Of all the reform movements that swept over England during the first half of the nineteenth century, the crusades against slavery did most to transform morals and opinions. The antislavery crusades gave to many people on various social levels a new sense of responsibility for the welfare of others at home and overseas. The methods of the Abolitionists and the pattern of their organizations were subsequently adopted by other reformers. Not even the Reform Bill—to which we shall now turn—can be fully comprehended without a knowledge of the antislavery movements.

# 5. *The Reform Bill of 1832*

The Parliamentary Reform Act of 1832, among other basic changes, disfranchised fifty-six small towns with fewer than two thousand people and enfranchised forty-three more populous places, chiefly in the cotton and woolen manufacturing districts. The Reform Act also gave the right to vote to all householders in the towns who paid £10 annual rent—a provision designed to increase the political power of the middle classes. For the first time the industrial cities, Manchester, Birmingham, and Leeds, where the Dissenters had their greatest numerical strength and moral influence, gained the right of representation. In these towns the Corporation Act had long prevented the Dissenters from participating in local government, and the Test Act had excluded them from Parliament. After repealing the Corporation and Test Acts in 1828, they moved forward to open the doors of Parliament and to purify the corrupt system of representation.

From the time of the French Revolution the Dissenters had identified the cause of religious liberty with the Whig proposals for the reform of Parliament. "We are to a man," David Bogue wrote in 1790, "the friends of civil as well as religious liberty."[1] Other eminent Dissenters, Joseph Priestley, Robert Hall, Richard Price, and Robert Robinson, agreed that the Dissenters must remain the steadfast friends of civil liberty—that is, a pure system of representation—in order to safeguard their religious freedom.

In a catechism prepared for the Dissenters, Robinson provided ample political as well as religious indoctrination. "Modern nonconformity leads us," he catechized, "to the study of government; Sidney, Locke, Montesquieu, and Beccaria teach the notions which we hold of government. All think the people, the origin of power; and the administrators, responsible trustees."[2]

Notes to this chapter begin on page 182.

Joseph Priestley, the Dissenting theorist, was foremost in the ranks of Parliamentary reformers during the last quarter of the eighteenth century. As early as 1769 he had written a tract in favor of reform. At the election of 1774, while the Dissenters were still suffering disfavor for having supported John Wilkes' campaign for reform, Priestley attempted to arouse them to action on behalf of civil and religious liberty. In his *Address to Protestant Dissenters* he reminded them that "the old Puritans and Nonconformists were always equally distinguished for their noble and strenuous exertions in favor of them both." [3] He further instructed them to vote only for those reformers who would pledge themselves to shorten the duration of Parliament and exclude "all placemen, court pensioners, and sons of nobility from the House of Commons." [4]

In 1791 Robert Hall, following the line laid down by Priestley, urged the Dissenters to act, because "a compact between priest and magistrate [threatens] to betray the liberties of mankind, both civil and religious." [5] Two years later, in *An Apology for the Freedom of the Press,* Hall again sounded the clarion of political action. "The connection between civil and religious liberty," he said, "is too intimate to make it surprising that they who are attracted to one, should be friendly to the other." [6]

Few Dissenters were more widely read or highly honored in their own day than Richard Price; and "as a practical economist he was more regarded than Adam Smith or Dean Tucker." [7] Price was also an eminent advocate of religious liberty.[8] In his *Observations on the Nature of Civil Liberty,* published in 1776, he argued that a man was free only when he could follow his conscience without interference from the magistrate. The greatest threat to liberty, he thought, was the corrupt system of Parliamentary representation. Owing to his prominence as the apostle of freedom, Price's sermon in 1790 on the *Love of Country* provoked Edmund Burke to reply with his *Reflections on the French Revolution.*

During the reaction which came with the wars against France, liberal reforms were identified with the enemy and made the object of contempt and suppression. Both civil and religious liberty were so eclipsed that the Dissenters dared not agitate for either the repeal of the Test Acts or the reform of Parliament. They felt, instead, constrained to make professions of loyalty to the King and the constitution.[9] For more than a decade it was unsafe to be an advocate of liberty, because the Tory rulers, intent upon waging war against France, prosecuted the leaders of reform organizations, proscribed public meetings, and suspended the Habeas Corpus Act.

While other doors were closing upon reform, the Dissenting chapels remained open to nurture liberal principles. The meeting-houses of the Friends, Baptists, Unitarians, Independents, and Presbyterians continued to cherish and practice the principles of popular self-government. Disdaining the need of bishops to guide them and repudiating the necessity of a religious hierarchy to rule over them, they steadfastly professed that the only adequate system of government was one truly representing the people. The essence of their Nonconforming zeal was the denial of divinely ordained orders in society, an attitude which the Quakers symbolized by their refusal to doff their hats in the House of Lords and to bend their knee to the King. While the Established clergymen were preaching on the scriptural text, "be subject unto higher powers . . . for the powers that be are ordained of God," the Dissenting preachers were exhorting their flocks to be obedient in civil affairs but to be superior to, and independent of, the magistrate in moral and religious affairs. Because Dissenting parents had been denied a proper place in local and national government, their children learned liberal political action about the Lord's Table, and so kept the lights of liberty burning.

During the long period of reaction the Whig followers of Charles James Fox kept alive the memories of liberal reform and waited patiently for a more favorable opportunity to advocate the principles of civil and religious liberty. The role of Fox as a Parliamentary reformer can hardly be exaggerated, for he was a voice in the wilderness making the way plain for later reformers.[10] When Fox died in 1806, Lord and Lady Holland, who were devoted to him and his principles, made Holland House a home for Whig reformers and for twenty years kept its doors open to the advocates of civil and religious liberty.[11]

In 1815 the war with France came to an end; but this happy event did not at once abet liberalism, for the Tories continued in office with prestige enhanced by victory. After fighting to defend a society and government, sanctified by wartime emotions, the Tories had no intention of changing their basic institutions by amending the system of representation. When peace brought with it the economic consequences of deflation, unemployment, and declining trade, the political agitators returned to their platforms and aroused a clamor for the radical reform of Parliament. These demonstrations of discontent the Tories answered by suspending the Habeas Corpus Act and restricting public meetings and freedom of speech. This course of reaction ended in 1819 with the Peterloo Massacre, but not before it had embittered a large part of the nation and had aroused the leaders of Birmingham, Leeds, and Manchester to a new determination to break the Tory monopoly of power in church and state.

During the 1820's the Parliamentary reformers took up the work where they had left it at the beginning of the French Revolution. In 1823 John T. Rutt, a Unitarian, edited and published Priestley's works in several volumes. Of the great rational Dissenters, who had defined the doctrines of civil and religious liberty before 1790, only Robert Hall lived to see the revival of reform and to achieve a position of leadership in the new movement. In 1821, after a lapse of thirty years, he republished his famous essay, *An Apology for the Freedom of the Press.* He did so because Anglican polemicists were saying that he had renounced his earlier political opinions. Pointedly refuting such allegations, Hall declared, "the effect of increasing years has been to augment, if possible, my attachment to the principles of civil and religious liberty and to the cause of reform as inseparately combined with their preservation." [12] When the new edition first appeared, the Churchmen who reviewed it censured Hall as "plainly and clearly a radical reformer" and as "a meddler in politics." To these charges he replied that "only radical reform could save the country from certain ruin"; and as for meddling in politics, he thought the Churchmen really meant he "meddled on the wrong side." [13]

During the decade prior to the passing of the Reform Bill, the Dissenting preachers proudly identified themselves with the middle-class reformers of the industrial cities of Manchester, Birmingham, and Leeds.[14] Growing rapidly and acquiring more wealth daily, these cities were the centers of a new industrial society. From the census of 1801 to that of 1831 their populations had more than doubled: Manchester had grown from 84,020 to 182,812; Birmingham had increased from 73,670 to 146,986; and Leeds had expanded from 53,162 to 123,393. In these cities both the Dissenters and the Methodists had their largest following.[15]

In the same areas the Established Church, on the other hand, suffered its worst weakness—a weakness which was not overcome until after the appointment of the Ecclesiastical Commission in 1836. Prior to this none of these cities had its own bishop. There was no bishop for the whole of Lancashire, the center of the new cotton industry; and none for the West Riding of Yorkshire, the center of the woolen industry.[16] In the dioceses of London, Chester, York, and Lichfield and Coventry, with a total population of more than 3,000,000, the Church had seats for only one ninth of the people. The Ecclesiastical Commission estimated in 1837 that the diocese of Chester, which included Lancashire, with a population of 860,000, had seats for only 97,000 persons; York, with a population of 502,000, could accommodate only 47,000; and the diocese of Lichfield and Coventry, with a population of 235,000, could house only 29,000.[17] On the other hand, in the rural areas of the southern counties the Church had more accommodations than was necessary. It was obvious, then, that the Established Church, apart from the Evangelicals, had failed to meet the needs of a new industrial society.

Although it was impossible to determine accurately the relative strength of Church and Dissent before the religious census of 1851, the reformers, who were pleading for civil and religious liberty, estimated the number of Dissenters as equal to, if not surpassing, that of the Church. Lord Holland supposed the Dissenters numbered more than 3,000,000, not including the Wesleyan Methodists.[18] Joseph Hume thought a majority of those seriously interested in religion were Dissenters.[19] O'Connell said Dissenters numbered 6,000,000.[20] *The Extraordinary Black Book,* the manual of radical reform, asserted that the chapels had more seating capacity and were better attended than the churches.[21]

The reformers, moreover, identified the Dissenters with the middle classes. When John Smith seconded Russell's motion repealing the Test Acts, he said, "The Dissenters of the present day were as intelligent, as loyal, as industrious, and as prosperous a class of people as any within His Majesty's dominions." [22]

The new industrial cities, because of the influence of Dissent, demanded first the repeal of the Corporation and Test Acts and then the reform of Parliament. From the beginning of the nineteenth century a new class of merchants and manufacturers, after gathering their fortunes from shops, factories, and warehouses, continually demanded a voice in local government. Prohibited in most cities and towns by the Corporation Act from holding such municipal offices as mayor, alderman, and common councilman, these new men pushed their way into the church vestries and the municipal commissions.[23] As a result, the vestry meetings frequently became the battleground for religious and political factions. At Leicester, for instance, where Dissenters outnumbered Churchmen, there was a coincidence of political and religious alignments.[24] At Coventry religion had long been a cause of contention and a badge of political partisanship.[25] At Sheffield the contestants over church rates resorted to physical violence and after 1824 refused to vote church rates.[26] At Bristol local government was divided between the Tory corporation and the Whig commissioners, between Dissenting churchwardens and church overseers.[27]

Although the Methodists and Dissenters had kept pace with the rapid growth of Leeds from 1801 to 1831, they were nevertheless excluded from the municipal corporation, which coopted itself from the leading Church families. The Dissenters, therefore, moved into the democratic vestry meetings and used them between 1822 and 1832 to become the controlling power in Leeds politics.[28]

At Birmingham the memory of the riots of 1791 was refreshed by the continued rivalry between Church and Dissent. Popular education was one cause of contention. When the Unitarians took the lead in 1825 in founding the Mechanics' Institutions at the Old Meeting House, the Tories denounced it as "a hotbed of sedition."[29] There was still another renewal of sectarian bitterness in 1830 when Churchmen unsuccessfully tried to exclude Dissenters from the management of the Birmingham Free Grammar School.[30] In the following year the Dissenters crowded into the vestry meeting, elected their own churchwardens, and angrily contended against the payment of church rates.[31] Such were the religious and political alignments that prevailed at Birmingham when the agitation for Parliamentary reform arose and gained the momentum to sweep everything before it.

At the time of the passing of the Reform Bill Manchester, still an unincorporated borough, was ruled from Rolleston Hall by Sir Oswald Mosley as the lord of the manor. Excluded from this anachronistic manorial government, the Dissenters, led by John Edward Taylor, Archibald Prentice, and the Potter brothers, contrived to manage the church vestry and the municipal commissions.[32] The contention in the vestry meetings over the payment of church rates was as acrimonious as any election of a Member of Parliament. At nearby Salford the Dissenters also refused to pay the rates, and as a result there was no tolling of church bells for religious services.[33]

In contrast to the northern cities, London permitted Dissenters to participate in local government, and they consequently became influential in metropolitan politics. Whereas the London Common Council had petitioned Parliament against the repeal of the Test Acts in 1790, it petitioned Parliament in favor of repealing them in 1828. London also elected Dissenters to Parliament; in 1830 three of the four members representing London were Dissenters.

In London and the new industrial cities the Dissenters established newspapers to proclaim their faith in religious liberty. These publications soon alarmed the Church. As early as 1790 Robert Southey in his essay, *Observations on the Conduct of Protestant Dissenters,* felt apprehensive because so many newspapers were in their hands. Writing in 1808, the historians of Dissent, David Bogue and James Bennett, acknowledged these journalistic enterprises only to lament that such careers were not conducive to pious living.[34] Observing at a later time the outpouring of Dissenting papers, Thomas Carlyle wrote disdainfully: "A preaching friar settles in every village and builds a pulpit, which he calls a newspaper." [35]

For Dissenting preachers it was only a step from the pulpit to the press. During the agitation for the Reform Bill, Josiah Conder, already busy with the *Eclectic Review,* started a weekly newspaper, *The Patriot,* to push Parliamentary reform and to urge the claims of full religious equality upon a friendly Whig Government. William Johnson Fox, who stepped easily from the pulpit to the press, proclaimed by the printed page the same opinions that he had preached to his Unitarian congregation. He began to contribute to *The Monthly Repository* in 1823 when it was the leading Unitarian magazine, and he later purchased and conducted it privately. In addition, he contributed to the London *Morning Chronicle* and *The True Sun.*[36] In all his activities, whether preaching or writing, he was more the crusader than the journalist, for reform meant to him "not an affair of business or party" but "a real spirit in the soul of man." [37]

Dissenters published several important provincial newspapers. Edward Baines owned and edited the *Leeds Mercury.* When he first came to Leeds in 1795, after transferring his apprenticeship from Preston, he joined the Congregational chapel because its members were the exponents of liberal reform.[38] As the foremost Whig paper of Yorkshire, the *Mercury* never ceased advocating civil and religious liberty.

John Edward Taylor followed a similar course at Manchester.

In 1821, with the aid of Unitarian friends, Taylor started the *Manchester Guardian.*[39] In the prospectus of the new weekly he addressed himself to the "friends of freedom" and dedicated his paper to "sincere and undeviating attachment to rational liberty." The *Guardian's* attachment to liberty, however, was not strong enough to satisfy Archibald Prentice. To advance the cause of liberty, Prentice bought *Cowdroy's Manchester Gazette* and conducted it after 1827 as the *Manchester Gazette and Times.* His guiding principles were religious liberty, free trade, and Parliamentary reform.[40] Differing more in degree than in principle, Taylor and Prentice were influenced by the memory of the Peterloo Massacre, which they had witnessed and reported to London newspapers.[41]

In 1819, when the reform agitators, led by Henry Hunt, planned a mass meeting at St. Peter's Field in Manchester, the local magistrates, declaring such a meeting revolutionary, tried to disperse the crowd and arrest the leaders.[42] They called in troops and swore in special constables for the occasion. When the crowd refused to disperse, the troops charged into the mass of people killing 11 and injuring 600.[43] Following this tragedy the Tory Government, fearful of other popular demonstrations, passed the "Six Acts" of repressive legislation depriving the people of their civil liberties. Though their activities were curtailed, the Manchester reformers kept steadily in view the practical measures, free trade, retrenchment, abolition of slavery, and full religious liberty, that might be expected from an amendment of the representative system.[44]

Religious loyalties at Birmingham were so strong that "they touched both politics and literature at every point." [45] The oldest and best-established newspaper, *Aris's Birmingham Gazette,* which had long avoided party conflicts, became in 1830 a strong Whig and reforming paper. The *Birmingham Journal,* originally a Tory paper, was bought by Jonathan Crow in 1830 and was made an organ of radical opinion. When Joshua Scholefield and Joseph Parkes took it over two years later, they continued to advocate civil and religious liberty.

The early reformers of Birmingham, like those in Manchester, suffered the heavy hand of Tory oppression. During the economic distress of 1817 George Edmonds, a local schoolteacher for twenty-six years, organized a Hampden Club to support Major Cartwright's plan of reform. A successful agitator, he assembled at Newhall Hill a huge crowd, estimated at 25,000, which petitioned Parliament in favor of reform.[46] When the Hampden Club organized a second demonstration in July 1819 to honor Cartwright, the Government arrested and imprisoned Edmonds. Once subdued by the Tory repression, the Birmingham reformers could not revive their agitation during the economic prosperity of the early 1820's. But in the depression of 1829 the agitators returned to their platforms and won a more popular hearing than ever before. With this encouragement the members of the Hampden Club, aided by Thomas Attwood, formed the Birmingham Political Union.

No one at Birmingham ever made economic distress more articulate than did Thomas Attwood. Attwood gained the confidence of artisans as well as the support of manufacturers, bankers, and merchants. Far from being a working-class agitator, he felt the interests of the middle and working classes were so closely bound together that one could not prosper without the other. Like other reformers of his time, Attwood had a remedy for the economic ills that harassed both the manufacturer and the artisan. His panacea was paper currency, liberally but carefully issued in place of gold. After fifteen years of writing and speaking on this subject, he had persuaded many Birmingham citizens of the merits of his currency scheme; and he had convinced the majority that he had their interests at heart. His petition to Parliament in 1829, recommending currency reform, was signed by 40,000 persons, who, if they did not understand the significance of paper currency, believed in the man who had proposed it.

But Attwood could not persuade the members of the Tory party, to which he belonged, to adopt his currency scheme. Both Huskisson and Peel refused to consider it; and when the Duke of Wellington rejected the Birmingham petition, Attwood left the Tories to join the ranks of the Parliamentary reformers. He resolved to send new men to Parliament to relieve the miseries of the people by a drastic reform of the currency.[47]

It was not easy for Attwood to sever connections with the Tory party. It meant separation from his brother Matthias, with whom, as a member of Parliament, he had worked for several years on currency reform. Nor was it easy for him to adopt Parliamentary reform, for he had previously opposed reform as a cause of mob violence. His conversion to reform, consequently, was a profound religious experience. "When I first assisted in the formation of the Political Union," he declared publicly, "it was not without long and anxious deliberation . . . I sat up all night in serious and anxious meditation and after I had made up my mind, I went down upon my knees in the gray of the morning and thanked Almighty God. . . ."[48]

Attwood endowed the Political Union with his own love for "peace, law, order, loyalty, and union," and conducted it in the manner of a Methodist outdoor meeting. He encouraged the singing of hymns and offered long, fervent prayers. His speeches were moral pleas for righteousness. Like an Old Testament prophet, he denounced wickedness in high places; and like the shepherd of a flock, he comforted and guided the people. He never pursued the course of a Whig or Tory politician. Rather than rejoice in partisan success, he found greater satisfaction in being in a minority, even in standing alone. A practical politician would have abandoned so unpopular a cause as paper currency, but the very loneliness of such a cause—since it was a righteous one—made him cling to it more tenaciously.[49]

Attwood's religion was that of Wilberforce's *Practical View*. He earnestly went about doing good and seriously tried to love his neighbor as himself. He joined in promoting the Bible Society and in campaigning against colonial slavery. His charity for the poor was so great that his grandson, writing as his biographer, apologized for his ignorance of political economy.[50] His religion, while reinforcing his virtues, aggravated certain defects in his character. It made him more suspicious and intolerant of his opponents. It also increased his melancholy. For many years he frequented graveyards to meditate on life and weep over the dead.

Born and reared in the Church of England, Attwood was not happy in its fellowship after he became the leader of the Political Union. His wife, who had close family connections with the Church, suffered the loss of many of her friends when he took up the cause of reform. Only one church clergyman, A. S. Wade, joined the Political Union, and none ever wrote him to commend or to discourage his undertaking. The Dissenters of Birmingham, on the other hand, accepted him gladly. In the midst of the agitation for Parliamentary reform, they elected him as their churchwarden to represent them in local affairs.[51]

The alliance of Whigs and Dissenters, which was so conspicuous in local politics, prevailed also on the national level. In their national agencies the Dissenters clearly identified themselves with the Whig reformers; and the latter never failed to point out the intimate relationship between civil and religious liberty.

Proud exponents of religious toleration, the Whigs won their first major political victory in a half century by repealing the Test Acts. That the Tories in desperation attempted to steal the principal plank from the Whig platform by accepting religious toleration did not conceal from anyone the vastness of the Whig victory. On the contrary, this ill-conceived stratagem of Peel proved to be the rock upon which the foundering Tory party burst asunder. The triumph of religious liberty was, indeed, the first installment of Parliamentary reform.

Lord John Russell, more than any other Whig, was responsible for the revival of a national enthusiasm for civil and religious liberty. The Russell family had long been distinguished and undeviating champions of liberty. The sixth Duke of Bedford, Lord John's father, wishing to give his son a more liberal education than could be had at either Cambridge or Oxford, sent him to the University of Edinburgh. When Lord John first entered Parliament in 1813, the Duke urged him to follow a liberal course: "The line I should recommend to you for your selection is that of foreign politics, and at home politics bearing on civil and religious liberty—a pretty wide range." [52]

After Lord John Russell had made himself the recognized leader of reform, the Dissenters frequently invited him to preside over their assemblies. Russell, on his part, gladly accepted their invitations because they gave him an opportunity to identify religious liberty with Parliamentary reform. When addressing the annual meeting of the Protestant Society in 1821 he pledged himself to support the claims of Dissenters; at the same time he reminded them that "religious liberty in this country was closely connected with civil liberty," for both were the children of the Revolution. "It becomes those who love either of these liberties," he concluded, "to bring those twin brethren close together as oft as it is possible, and teach them to seek from each other their best support." [53]

The Dissenters' national organizations annually brought together "those twin brethren" and afforded the Whig politicians and the Dissenting preachers opportunities to pledge themselves mutually to civil and religious liberty. The Protestant Society, the Dissenting Deputies, and the British and Foreign School Society were organizations promoting the national interests of Dissent; and of the three, the Protestant Society had become politically the most important by 1830; in fact, it had acquired such influence that it could command the leading Whigs to take the pledge of religious liberty. The important role of the Protestant Society was summarized in 1834 by Secretary John Wilks:

> Lord Holland needed no solicitation; ever ready to promote the social happiness of man, he needed no urging to come among us; and on three occasions he assured us from the conviction of his soul, that he was attached to our good cause, and that there was no indignity by which Dissenters were oppressed, no chain which galled and wrung them which he was not anxious should be instantly broken and eternally removed. He became our champion upon all occasions, and prevailed successively on Mr. Whitbread, on Lord John Russell, on the Marquis of Lansdowne, Lord Dacre, Earl Fitzwilliam, Viscount Ebrington, and Lord Nugent to charm us by their eloquence and spirit, and to ensure us that they deemed the rights of conscience, the most momentous of all human rights. . . .[54]

The Dissenting Ministers of the Three Denominations of London, and their agency, the Dissenting Deputies, had fought for religious and civil liberty for more than a century. In 1827 these Ministers formed a committee of Dissenting laymen and twenty-eight Members of Parliament to devise means of repealing the Corporation and Test Acts. The members of this Committee, with hardly an exception, were Parliamentary reformers.[55]

The Dissenters also cooperated with the Evangelicals of the Church and the Wesleyan Methodists in the May Meeting to promote Christian missions and humanitarian reform. During the late 1820's the Wesleyans and the Evangelicals repudiated the Tories for failing to abolish slavery.

In the elections of 1830 the Evangelicals, Methodists, and Dissenters entered into many contests to pledge candidates to the total abolition of slavery. The Dissenting Deputies promised "every assistance in its power against slavery," and urged their London congregations to petition Parliament for total and immediate emancipation.[56] The Baptists, who were in a rage against the Tory Government because their missionaries were being persecuted in Jamaica, sent circular letters to their congregations urging them to pledge all candidates against slavery.[57] Inasmuch as Wesleyan missionaries were also being persecuted in the West Indies, the Conference urged the Methodists in 1830 to join in the great crusade against slavery.[58] Thus piety drew men into the political campaign that elected the Parliamentary reformers.

The Anti-Slavery Society, which was led by the Quakers and Clapham Evangelicals, had grown increasingly hostile to the Tories.

The Abolitionists felt that they had been betrayed by the Tory promises of 1823 to ameliorate the conditions of slavery. They also believed that a government, dependent upon a corrupt system of representation, would continue subservient to the West Indian interest. For these reasons the Abolitionists, with hardly an exception, were Parliamentary reformers. At the annual meeting of the Society in May 1830 the Members of Parliament, who were invited to speak and take places of honor, were reformers.[59]

Both the Tories and the Whigs recognized the close connection between abolition and reform. For this reason the Tory Ministers tried to defeat Charles and Robert Grant in 1830, but these "Saints" were returned in spite of the ministerial opposition.[60]

One of the most important political contests of 1830 was that of Henry Brougham for Yorkshire. Expecting an early dissolution of Parliament, Brougham introduced a motion against slavery. In debating this question he assailed the Tories for failing to abolish slavery and he defended the Dissenting missionaries against the intolerance of the Anglican clergy. By this speech he expected to win the confidence of those pious voters who had previously given their votes to Wilberforce.[61] Brougham was not disappointed, for as a result of the speech the Dissenters and Methodists placed him in company with the "Saints" and bore the financial burden of his campaign. From Yorkshire George Strickland wrote him this good news: "All the sects are united for you, and the abolition of slavery, which is your stronghold. . . ." [62]

The Anti-Slavery Society interpreted the results of the election of 1830 as a guarantee that slavery would be abolished.[63] The Dissenters, moreover, rejoiced in the return of John Wilks from Boston as their Parliamentary spokesman. By electing Robert Waithman, a member of the Dissenting Deputies, and Matthew Wood, a member of the Protestant Society, the Dissenters felt assured that their interests would be represented.

As a result of the elections the Whigs, for the first time since the French Revolution, had power to drive the Tories from office and to introduce a Reform Bill. Of 236 Members returned by English constituencies somewhat popular, only 79 supported the Tory Government, while 141 opposed it and 16 remained uncommitted.[64] It was thus clear from the returns that if the Whigs were to remain in office—and even survive as a party—they must put an end to the aristocratic control of the House of Commons.[65]

Many Tories, recognizing the need of reforming the system of representation, were willing, even at the expense of reducing their own personal influence, to modify the system of rotten boroughs. A few Tories desired to enfranchise the industrial cities, but the majority of Tories were unwilling to lessen the power of the landed interest and enlarge that of the manufacturers. Moreover, the Duke of Wellington, who was anxious for the security of the Established Church, refused to enfranchise the Dissenters. His declaration, upholding the constitution as nearly perfect, prevented the Tories from introducing a moderate reform bill.[66]

Instead of quieting the noisy demand for reform, Wellington's declaration filled the reformers with consternation. At the opening of Parliament in February 1831 they circulated petitions and obtained thousands of signatures. On February 26 Lord Althorp presented a petition from Manchester signed by 12,000 persons and one from Bristol with a large number of signatures.[67] Hundreds of petitions from nearly every part of the country reached Parliament.

On March 1, 1831, Lord John Russell introduced the first Whig Reform Bill, so bold and sweeping in scope as to astonish some Tories and outrage others. He proposed "utterly to disfranchise sixty boroughs" having fewer than 2,000 inhabitants, and to limit forty-seven other boroughs, with less than 4,000 persons, to one seat in Parliament. Altogether he proposed boldly—and it seemed to the Tories brazenly—to deprive 168 Members of their seats. He intended to grant London and the Metropolitan area 8 additional seats, to give 34 seats to the new industrial towns heretofore unrepresented, including 2 each to the large industrial cities such as Manchester, Birmingham, Leeds, and Sheffield, and to add 65 seats to the more populous counties.[68] By broadening the county franchise to include leaseholders of property worth £50 and by extending the right to vote to householders in the towns paying an annual rent of £10, he increased the number of voters by 455,000. The first Reform Bill granted the middle classes the right to vote and enfranchised those towns where the Dissenters exercised their greatest influence.

The middle-class representatives, consequently, accepted the Reform Bill readily and supported it with enthusiasm. Only Henry Hunt, the working-class orator, held back. The Benthamite Radicals of London, although they continued to favor the ballot, a broader franchise, and shorter parliaments, accepted the Whig Bill. Speaking on their behalf, Joseph Hume declared that the

Whig plan "exceeded by far all the expectations that he had found," and he thought the adoption of the ballot "had been wisely deferred until . . . the present measure was tried." [69]

Outside Parliament, the Dissenters, who carried in their magazines and newspapers accounts of the proceedings, fully endorsed the bill; and Clapham Evangelicals saw in it "nothing unjust, inexpedient, or unconstitutional." [70] When the bill passed its second reading by the narrow margin of 302 votes to 301, the editor of the *Baptist Magazine* saw in this event the "finger of God," inasmuch as the House of Brunswick had also come to the throne by a single vote.[71]

Lacking a decisive majority in the House of Commons, the Whigs welcomed the first opportunity for a general election. After being defeated on General Gascoyne's motion not to reduce the number of English members—a minor phase of the bill—they dissolved Parliament and went to the country with the cry, "The bill, the whole bill, and nothing but the bill." The Tories, however, viewed such an early election as little less than a calamity, for the preceding campaign had ruined family fortunes. The Liverpool contest, for example, where votes sold as high as £100 apiece, cost the contestants £100,000.[72] While some Tories could not afford to stand for re-election in 1831, Whig reformers were being returned without the expense and burden of electioneering.

The Dissenting Deputies significantly undertook the return of Lord John Russell for the important county seat of Devon. After obtaining his ready consent, they called a general meeting of the London Dissenters, adopted a resolution favoring his candidacy, and raised funds to defray his expenses. The Deputies began the donation of funds with £500, and the Protestant Society followed with "a handsome subscription." [73] These official acts of the two national Dissenting organizations, which set the example for Dissenters elsewhere, must have influenced the outcome of other contests.

While the Dissenters engaged in returning Whig reformers, the church clergy strove hard to return Tory antireformers. Under the Church's influence both universities elected opponents of the Reform Bill. At Cambridge University the clergy raised the old cry of "Church in danger" to defeat Lord Palmerston, who had represented them for twenty years. Oxford University re-elected Sir Robert Inglis as a foe of the Reform Bill.[74]

The coincidence of reform and the abolition of slavery brought into the campaign of 1831 pious men who otherwise would have refrained from the clamor of partisan politics. Joseph John Gurney, an Evangelical Quaker, saw nothing political in his efforts to free the Negro, for he considered the question of slavery settled by the plain precept, "Do unto others as ye would that others should do unto you." [75] Other Dissenters saw abolition as a question of great principle, "the issue of which the destinies of Great Britain and of the world are involved." Since Lord Brougham had eloquently espoused the cause of the Negro, his party had become in the eyes of many Dissenters "a great moral party composed of the friends of knowledge, and freedom, and justice all over the world." [76]

With help from many quarters the Whigs returned from the elections of 1831 with a majority sufficient to assure the rapid passage of the Reform Bill. The results showed that the English counties had elected 76 Whigs and only 6 Tories; and that the English boroughs, with popular elections, had returned 162 Whigs against 34 Tories. On the other hand, the nomination boroughs elected 164 members opposed to reform and only 76 in favor of it. As estimated by *The Times*, there were 394 members for reform and 258 in the opposition.[77] The elections had "for the first time since the establishment of the monarchy," Wellington woefully declared, "put the King in the ranks with the Radicals, the mob, and the Dissenters. . . ." [78]

With increased strength at his command, Lord John Russell introduced on June 24, 1831, his second Reform Bill, only slightly different from the first. The Dissenters again endorsed it. The Clapham Evangelicals approved it because they thought the new bill would enfranchise "the great bulk of the middle classes of society, among whom, rather than among the very high or the very low, lies most of the piety and good sense and right feeling." [79]

After the Reform Bill had passed its second reading in the House of Commons by the decisive majority of 367 votes to 231, it went into committee where Tory tactics of obstruction detained it for forty days. During this tedious wrangling the Dissenting representatives, John Wilks, Matthew Wood, and Robert Waithman, patiently safeguarded the interests of cities which they represented. As members popularly elected, they shielded the Whig Ministers from the attacks of Henry Hunt who presumed to speak for the great body of reformers. Despite Hunt's harangues and Tory obstruction, the Reform Bill eventually passed its third reading and went to the House of Lords.[80]

When Lord Grey presented it to the Upper House on October 3,

1831, he justified his action by declaring that since the schoolmaster was abroad, the growing intelligence of all classes of the community had made the old system of representation one of "universal derision and contempt." [81] He advised the Lords rather pointedly that the time had come for them to distinguish between their private property and public trusts, for the latter carried obligations not attached to the former. He denied that he was consciously weakening the landed interests; rather, he thought that by granting 65 additional members to the counties he had sufficiently maintained the importance and weight of the aristocracy. In a direct appeal to the bishops, he asked them what their situation would be "if this bill should be rejected by a narrow majority of lay peers" and "its fate should thus be decided, within a few votes, by the heads of the Church." He earnestly pleaded with them, because they were ministers of peace, not to be "in opposition to the feelings and wishes of the people." [82]

To sustain the Whig Ministers against the Lords' intransigence, the Political Unions increased the popular clamor for reform. In many towns and cities they held mass meetings, made endless speeches, and circulated hundreds of petitions. Bristol sent in a petition with 25,000 names, Glasgow one with 45,000, and Manchester one with 33,000.[83]

On the day Lord Grey introduced the Reform Bill in the House of Lords, the Birmingham Political Union staged a demonstration of 150,000 persons. In the name of "peace, order, and legality" Thomas Attwood urged the great throng "to put a hook in the nose of Leviathan" and bring an end to the "atrocious influence of the oligarchy." Like bad shepherds the oligarchs had not "fed the hungry" or "rendered justice to the poor and oppressed." In an address full of allusions to the Holy Scriptures, Attwood identified the Reform Bill as a righteous cause and won for it, therefore, the passionate loyalty of the Birmingham people.[84]

Attwood kept the huge crowd well in hand by conducting the demonstration with the sobriety and solemnity of a Methodist revival meeting. He concluded it with the following religious ceremony: "I am about to ask you to cry out the words, 'God save the King;' I therefore desire that you will, all of you, take off your hats, and that you will look up to heaven, where the Just God rules heaven and earth, and that you will cry out with one heart and one voice, 'God bless the King.'" After this benediction, Attwood felt contentment in seeing his "150,000 friends disperse to their homes as quietly as a few school children from a village school," the people going their way feeling that God and King and constitution were on their side.

The demonstration of the Birmingham Political Union relieved Whig anxiety lest mob violence should impede the progress of reform. When Lord Brougham presented the Birmingham petition, he cited the prayers for the welfare of the King as proof that the people had "conducted themselves with as much decorum as the House of Lords itself. . . ." [85] But the peaceful assembly of people and their petitions with hundreds of signatures did not lessen the opposition of the bishops. On the fifth day of debate, just prior to the important division on the second reading of the bill, the Archbishop of Canterbury declared that he would vote against it because "it was mischievous in its tendency and would be extremely dangerous to the fabric of the constitution." [86] The Lords then rejected the bill by 199 votes to 158. Only one bishop present, and one by proxy, voted in the minority. It was observed at once that if the twenty-one bishops who had voted against it had, instead, voted for it, the bill would have carried by a majority of one.

Following the defeat of the Reform Bill in the House of Lords there was an outburst of resentment against the bishops. Lord Suffield, the leader of the Abolitionists and a devout Evangelical Churchman, severely reprimanded them for their partisan conduct: "I saw them willing to support every administration until now . . ." he said. "So long as the Government of the country was arbitrary and oppressive, so long do I find the right reverend prelates giving it their support; but as soon as a liberal Government produces a measure for the benefit of the people at large . . . so soon do I find the right reverend bench deserting that administration and throwing all its power into action against it." [87]

Outside Parliament similarly inflammatory language incited mob violence against the bishops and other antireformers. At Plymouth such dire threats were made against the Bishop of Exeter that he dared not approach the town to consecrate a place of worship.[88] At Derby the mob attacked the homes of the antireformers, broke open the local jails, and did other violence, causing the loss of several lives. Resentful of the Duke of Newcastle, a mob at Nottingham burned down his castle.[89] The most destructive of the riots occurred at Bristol, where the mob set fire to the bishop's palace and destroyed other property.[90]

When the news of the defeat of the Reform Bill reached Birmingham, muffled church bells rang all night as a dirge for the House of Lords. Fortunately, the Political Union, by exercising a positive leadership, prevented the outbreak of violence. Fearful of such an event, Lord John Russell wrote to Attwood beseeching him to use his influence "not merely to prevent any acts of violence but any such resistance to the laws as is threatened by the refusal to pay taxes." [91] This plea led Attwood to abandon his plan of organizing the Union in a military fashion, and to reject a proposal for a national federation of political unions. When the Whig Government subsequently issued a proclamation on November 22 against political unions, they found the Birmingham Political Union, and similarly organized unions, to be within the limits of the law.[92] Thus the good judgment of Attwood and other leaders saved the Whigs from the fiasco of having to prosecute the friends of the Reform Bill.

After passing this crisis, the Whigs introduced a third Reform Bill, hopeful of a better reception in the House of Lords. At the first reading, several of the Lords manifested a more conciliatory spirit. Lord Harrowby, who had long been counted as one of the "Saints," and the Bishop of London declared their intention of voting for the second reading. Notwithstanding the softer opinion of the "waverers," the Tories defeated the bill in committee. Whereupon the Whig Ministers resigned and brought the country to another crisis.

When the King turned to the Tories for a new government, the Political Unions began to consider stronger action against the Tories. At Manchester a crowded meeting of 25,000 adopted resolutions and sent off a deputation posthaste to London with their demands that the House of Commons withhold supplies. The London Common Council made a similar demand. At Birmingham, the Council of the Political Union, expecting the arrest of their leaders, drew up a "Solemn Declaration" against the Duke of Wellington. Fortunately, the Duke was unable to form a government, and the country passed a second crisis without bloodshed. When this news of the return of the Whig Ministry reached Attwood, he assembled the Political Union in a great prayer meeting, 40,000 strong, "to express gratitude to Almighty God for the escape which the nation has had from a tremendous revolution." To this prayer of gratitude thousands of voices echoed, "Amen!" [93]

Recalled by the King, Lord Grey returned to the Upper House with the threat of creating enough new Peers to pass the Reform

Bill. To prevent this action that would have meant their own degradation, the Lords gave way and the bill then passed with only slight opposition. On June 7, 1832, it received the royal assent.[94]

The passing of the Reform Bill filled the Tories with forebodings. For John Croker, the editor of *The Quarterly Review*, it was frightful to see familiar institutions confused and changing color. Depressed by these dismal prospects, he retired from Parliament rather than "take an active share in a system which must . . . subvert the Church, the Peerage, and the Throne—in one word the constitution of England." [95] Sir Robert Peel and the Duke of Wellington, because of the Reform Bill, felt great anxiety for the security of the Established Church.

The middle classes everywhere celebrated the passage of the Reform Bill. The Lord Mayor of London, at a victory dinner for the reformers, gave the keys of the city to Thomas Attwood. The Dissenters rejoiced in many places that "the long conflict with corruption is over." [96] The Methodists felt that the "Reform Bill affords an opportunity for pious people to express themselves." [97] The Clapham Evangelicals confidently declared that "we now have a constituency which must include the great mass of property and intelligence." [98] These religious groups, encouraged by the acquisition of greater political influence, returned with renewed zeal to their first love—the crusade against colonial slavery. The Dissenters, in particular, confidently expected a friendly Whig government to remove the religious disabilities under which they had long suffered.

# 6. *The Redress of Religious Grievances*

In the first general election under the Reform Bill, the Dissenting preachers felt it to be their duty to make the new law work effectively. They earnestly urged their congregations to take part in the elections in order to restore "our invaluable constitution to all its pristine vigor and beauty." [1] The Baptists of Yorkshire, for example, sent *An Appeal to the Christian Electors of the United Kingdom on Their Obligations in Reference to the Ensuing Elections.* The *Appeal* instructed the voters to take pledges from all candidates on the redress of religious grievances and the abolition of slavery.[2]

The question of slavery, above all others, drew religious men into the heat of partisan politics. In several newly enfranchised industrial cities, the Dissenters pledged both Whig and Radical candidates to "immediate and total abolition." The Agency Committee of the Anti-Slavery Society, which was financially supported and fully endorsed by the Dissenting organizations, pledged 150 candidates to the emancipation of the West Indian slaves.[3]

As a result of the elections of 1832, the Dissenters were better represented in the first reformed Parliament than they had ever been in the old House of Commons.[4] Their principal spokesmen, John Wilks, Matthew Wood, and Daniel Harvey, who had represented them previously, exercised a greater influence in the new Parliament. In addition to them, the newly enfranchised towns of Lancashire elected the Dissenters John Fielden, Joseph Brotherton, George W. Wood, and Richard Potter to represent their interests. The Yorkshire Dissenters, after the retirement of Macaulay, elected Edward Baines to be their representative. Though elected as Whigs, the Dissenters in Parliament frequently united with the Benthamite

Notes to this chapter begin on page 188.

Radicals and the Irish Catholics to form an opposition almost as powerful as the Tories.[5]

The Tories, who greatly feared the Dissenters, were fully aware of their power in the reformed House of Commons. Shortly after the new Parliament had met, the Duke of Wellington explained the political situation resulting from the first election under the Reform Bill:

> A new democratic influence has been introduced into elections, the copy-holders and free-holders and lease-holders residing in the towns which do not themselves return members to Parliament. These are all Dissenters from the Church, and are everywhere a formidably active party against the aristocratic influence of the landed gentry. But this is not all. There are Dissenters in every village in the country; they are the blacksmith, the carpenter, the mason, etc. The new influence established in the towns has drawn these to their party; and it is curious to what a degree it is a Dissenting interest.[6]

The Dissenters soon demonstrated their political power. They won their first victory for religious freedom when Joseph Pease, a conscientious Quaker, gained the right to sit in Parliament without taking an oath. After study of Parliamentary precedents and court records, the House voted to allow Pease to take his seat by affirmation.[7] Later in the same session Parliament enacted a law, initiated by Grote and supported by Hume and Warburton, "to allow people called Separatists to make a solemn affirmation and declaration instead of an oath."[8] The friends of religious liberty in the new Parliament, however, were not strong enough to emancipate the Jews. The question arose early in the session when John Wilks presented a petition from the Protestant Society praying for their emancipation. The petitioners denounced the exclusion of the Jews from public affairs as "the last fragment of a barbarous system."[9] After having presented several petitions from both Dissenters and Jews, Robert Grant proposed the resolution: "That it is expedient to remove all civil disabilities respecting His Majesty's subjects of Jewish persuasion. . . ."[10] The Jewish relief bill passed the House of Commons in spite of the opposition of the devout Churchmen, Sir Robert Inglis, Sir Andrew Agnew, and Lord Ashley. But when it reached the Upper House, the Duke of Wellington expressed the consensus of the Lords by simply declaring that to admit the Jews would destroy the Christian constitution. The Lords then defeated the motion by a decisive majority, 20 bishops voting against the Jews and only 3 consenting to admit them to Parliament.[11]

Though the Dissenters failed to liberate the Jews, they joyfully celebrated the abolition of slavery in 1833 and esteemed it a triumph for religious liberty. At the beginning of the new Parliament they had deliberately delayed the redress of their own grievances until the Whig Ministers had undertaken the emancipation of the slaves. After the antislavery bill was well on its way through Parliament, they turned to redress their own grievances. The Protestant Society, the Dissenting Deputies of London, and several denominational bodies formed the United Committee, as they had previously done in 1828, in order to press their claims upon the Whig Ministers. The Committee published their demands in a pamphlet entitled *The Claims of the Protestant Dissenters.* Recognizing "the glorious change in the state of representation" which had brought a friendly Government into office, they thought the time for the repeal of religious penalties was at hand.[12] They clearly indicated what they expected of the Whigs. They demanded marriage according to rites of their own choosing, freedom to bury their dead in the parish graveyards, admission to the universities, and a civil registry of births, marriages, and deaths. Finally, they demanded the abolition of church rates and the voluntary support of all churches.[13] To achieve social and political equality the United Committee promoted a national agitation for religious liberty. The Committee urged the Dissenting chapels to petition Parliament for the removal of religious penalties and instructed them to request the Government specifically to redress religious grievances before it undertook the reform of the Established Church.[14]

In 1832 the Dissenters were somewhat divided on the best course of action, whether to ask timidly for several pieces of reform or to demand boldly the whole loaf of disestablishment. Many Baptists and Congregationalists among the militant crusaders of the north, especially in Yorkshire, demanded complete separation of church and state. The Wesleyan Methodists, of course, did not share this extreme view, for they continued to believe in their ability to evangelize the Establishment. Wisest in the ways of politics, the Unitarians favored a course of expediency. Knowing that the Whig aristocrats would not consent to disestablishment, the Unitarians recommended the moderate course of redressing grievances. The majority of the Dissenters accepted this prudent course and looked steadily to the Whigs for the removal of their religious disabilities.

Because they were divided on the question of disestablishment, the Dissenters gained very little satisfaction from the first reformed

Parliament. George Faithful's resolution "that the Church as by law established is not recommended by practical utility," provoked only an angry response from the Whig leaders.[15] Likewise, Benjamin Hall's motion against the abuses of the Welsh Church was defeated without a division. By summarily rejecting these two resolutions the Whigs clearly indicated their unwillingness to discuss the question of disestablishment.

The Whigs failed to redress Dissenters' grievances because Ireland was in a state of insurrection. Irish peasants would not pay church tithes and Irish juries would not convict their countrymen for disobeying the law. While seeking a remedy for these conditions, the Whig Ministers pulled in opposite directions.[16] Lord Stanley, on the one hand, favored stronger coercion; Lord Anglesey, on the other hand, recommended a drastic reform of the Anglican Church which was the Established Church of Ireland. Lord Stanley's Peace Preservation Act deprived the Irish people of their civil liberties and established military courts to mete out swift penalties. A majority of Whigs and Tories enacted this harsh law against the combined opposition of the Dissenters, Radicals, and Irish Catholics.[17] Besides coercing the Irish people, the Whigs tried to pacify Ireland by reforming the Established Church. They proposed to abolish church rates, tax the richer benefices, and reduce the number of archbishops from four to two and the number of bishops from 18 to 10. They further proposed to end the scandal of sinecures.[18]

During the debates on the Irish Church it soon appeared that the Whigs differed among themselves on the question of appropriating the Church's surplus revenues. Loyal Churchmen among the Whigs wished only to strengthen religion by redistributing church revenues more equitably among the parishes. The Dissenters, on the other hand, believing the revenues of the Irish Church to be larger than necessary, wished to appropriate the surplus for general education.[19] From quite a different angle, the Radicals saw in the appropriation clause a means—along with the pension lists—of attacking the vested interests of the aristocracy. In this confused political situation the Tories, who were unable to defeat the bill themselves, divided the aristocratic Whigs against the middle-class Dissenters and Radicals.

When the Irish Church bill went into committee, William Dillon, a Dissenter, moved an amendment "that the revenues of the Irish Church be applied to purposes of general utility." In support of this proposition, which meant the virtual disestablishment of the Irish Church, Cuthbert Rippon declared that Dissenters and Catholics, since they comprised a majority of the United Empire, should be freed from the burden of religious establishments. The motion, however, gained a small minority of only 18 votes.[20] Following the overwhelming defeat of disestablishment, Lord Stanley's counter-motion, that the surplus revenues be used solely for the benefit of the Established Church, gained the support of both Whigs and Tories, and together they triumphed over the combined strength of Dissenters, Radicals, and Irish Catholics. After thus securing the revenues of the Irish Church, the Whigs were able to carry their bill effecting a beneficial reform of the Irish Church.

Since the Irish question had prevented the redress of Dissenters' grievances during the first session of the reformed Parliament, the Whig Ministers hastened to defend their conduct.[21] In a political pamphlet, *The Reformed Ministry and Parliament,* they tried to placate the hostility of the Dissenters by promising to redress their grievances in the ensuing session.[22]

In preparation for a new session of Parliament, the United Committee began another agitation for religious liberty. The Committee formed associations in principal towns, held public meetings, and sent petitions to Parliament.[23] In March 1834 the delegates from these associations, representing several thousand chapels, met at Manchester and demanded the disestablishment of the Church and the exclusion of bishops from the House of Lords.[24] The Whig Ministers, however, did not countenance disestablishment. When a delegation of Dissenters from Nottingham, in an interview with Lord Grey, boldly demanded the separation of church and state, he rebuked them for their extreme demand and frankly declared that his Ministry, though willing to remove religious penalties, would do nothing to hinder the Established Church.[25]

Opposed to disestablishment, the Whig Ministers tried to redeem their election pledges to the Dissenters by admitting them to the universities. Lord Grey fired the opening shot in this battle when he presented a petition from Cambridge University favoring the admission of Dissenters. This Whig petition, which had been signed by 63 persons, caused a lengthy debate in the House of Lords. Not to be outdone by the Whigs, the Tories whipped up counterpetitions at both universities. After debating these petitions for three days in the House of Commons, the Whigs passed a bill to admit the Dissenters to the universities. The House of Lords, however, rejected it, only 2 bishops voting to admit the Dissenters and 22 voting to exclude them.[26]

The Whigs then undertook the reform of the marriage laws. When Lord John Russell introduced his bill "for the relief of persons dissenting from the Church of England in regard to the celebration of marriages," he recognized the Dissenters' view that marriage "should be entirely a civil contract with liberty to the parties afterward to celebrate such religious ceremonies as were most agreeable to their feelings." But he could not accept a view that was "so repugnant to the feelings of the country." [27] When Russell, therefore, brought in a bill designed more to please the Anglican clergy than to relieve the Dissenters, the latter protested so angrily that the Whigs had to give up their bill without a second reading.

In the session of 1834 the Whig Ministers likewise failed to produce a satisfactory bill on church rates. Lord Althorp proposed "that church rates be entirely abolished and that in lieu of them the sum of £250,000 should be an annual charge on the land tax." [28] Though intended as relief for Dissenters this proposal only goaded them into stronger opposition. Wilks, Harvey, and Baines denounced the Whig measure; in this outcry they were joined by the Radicals Gisborne, Hume, and others. When the Dissenters objected to paying church rates, not as a burden, but on principle, Lord Althorp decided not to proceed with his bill.

During the second session of the reformed Parliament the Whig party foundered on the Irish question. The disruption of the Ministry, which occurred during the debates on the Irish Tithe Bill, was caused by Russell's declaration "that the revenues of the Church of Ireland were larger than necessary for the religious and moral instruction of persons belonging to that Church. . . ." [29] At this point in the speech Lord Stanley passed a note to Graham, "John Russell has upset the coach. We cannot go on after his declaration that 'if a nation ever had a right to complain of a grievance, it is the people of Ireland of the Church of Ireland.' " [30] Inasmuch as Russell had dared to appropriate the revenues of the Anglican Church in Ireland, Stanley, Graham, Richmond, and Ripon announced their resignation from the Government. The divisions within the Cabinet over this question eventually led Lord Grey to resign and gave Lord Melbourne an opportunity to form a government.

When the King appointed Melbourne, he advised him to base his Government upon the principle of "firmly maintaining the civil and religious establishments. . . ."[31] During Melbourne's brief ministry he devoted his attention chiefly to the vexatious problem of Dissenters' marriages. If he could not find a solution to satisfy the Dissenters, he thought that he might devise a plan to win the support of the Wesleyan Methodists. But he had no opportunity to mature his scheme. When Lord Althorp went to the House of Lords, the King objected to Russell as leader of the House of Commons and requested Peel to form a government.[32]

Sir Robert Peel at once turned his attention to the problems of reforming the Church and redressing religious grievances. He wished to reform the Established Church by abolishing sinecures and pluralities.[33] But the Anglican clergy prevented him from redistributing the income of the Church.[34] Peel then attempted to conciliate the Dissenters. In his declaration to the Tamworth electors he not only accepted the Reform Bill but also conceded to the Dissenters the abolition of church rates, admission to the universities, and marriage rites performed by their own ministers.

The Dissenters, however, spurned Peel's hand of conciliation and denounced his concessions as a maneuver to divide them at the forthcoming elections. They called the *Manifesto* a "policy limited to pleasing this party and neutralizing that, propitiating the Church and cajoling the Dissenters. . . ."[35] Shortly after Peel had addressed his Tamworth electors, the Dissenting Deputies published the following resolutions:

> That the declaration of the line of policy intended to be pursued by the administration of Sir Robert Peel, as contained in his address to the electors of Tamworth, is most unsatisfactory to Dissenters, and affords no prospect of the adoption of liberal measures on the part of the Cabinet of which he is the head.
>
> That this deputation cannot but record its total want of reliance on the granting of any effectual relief to Dissenters by a political party which has ever been opposed to affording to that numerous and important body their just and equal rights as subjects of the Realm.[36]

Alerted and guided by the Deputies' resolutions, the Dissenters participated in electing the second reformed Parliament.[37] In London and other cities they enabled the Radicals and the liberal Whigs to retain their hold on the middle classes.[38] The lowest Whig of London defeated the highest Tory by 1,400 votes. At Finsbury the Dissenters and even the quiet Quakers arose with "frantic passion" against the Tories.[39]

Churchmen, meanwhile, campaigned for the Tories with a vigor that brought success. In several contests the old cry of "Church in danger" drove the Tories to the polls in sufficient numbers to turn defeat into victory.[40] By carrying the counties the Tories increased their strength from 150 members to 270 in the second reformed Parliament.[41] The Whigs estimated their own numbers as a majority of 25 to 40.[42]

Shortly after the elections of 1835 Peel introduced a bill making marriage a civil contract for Dissenters without changing the ceremony for Churchmen. When the Dissenters objected to this proposal because it carried the stigma of a second-class citizenship, Peel could proceed no further with the reform of the Marriage Laws.[43] Peel not merely failed to satisfy the Dissenters, but he also failed to satisfy the Irish Catholics with his bill to commute the Irish tithes. When he made the Irish tithes a stand-or-fall question, the Whigs forced him to resign.[44] Thus Peel was driven from office after having devoted himself unsuccessfully to such religious questions as Irish and English tithes, the reform of the English Church, and Dissenters' marriages.[45]

Lord Melbourne then formed a second ministry on principles hardly less conservative than Peel's. He flatly rejected Durham, Brougham, and O'Connell, but he could not do without Russell as leader in the House of Commons.[46]

Lord John Russell at once promised the Protestant Society that he would introduce a marriage bill more to their liking, but he requested at the same time that they postpone the agitation for the redress of grievances until he had reformed the municipal corporations.[47] Knowing that most Dissenters desired the abolition of the old municipal corporations, Wilks replied to Lord John that he had no doubt that they would "wait patiently" for the removal of church rates.[48] Outside Parliament the Dissenters, following Wilks' advice, linked municipal reform with the redress of religious grievances, even giving preference to the former over the latter. They presented petitions to the House of Commons praying for the reform of municipal corporations as well as for the abolition of church rates, admission to the universities, and civil registration of births, deaths, and marriages.[49]

The municipal corporations had long been a source of political rivalry and religious bitterness in cities where Dissenters were numerically strongest. The Corporation Act, which had originated in the seventeenth century, destroyed their political influence in the towns. Even though annual Indemnity Acts after 1760 eliminated the penalties of nonconformity, political partisanship and social status combined to exclude most Dissenters from municipal government.[50] The authority of local government in many of its functions, moreover, was lodged in close corporations whose members were either appointed by cooptation or elected by a small number of freemen who sold their votes like produce. Whether elected or appointed, the corporations were the citadels of nepotism. Almost exclusively Anglican in religion and Tory in politics, except in a few towns such as Nottingham, London, and Bristol, the corporations perpetuated the bigotry and injustice which poisoned the social life of many communities.

When Lord John Russell introduced the municipal reform bill in 1835 he explained it as follows: "The measure we propose . . . is in strict accordance with the spirit of the Reform Act. It is a measure in strict conformity with the declaration . . . that our municipal corporations ought to be subject to vigilant, popular control." [51] During the debates on the municipal reform bill the Dissenters stood with the Radicals for a broader suffrage than the Whigs had provided. Pulling hard in the opposite direction, the Tories struggled to delete the democratic aspects of the municipal reform bill.[52]

In spite of Tory opposition, the Municipal Corporation Act of 1835 provided a uniform constitution for 178 towns and created elected bodies as the source of municipal authority. The Act enabled the Dissenters for the first time to participate freely in city government and they, therefore, rejoiced in it as "the greatest advance yet made toward a practical recognition of the principle of religious equality." [53] While they were celebrating what they esteemed to be a victory for religious liberty, the Dissenters did not permit the Whigs to forget their promises to redress religious grievances. The United Committee called on Lord Melbourne to warn him of the "dire consequences of the Dissenters' wrath at the next general election" if the Whigs failed to remove religious disabilities.[54] Although the Dissenting Deputies expressed confidence in the Whigs, they nevertheless urged their congregations to continue petitioning for the redress of grievances.[55]

In 1836 Lord John Russell introduced two bills which the Dissenters were demanding, one providing a national civil registration of births, marriages, and deaths, and the other amending the Marriage Act of 1754.[56] The Tories, to win favor with the Anglican clergy, attempted to amend both bills to the advantage of the Established Church.

Henry Goulburn and Sir Robert Inglis, speaking for the Anglican clergy, led the fight in the House of Commons against the civil registration of births, marriages, and deaths. Goulburn frankly acknowledged that his object was to protect the religious advantages of the Establishment.[57] When the registration bill reached its third reading, he moved an amendment to prevent the naming of infants before baptism. In effect, his amendment would have forced the religiously indifferent masses into the Church for baptism. Sir Robert Inglis further proposed that every congregation should maintain a separate register. This amendment, in effect, would have benefited the Church, which already had registers, and would have greatly burdened the Dissenters, many of whom had no registers and some of whom did not practice infant baptism. The Dissenters, with the aid of the Radicals, opposed and defeated both Tory amendments to the civil registration bill.

The Tories, notwithstanding their defeat on registration, sought to amend the marriage bill in order to increase the authority of the Church. Goulburn would have achieved this by imposing on all non-Anglicans another religious test: "I do solemnly declare that I have conscientious scruples against the solemnization of marriage according to the rites and ceremonies of the Church of England." If he had been successful in this move, he would have forced the indifferent masses of people into the Church for marriage. Successfully opposing this amendment, Stephen Lushington and Edward Baines insisted that the Dissenters would prefer the old law to one imposing a new religious test. After the bill had passed the House of Commons, the Tories in the Upper House amended it to stigmatize the Dissenters, compelling them to have their marriages announced before the Guardians of the Poor. Although the Dissenters wished to fight on against this humiliating amendment, they yielded reluctantly on Russell's advice that they could obtain nothing better from the House of Lords.[58]

The Dissenters celebrated the passage of the Marriage Act of 1836, despite its defects, as a victory for religious liberty. After the adjournment of Parliament, the General Body of Dissenting Ministers hailed the new law as evidence of the "increasing energy and zeal of the friends of religious liberty."[59] Many Evangelical Dissenters, however, were not happy over the loss of religious registers; they felt that some Dissenters had sponsored civil registration and marriage as a means of weakening the Established Church rather than as a measure for strengthening religion.[60]

On the question of admitting Dissenters to the universities, the Whigs were willing to concede only a charter to University College. After obtaining the charter, the Dissenting Deputies again visited Russell to demand admission to the older universities, but Lord Melbourne refused further concession.[61] Consequently, the Dissenters were required to wait many years before they gained admission to the national universities.

The Dissenters did not oppose the English Tithe Act of 1836, which greatly benefited the Anglican clergy. But they did object to and defeat Russell's proposal that church rates be paid from the national purse. Moreover, they showed little forbearance of the Whigs' English Church reform which equalized the income of the bishops and created the new dioceses of Manchester and Ripon. They labeled the bill a bishop's bill and attacked it at many points. They especially resented the creation of the new dioceses, for they considered this an invasion of their own strongholds. John Bowring, opposing the new sees, expressed the sentiment of many Dissenters when he said that "rich and gorgeous establishments were unlikely to advance the great interest of truth and Christianity. . . . From his cradle he had been taught to believe that not worldly pomp and power . . . but the quiet unostentatious exercise of clerical duty was most acceptable." [62]

Although defeated in Parliament on the question of church reform, the Dissenters began in 1836 a new agitation against the payment of church rates. To carry on this movement they organized the Church Rates Abolition Society. The new Society began when a group of leaders, including Radical and Dissenting Members of Parliament, constituted themselves a provisional committee and issued *An Address* to the Dissenting chapels, recommending the formation of a new national society. Responding to the *Address*, the chapels elected delegates who established the new Society on a permanent basis.[63]

Early in 1837 more than 400 delegates of the Church Rates Abolition Society came to London for the opening of Parliament. They conferred with the Whig Ministers and scrutinized the voting of Whig Members in the House of Commons. During this new agitation against church rates the Dissenters sent 2,328 petitions to Parliament bearing thousands of signatures. Their noisy campaign had the desired effect upon Lord Melbourne, and he consented to a new church rates bill in order to quiet "much unseemly discord and contention." [64]

The Whigs proposed in 1837, in lieu of church rates, to raise an equal amount of revenue, £250,000 annually, from the better management of church lands and from additional pew rents. As the Whigs had anticipated, this bill won the full approval of the Dissenters; but the Church Tories, refusing to debate so extreme a proposition, chose to argue the general question of religious establishments. After debating the question of religious establishments for three days, the Whigs carried the first reading of the church rates bill by a vote of 273 ayes to 250 noes.[65]

The bishops, however, who became alarmed by these events, denounced the church rates bill in the House of Lords as "a spoliation of church property." The Archbishop of Canterbury, in particular, woefully declared that its effect "would be to make the dignitaries of the Church . . . mere annuitants, to deprive them of all the influence and advantages which were annexed to the possession of land. . . ." [66] Insisting that the plan violated Lord Melbourne's promise to oppose hostile legislation, the bishops refused to serve on the Ecclesiastical Commission. Their stand achieved its purpose. When the church rates bill came to its second reading in the House of Commons, the majority favoring it dwindled from 23 to 5. The Whig Ministers, consequently, decided not to proceed with a bill that had stirred up so much religious animosity.

The general election of 1837, which came at the death of the King, contested the relative strength of Church and Dissent in many constituencies.[67]

Soon after the King's death, the United Committee issued an *Address . . . to the Protestant Dissenters* calling them to the polls in order to counteract the influence of the Lay Union for the Defense of the Established Church.[68] The *Eclectic Review, The Patriot,* and other Dissenting periodicals urged their readers to pledge candidates to redress religious grievances and to exclude the bishops from the House of Lords. In several northern constituencies the Dissenters manifested their preference for Radicals such as Joseph Hume to Whigs such as Lord John Russell. At Leeds they voted for Edward Baines and Sir William Molesworth, who had campaigned on the platform of full religious liberty, repeal of the Corn Laws, and retention of the new Poor Law.[69] At Sheffield they returned H. G. Ward, whose name was synonymous with the appropriation of the surplus revenues of the Church. During the election of 1837, the union of Radicals and Dissenters on a platform of the ballot, triennial Parliaments, and the exclusion of bishops was strong enough to win several important constituencies.[70]

In 1837 the Whigs openly forsook the role of reformers to become the conservative defenders of Church, Crown, and Parliament. They made the most of the young Queen's popularity. Even Lord Durham gave a conservative confession of faith in upholding the Queen, Church, and Lords. In a declaration to the electors of Stroud Lord John Russell said: "I must declare to you freely and frankly that I see no sufficient cause for altering the ancient constitution of this country . . . and by that constitution I for one am prepared to abide." [71]

The elections of 1837 changed very little the relative strength of Whigs and Tories in the borough constituencies; but in the counties the Tories were everywhere successful. According to Russell's estimate, the elections returned 340 members supporting the Government and 313 in the opposition. As soon as Parliament met, Russell repeated the conservative declaration which he had made to the Stroud electors. Additional reform of Parliament, he said, would be a breach of faith with those Lords—Grey and others—with whom he had acted on the Reform Bill. The Reform Bill was final. The Whig Ministers also abandoned religious reform. After having contended for the appropriation of the surplus revenues of the Irish Church in five sessions of Parliament, they permitted an Irish tithes bill to pass in 1838 without the appropriation clause. At the same time, the Whigs gave up the question of church rates and refused further redress of Dissenters' grievances.

The Dissenters, therefore, had no choice but to turn to the Radicals as the exponents of religious liberty. The election of 1837 seriously weakened the political alliance between the Whigs and the Dissenters, which had dated from the Toleration Act of 1689. Having moved beyond toleration, the Dissenters demanded full religious freedom. This meant the disestablishment of the Episcopal Churches of England and Ireland. To this extreme the Whigs would not go. The Dissenters, consequently, turned from the Whigs, who were led by aristocrats, and undertook the formation of a more liberal party under middle-class leadership.

# 7. *The Radical Reform of Parliament*

The Dissenters and the Benthamite Radicals regarded the Reform Bill of 1832 not as the end, but as the beginning, of Parliamentary reform. They desired a more democratic franchise that they might eliminate the political corruption which was practiced unblushingly by both Whig and Tory leaders.

The Dissenters' tradition of radical political reform went back to the seventeenth century to the *Instrument of Government* and to the Independents in Cromwell's army. Their political ideas were cognates of their religious doctrine of the competence of the individual to know and do the will of God. They not merely believed in democratic principles but they practiced democracy in governing their own congregations. Since every Baptist, Independent, Unitarian, and Quaker meetinghouse was a school of democracy, it is here that one must look for the origins of modern radical and democratic ideas.[1]

Jeremy Bentham gave to the Dissenters a rational basis for their beliefs in democracy. Not a Dissenter by religious conviction, Bentham was second only to Joseph Priestley as an opponent of religious establishments. His profound antagonism against the aristocratic domination of church and state he expressed in a bitter letter to O'Connell: "cold, selfish, priest-ridden, lawyer-ridden, lord-ridden, squire-ridden, soldier-ridden England." [2] At every opportunity he opposed the Established Church and often denounced its National School Society as a "school of perjury." [3]

Bentham's political weapons against the aristocracy were the broad franchise, a secret ballot, and shorter parliaments.[4] As early as 1817 he published his *Plan of Parliamentary Reform . . . Showing the Necessity of Radical, and the Inadequacy of Moderate,*

Notes to this chapter begin on page 192.

*Reform.* During the 1820's he continued to advocate his *Plan of Parliamentary Reform;* "a reform which is not Radical," he wrote to O'Connell in 1828, "is moderate reform, is Whig reform." [5]

The Benthamite Radicals arose to political prominence because they advocated Parliamentary reforms more extreme than those proposed by the Whigs. In 1824 they started the *Westminster Review* as a rival of the *Edinburgh* and the *Quarterly* which they considered to be organs of the aristocracy.[6] The *Westminster Review* also rivaled the Dissenters' *Eclectic Review* in its opposition to religious establishments; and the latter, to meet this competition, began to advocate the ballot as a necessary reform of the representative system.

The Benthamite Radicals had their greatest triumph in the election of 1832. George Grote, a banker and a disciple of Bentham, was returned by London at the head of the poll.[7] Two other successful London candidates, Wood and Waithman, who were Dissenters, stood on the platform of Radical reform.[8] In several neighboring constituencies the successful candidates pledged themselves to the secret ballot and triennial parliaments. At Lambeth Tennyson promised to support household suffrage, vote by ballot, and triennial parliaments.[9] At Westminster the Radicals objected to Sir John Hobhouse, who refused to take the Radical pledge; [10] and early the next year, when he accepted a place in the Whig government, they defeated him and elected De Lacy Evans.

In the northern industrial cities, the candidates, appealing to the newly enfranchised middle-class voters, advocated the thorough reform of both Church and Parliament. At Liverpool the successful candidate, Ewart, and the unsuccessful one, Thornley, pledged themselves to the secret ballot and shorter parliaments.[11] At Manchester Philips and Thomson promised to reform Parliament and redress Dissenters' grievances. At Birmingham Attwood promised "to do his utmost to improve and enlarge the Reform Bill." [12]

As soon as the reformed Parliament met, the Radicals began to reform the Reform Bill. Their leaders, Hume and Roebuck, signifying their desire for further reform, took their seats with the opposition.[13] Early in the session they designated George Grote as sponsor of the motion for the ballot.[14] When he introduced his first motion, he said he did so in order "to eliminate the pressure of the powerful upon the weak, the corruption of the poor by the rich." [15] The Whig Ministers, however, were fully prepared for this democratic motion; and on their behalf Lord Althorp said they could not support the measure because they were bound by "a gentleman's agreement." Those who had worked for the passing of the Reform Bill, he said, had proposed it "as a final measure of reform." [16] With the solid support of the Tories, the Whig Ministers easily defeated Grote's motion for a secret ballot.

Notwithstanding this defeat, the Radicals sponsored a second measure of Radical reform. Charles Tennyson proposed to shorten the duration of Parliament by repealing the Septennial Act.[17] When debating his proposition, he attacked the Whigs' agreement on the Reform Bill as a final measure and asserted that Parliamentary reform was only half done. In reply to Tennyson Lord Stanley reinforced "the gentleman's agreement." "The Government," he said, "having carried a large and sweeping and extensive reform, were justified in looking upon it as final." [18] On the division which followed Stanley's declaration, the Tories again united with the Whigs to overwhelm the Radicals, Dissenters, and Irish Catholics.

The Radicals, making their third attempt to reform the Reform Bill, moved to broaden the elective franchise. De Lacy Evans, who had recently supplanted Hobhouse, the turncoat Radical, proposed to eliminate the payment of rates as qualifications for voting and thus enfranchise not fewer than 300,000 additional voters.[19] But the leaders of both major parties, continuing their cooperation against the Radicals, refused to make the slightest concession to Parliamentary reform.

During the second session of the first reformed Parliament the Radicals were again overwhelmed by the union of the Whigs and Tories. Tennyson's motion in 1834 to repeal the Septennial Act mustered only 185 ayes to 235 noes; [20] and Grote's motion in 1835 for the ballot gained a minority of only 144 ayes against 317 noes.[21]

Defeated in the reformed parliaments, the Radicals in 1836 devised a new strategy. They initiated three national campaigns to marshal public opinion against the Whigs and compel them to take a more liberal course. Henry Warburton outlined the new strategy in a letter to Grote: "Expression is to be given to public opinion and the Whigs are to be made to feel the force of it in constituencies by keeping them in a constant state of alarm by being ousted by Radical competitors—in Parliament by occasional threats of being voted against by their Radical allies." [22] Pursuing this policy, they instigated three national propaganda organizations. To arouse a national sentiment against the Corn Laws, they organized the Anti-Corn-Law Association.[23] To abolish church rates they initiated the Church Rate Abolition Society.[24] To augment the agitation for the Radical reform of Parliament, they turned to Francis Place and the workingmen of London with whom they had cooperated in abolishing the stamp duty on newspapers.[25]

In 1836 Francis Place and William Lovett, at the suggestion of the London Radicals, organized the London Working Men's Association.[26] Although its members were exclusively working class, the Association depended on the Benthamite Radicals for guidance and financial support.[27] Among its members William Lovett "was the ablest writer and man of business." [28] Lovett's earliest recollections were the religious impressions made upon his mind by his devout Methodist mother, who taught him to attend chapel three times every Sunday. Although Lovett never became a member of the Methodist chapel, he did unite with the Evangelical Bryanite sect.[29] Like other persons of Evangelical upbringing, he had unlimited faith in education; and, like them, he adopted temperance as a means of redeeming the working classes. His religious sympathies and early training led him to favor peaceful agitation and to oppose the use of violence.[30]

After Lovett and Place had organized the London Working Men's Association, they continued to cooperate with Parliamentary Radicals. In February 1837 the two groups came together to honor Thomas Wakley, the Radical member for Finsbury; [31] and in May they met to discuss a tentative bill of Radical reform.[32] At the later meeting they appointed a committee of twelve, six from each group, to write the bill. Early in June the committee of twelve members started to work, but soon the general election occupied the attention of the Radicals and they left the writing of the bill to William Lovett. When finally published, the People's Charter had six points of Parliamentary reform: universal suffrage, voting by secret ballot, the annual election of Parliament, payment of Members, equal electoral districts, and no property qualifications for Members of Parliament.[33]

While the Radicals of London were reviving the agitation for Parliamentary reform, middle-class Radicals in northern cities were reviving the Political Unions. At Liverpool William Ewart appealed to the Dissenters by linking Radical reform with religious liberty. In his Radical tract, *The Reform of the Reform Bill,* he also advocated the removal of the bishops from the House of Lords and the disestablishment of the Church. "The abstract idea of religion existing in the minds of men," he said, "becomes too elevated to endure the union of temporal pomp and political power with the profession of a purely spiritual calling. Nor indeed could there be a more permanent benefit to the Church than the withdrawal of its political power, and the equalization, as far as possible, of the payment of the clergy."

In other cities the Dissenters helped to revive the Political Unions. At Todmorden John Fielden, a rich manufacturer and a benevolent Dissenter, headed the Political Union.[34] At Birmingham Attwood had the financial support of G. F. Muntz and the Church Rates Abolition Society.[35]

During 1837 the London Working Men's Association supplemented the activities of the Political Unions by organizing more than a hundred associations in many parts of the country. Based on Lovett's *Address and Rules,* the local associations sent out missionaries, held mass meetings, and formed classes to study political principles.[36] Among the missionaries were devout men who made Radical reform a religious cause. The ablest missionary, Henry Vincent, a Quaker by conviction, hoped to uplift the working classes through education and moral regeneration. Another missionary, George Binns, favored Radical reform because he believed that Jesus had been the first democrat. In Durham Robert Lowery proclaimed democracy as the "political law of God." [37]

When the missionaries of the London Working Men's Association went into Yorkshire and Lancashire in 1837, they were overwhelmed by the storm raging against the new Poor Law. The severe economic depression had caused such general unemployment that the Poor Law Commissioners, when they went north to build workhouses and cut off outdoor relief, encountered the most virulent hostility.[38]

The Methodists of Yorkshire, who eschewed Radical reform, led the struggle against the new Poor Law. Michael Thomas Sadler's attacks upon Malthus' *Essay on Population* formed the theoretical basis for the movement against this inhumane law. In 1837 Richard Oastler, another Methodist, turning from his crusade against the factory system, took up the cry against the "dismal science" of the political economists and the new system of poor relief which they had instituted. These Methodist agitators of Yorkshire were deeply convinced that the Poor Law violated biblical teaching and Christian charity.[39]

In Lancashire Joseph Rayner Stephens was the principal anti-Poor Law agitator. After having received pious instruction from his father, a Methodist preacher, Stephens dedicated himself at the age of twenty to the Methodist ministry. He spent the early years of his ministry preaching the biblical commandments to feed the hungry, clothe the naked, visit the sick, and house the stranger. Along with his Methodist humanitarianism he preached the Dissenters' doctrine of religious freedom. These views eventually brought him into conflict with the Wesleyan Conference, which expelled him for advocating the separation of church and state.[40] Nevertheless, Stephens continued to preach extreme doctrines. "If all ministers would openly preach an equal Gospel to the rich and the poor," he said, "if the Gospel were thus faithfully, impartially, divinely preached in England for seven days, the end of the seventh day would end social tyranny as it affects the people." [41]

Stephens first preached against the Poor Law in his chapel at Ashton-under-Lyne. Infuriated by a sense of injustice and carried away by strong emotions, he frequently gave utterance to such ranting as this: "If the rights of the people are trampled under foot, then down with the throne, down with the aristocracy, down with the bishops, down with the clergy, burn the Church, down with all rank, all title, and all dignity." [42] Such violent outbursts soon extended his influence beyond his own chapel and community into the ranks of the unemployed and the discontented everywhere.

The popularity of Stephens' anti-Poor Law agitation attracted the attention of Feargus O'Connor, who left London in the summer of 1836, came to Leeds, and identified himself with the rebellion against the Poor Law. O'Connor had already learned the lessons of demagoguery in the Irish school of sedition and insurrection. Elected on O'Connell's "tail" in 1832, he was repudiated by the great Irish leader three years later. He then joined the London Working Men's Association but found it too moderate and moralistic. Before going to Leeds he denounced Lovett as "an old woman" and helped to organize the more violent London Democratic Association. He took with him to Leeds as his lieutenant H. A. Beaumont, a young man of superior birth and wealth but "vehement to the verge of madness." [43] Together they founded *The Northern Star* and soon made it exceedingly popular among the working classes. At Leeds O'Connor found the soil fallow for the seeds of insurrection which he sowed unsparingly.

Neither the anti-Poor Law agitation nor the reform movement of the London Working Men's Association induced the Whigs to undertake further reform. On the contrary, the Government resolved to carry out the new Poor Law in the face of all opposition. When the newly elected Parliament met in November 1837 Lord John Russell reaffirmed "the gentleman's agreement" and declared the Reform Bill "a final measure." The Radicals again failed to carry their reforms; Grote's annual motion for the ballot was defeated decisively—198 ayes to 315 noes.[44]

Outside Parliament, meanwhile, the campaigns for Radical reform and the crusade against the Poor Law grew louder and more menacing. In 1838 the economic depression, having reached its nadir, filled the city with hungry unemployed men, idly roaming the streets and listening to inflammatory harangues. The strong meat of violence, preached by Stephens and O'Connor, satisfied their appetites better than the milk of moral reform proclaimed by Lovett and Attwood.

During the first half of 1838 the campaign for the Charter and the crusade against the Poor Law continued separately. Fearful that his own cause might be lost, Stephens denounced both the Working Men's Association and the Political Unions. Rather than unite with the Chartists he preferred to threaten those who enforced the Poor Laws with declarations such as:

> For children and wife we'll war to the knife,
> He that hath no sword, let him sell his garment and buy one,
> Tyrants, believe and tremble.

This kind of preaching finally led to his arrest at Manchester in December 1838 on the charge of sedition. When questioned by the police, he denied being a Chartist and asserted that all his politics were summed up in two principles—"the justice of God and the comfort of the people." [45]

While Stephens and O'Connor were pouring out their words of violence, the Birmingham Political Union, under Attwood's guidance, carried on its agitation in a lawful manner. The Political Union incorporated its program of reform in the National Petition, which appealed to the depressed among the middle classes as well as among working classes. It demanded the reform of Parliament in order to abolish the Corn Laws and the Poor Law and to amend the money laws.[46] It acknowledged the depressed state of the nation and asked, What is the cause of this condition? "We find none in nature or in Providence," it replied. "Heaven has dealt graciously by the people, but the foolishness of our rulers has made the goodness of God of none effect." [47]

The Birmingham Political Union, with Attwood at the helm, carried its National Petition to the industrial cities of Lancashire and Yorkshire, and gained the signatures of the unemployed and discontented.[48] At Glasgow the Union achieved its greatest triumph. When addressing the great throng of Scottish workingmen, Attwood identified his reform movement as anti-Church and anti-aristocracy. "We have against us," he said, "the whole of the aristocracy, nine tenths of the gentry, and the great body of the clergy, and all the pensioners, sinecurists, and bloodsuckers that feed on the vitals of the people." [49]

At Glasgow the Birmingham Political Union joined forces with the London Working Men's Association, and together they presented the People's Charter along with the National Petition. They also planned a convention of the working classes in order to adopt the National Petition and the People's Charter.

In August 1838 the General Convention of the working classes assembled at Birmingham.[50] A great crowd of discontented people, which was estimated at 200,000, listened to Attwood and Lovett uphold political reform as a means of getting jobs and bread. After adopting the National Petition the delegates resolved to hold another convention in London and to present the Petition to Parliament. The working classes, however, did not follow the peaceful course proposed by Attwood and Lovett, for the anti-Poor Law agitators, led by O'Connor, moved into the Birmingham Convention and adopted the Charter and the National Petition as their own. By speaking of "fleshing the sword to the hilt," O'Connor became the hero of the working classes.[51] In the great contest for the leadership of the working classes Attwood was no match for the Irishman.

During the winter of 1838 Chartism reached the pinnacle of its popularity. O'Connor went everywhere threatening the violent overthrow of established institutions. "This, in proportion as it excited the people," Francis Place said, "made their leaders crazy and they committed wonderfully foolish extravagances." [52]

The talk of revolution quickly alienated the respectable middle classes and deprived them of the reform movement which they had initiated and carried on. In Parliament the Benthamite Radicals repudiated the Charter.[53] O'Connell denounced O'Connor with unqualified invective; and Sharman Crawford, the persistent friend of reform, rebuked Beaumont for his incendiary language. For the same reason Place and Roebuck withdrew their support from the Charter.

The withdrawal of the Radicals, however, did not put an end to Chartism. At the opening of Parliament in February 1839 the National Convention came to London to collect signatures and to present the National Petition. Discord and resentment prevailed from the beginning. The members could agree long enough to elect Lovett secretary, but they fell into a controversy over who should be doorkeeper. Unable to elect a permanent chairman, they appointed a different presiding officer each day. O'Connor's physical-force followers dominated the meetings with their bluster. "Love of talk," said Lovett, "was the bane of the convention." [54] As the irresponsible talk went on, the reputation of the Convention fell lower and lower. Attwood's party, representing the Political Unions, resigned, and the Christian Chartists also gave up their seats.[55] Eventually the National Convention, having obtained a sufficient number of signatures, adjourned to the more congenial atmosphere of Birmingham and began contemplating "ulterior measures" if Parliament refused to act on their Petition.

On June 14, 1839, Thomas Attwood finally presented the National Petition in the House of Commons.[56] When doing so, he made a passionate plea for the workingmen who had signed it but denounced the violence of those who had advocated it. Another month passed, however, before the House of Commons would consent to debate the question of Parliamentary reform. On July 11 Attwood was allowed to introduce a motion to consider the National Petition. In the debate on this motion, Fielden, Hume, Warburton, and O'Connell urged further reform. Opposing Attwood's motion, Lord John Russell reminded the House that the Chartist leaders were "going through the countryside, from town to town . . . exhorting people in the most violent and revolutionary language . . . to subvert the laws by force of arms." [57] Russell concluded, therefore, that further consideration of the Petition would cause alarm among all classes. In the division that followed only 46 Members voted to consider the Petition, while 246 voted against it. In the minority were the Irish Catholics, the Radicals, and the Dissenters.

After Parliament's summary rejection of the National Petition a rump National Convention, having reconvened in Birmingham, openly advocated such "ulterior measures" as a general strike, a run on the banks, and a resort to arms to defend their constitutional privileges. Even these physical-force measures, all of which the Convention failed to execute, were too timid for Julian Harney, who wanted nothing less than a reign of terror.[58] His loud and loose talk, without frightening the Government, made the Chartists easy targets for the police and assured their speedy conviction on charges of sedition.

The Whig Government's suppression of Chartists was thorough and indiscriminate. The police and the courts made little distinction between those who had used only peaceful methods of persuasion and those who had incited mob violence. Henry Vincent, the temperance crusader, for instance, was arrested in Monmouth and sentenced to a year in prison. The Birmingham Sunday-school teacher, Collins, and the peaceful leader of the Working Men's Association, Lovett, were incarcerated at Warwick. Twenty or more members of the Convention were arrested and sent to prison. The most severe treatment fell on the leaders of the Newport uprising. The Chartists responsible for this outburst, Frost, Williams, and Jones, were sentenced to hang but this was later commuted to a life of exile.[59] Altogether 443 persons were imprisoned for Chartism.[60]

By the summer of 1840 the physical-force phase of Chartism had come to an end, for the Chartist leaders were in prison. Eventually the Government caught up with O'Connor, who had studiously avoided arrest, and imprisoned him.[61] At last the loud mouths were shut and the threats of violence silenced.

With the river of discontent dammed up, the stream of political reform began to flow again. The Dissenters and Radicals eagerly wished to regain the principles of Parliamentary reform which had been so badly damaged by the advocates of physical force. Although both groups were now fully occupied with their campaign against the Corn Laws, there were many among them who believed that the Corn Laws would never be abolished by an aristocratic Parliament. Moreover, among the working classes there were devout men who wished to redeem the people from their sins of sloth, ignorance, and drunkenness. Several reform movements for education, temperance, and feminism began to parade with the Charter as their banner. This new period of moral-force Chartism, which was something quite different from physical-force Chartism, culminated in the complete suffrage movement.

# 8. *Christian Chartists and Complete Suffrage*

Moral-force Chartism revived in Scotland even while the Whig Government was taking the strongest measures to suppress the movement in England. Seventy Chartist delegates representing fifty different places met in August 1839 at the Universalist Chapel of Glasgow to protest against the harsh treatment of the Chartists. Acknowledging that prosecution had been the result of "the injudicious conduct" of some of the Chartists, they resolved to devise "a system of enlightened organization . . . to promote sound and constitutional agitation. . . ." [1] To this end, they addressed *An Appeal to the People of Scotland* in which they asserted the moral and religious character of political reform: "The great question of national liberty is the people's Charter. . . . The cause of liberty is the cause of mankind and of God." Finally, they recommended the use of moral force only: "Let peace, order, and union be your watchword, and the day of our emancipation will soon be proclaimed amongst men, and registered in heaven." [2]

To launch the new movement for Radical reform, the Christian Chartists formed the Universal Suffrage Central Committee and delegated to it the responsibility of leading the crusade. They instructed the Central Committee to employ "political missionaries not to incite to insurrection" but to "disseminate through he medium of small tracts a complete body of sound political information . . . which we inherit from our Creator." In order to dissociate themselves from the physical-force Chartists, they took as their slogan the cry of the old reformers for "full, fair, and free representation." They plainly denounced O'Connor's tactics, refusing to indulge in "vituperation or mean abuse . . . or immoral anecdote." [3] Furthermore, they expressed their desire "to

Notes to this chapter begin on page 196.

breathe into the present agitation principles of brotherly love, union, justice, liberality, and freedom." [4]

The Christian Chartists, who were thorough Dissenters in their religious views, advocated voluntary education, abolition of slavery, and the disestablishment of state churches. "There is no tyranny," said one writer for the *Chartist Circular,* "so paralyzing to the public mind as the despotism of priestcraft." [5] Another writer denounced the Anglican clergy as "a time-serving sycophantic class," guilty of "selfishness, illiberality, and duplicity." Still another asked, "In the name of all that folly ever worshipped . . . what is the good of a Bishop? What does the animal ever do? What charities does it nurture?" [6] Inasmuch as the Scottish Chartists had fully identified themselves as Dissenters, they sanguinely expected approval and financial help from the Dissenting chapels; and with this in mind, they sent *An Address to the United Secession Synod* with the plea, "Come forward, then, Reverend Sirs, and unite with us in the labor of universal love; and may our Heavenly Father, to whom we are all responsible, direct and bless our concentrated efforts. . . ." [7]

When Dissenting Ministers did not respond to their plea, the Scottish Chartists boldly resolved to establish their own chapels. The Central Committee issued the following instructions: "It may be a private house, a school, or a public hall rented by an association for public meetings, education, and religious worship; and every Sabbath day the Gospel should be preached in it by a religious, honest missionary chosen by the Chartists." According to the instructions, schools were to be connected with the churches and the preacher was to be primarily a teacher "to elucidate all the principles of the Charter." To aid the indoctrination of young Chartists the Committee supplied a *Catechism* of political principles.

During the fall of 1840 the Central Committee had so much success in establishing schools and churches that it claimed at the end of the year that the Chartists "have now planted their humble places of Christian worship in almost every corner of the land." Their progress was sufficiently great to arouse the hostility of the older chapels, which denounced them as infidels. The Chartists, of course, denied the charges. "Our enemies know well that we are not infidels; they know also that we are sincere Christians, worshipping God like the primitive believers, in our humble churches without paid priests. . . ." [8] The opposition of the chapels, however, proved effective, for during the next year the Central Committee abandoned the project of establishing Chartist churches.

Meanwhile, Christian Chartism spread from Scotland to the industrial sections of northern England and found some acceptance among the working-class members of Baptist and Methodist chapels.[9] At Birmingham Arthur O'Neil and John Collins established a Chartist Church. At Leeds J. B. Smith formed Sunday schools and supplied them with Chartist lessons.[10] William Hill, editor of *The Northern Star,* prepared a Christian Chartist creed to be taught in Chartist schools and a list of nonsectarian hymns to be sung.[11] In the Midlands the Chartists, especially among the miners, held prayer meetings and sang Chartist hymns.[12] Christian Chartism, however, like other phases of moral-force Chartism, was denounced by O'Connor and ultimately brought to an end by his opposition.[13]

William Lovett and John Collins, on the other hand, tried to encourage Christian Chartism. While in prison at Warwick they proposed a new moral-force program in their pamphlet, *Chartism, a New Organization of the People: Embracing a Plan for the Education and Improvement of the People Politically and Socially.* In the preface to this work the authors repented of the conduct that had brought them to prison and expressed their confidence "that no other means are likely to be so effective as a peaceful combination of the millions, founding their hopes on the might and influence of intellectual and moral progress." [14] In detail they explained the "Plan, Rules, and Regulations" for the establishment of a National Association of the United Kingdom for Promoting the Political and Social Improvement of the People. They further proposed "the appointment of missionaries, the printing of tracts, the establishment of circulating libraries, the erection of public halls and schools for the education of the people in physical, mental, moral, and political science, and the establishment of normal schools for the training of teachers of both sexes." [15]

Lovett and Collins were greatly optimistic about the success of educational Chartism, for they assumed that a million persons who had signed the National Petition would subscribe funds to support the National Association. But the working classes, as Francis Place had expected, failed to support the project. Subscriptions came chiefly from the Parliamentary Radicals, Hume, Easthope, Wood, Grote, and from other middle-class sympathizers. Eventually the National Association opened one hall in London and obtained

William J. Fox as lecturer. Even with Fox's help, the National Association had so little success that Lovett lost faith in the workingman's ability to bring about his own moral improvement.[16]

Teetotalism, another phase of Christian Chartism, was more successful than Lovett's educational Chartism. Henry Vincent was the devoted exponent of this cause. Upon his release from prison, he began to organize temperance unions. As the preacher of the Chartist Church at Bath he proclaimed this panacea; and as an itinerant preacher he traveled extensively lecturing on temperance, obtaining teetotal pledges, and organizing public libraries and lecture rooms.[17] The enthusiastic response to his oratory led him to believe that "The formation of Chartist Teetotal Societies will be one of the most powerful means of advancing the cause of liberty."[18]

As a consequence of the peaceful methods and the moral attitudes of the Christian Chartists, several middle-class leaders attempted to recover the principles of Radical reform and to reconcile the working classes with the middle classes. The reconciliation of the two classes meant especially the cooperation of the Chartists with the Anti-Corn-Law League.

The first attempt to reconcile the two classes occurred at Leeds where political parties were most bitterly divided. The younger Edward Baines at first opposed this because O'Connor's Chartists continued to make life miserable for all political leaders. In spite of these difficulties John Marshall, the philanthropist, tried to foster more friendly relations between the two classes. With the help of Hamer Stansfield, Marshall organized the Leeds Complete Suffrage Association, which included both Chartists and free traders.[19] The platform of the new Association consisted of the repeal of the Corn Laws, complete suffrage, and the expansion of elementary education.[20]

In January 1841 the representatives of the two classes came together at Leeds for the first time. The Parliamentary Radicals, Hume, Strickland, and Crawford, represented the middle classes; and the Christian Chartists, Lowery and O'Neil, represented the working classes. The meeting, however, failed to reconcile the two classes, for the O'Connor ruffians were on hand to shout down the middle-class Radicals.[21]

Despite O'Connor's physical-force tactics the Christian Chartists began to work zealously for a union of the classes. In a plea for unity, Collins and O'Neil declared that the time had come for employer and employee to meet together to consult on matters of common interest, for "every day and every hour the commercial prospects become more gloomy . . . universal bankruptcy is inevitable. . . . There is no hope but in a union of the oppressed classes to secure for themselves virtual instead of nominal representation." [22]

Although the Leeds experiment was discouraging, the cause of reconciliation found a new advocate in Edward Miall and his militant Dissenting journal, the *Nonconformist.* From the beginning of the *Nonconformist,* Miall honored Lovett, Collins, and Vincent in its columns. He emphasized what he considered the main point of the Charter—the extension of suffrage—and by this he endeavored to unite the middle and lower classes. After the Conservative victory of 1841, he was convinced that the union of the lower classes was necessary to repeal the Corn Laws and remove religious disabilities.

Miall furthered the cause of reconciliation when he obtained the assistance of Joseph Sturge, the Quaker philanthropist and an antislavery advocate, who was esteemed by both the middle and the working classes of Birmingham. Sturge began the complete suffrage movement when he published, during the fall of 1841, a series of articles entitled "Reconciliation between the Middle and Working Classes."

Born in 1793 near Bristol, Sturge spent his childhood and received his elementary education in that vital center of Quakerism. At the age of twenty-one he became the apprentice of a Quaker merchant, and after spending eight years learning that trade, he moved to Birmingham and established his own enterprise.

Sturge freely participated in the political and religious activities of the middle classes at Birmingham.[23] He shared in the work of the Bible Society, the Peace Society, and other Evangelical organizations. The questions of slavery and religious liberty brought him and other Quakers into the arena of political combat. As early as 1824 the Society of Friends had taken their stand for religious liberty by refusing to pay church rates; and in keeping this Quaker testimony Sturge had lost property on several occasions.[24]

The "white slaves" in the factories of England, as well as the black slaves of the West Indies, aroused Sturge's sympathy, and he labored untiringly to improve their lot. Owing to his benevolent labors on behalf of the working classes, the Chartists addressed a letter to him in the Birmingham *Journal* on September 15, 1838, challenging him to become the "professed and fearless advocate of English freedom."[25] At first Sturge refused to take up the working-class challenge, for he believed the repeal of the Corn Laws would bring quicker relief to hungry people. But the persistent opposition to free trade in Parliament eventually convinced him that only a thoroughly reformed House of Commons would repeal the Corn Laws.[26] After reaching this conviction, he began to work for a union of Chartists and free traders. He first clearly defined his principles of reconciliation in the pages of the *Nonconformist,* and then he persuaded members of the Anti-Corn-Law League to declare themselves in favor of Radical reform.

In November 1841 Sturge took another step in mediation between the League and the Chartists. After the free-trade delegates had finished the League's business, he invited them to consider the Radical reform of the representative system. The Radicals and other members of the League who participated in the discussion agreed to endorse the agitation for complete suffrage, provided the new movement be conducted separately from free trade. At the same time they authorized Sharman Crawford to cooperate with Sturge in drawing up a *Declaration* favoring Radical reform. In keeping with the League's instructions, Sturge and Crawford drew up a *Declaration* recommending "fair, full, and free exercise of the elective franchise" and introduced it at subsequent Anti-Corn Law conferences in London and Edinburgh.[27] Moreover, Sturge addressed a *Memorial* to the Queen, requesting her favor upon "full, fair, and free representation of the people in the House of Commons," and circulated it among the members of the London Working Men's Association. Soon thereafter members of the Association, Lovett, Hetherington, and Parry, met with members of the League, Sturge, Crawford, Miall, Spencer, and Thompson, to consider a joint program for the extension of suffrage.[28]

The first Complete Suffrage Union, consisting of the signers of the *Declaration,* was organized in Birmingham. The Birmingham Union, serving as a provisional committee, then organized more than fifty Complete Suffrage Unions. The committee carried on correspondence with the friends of Radical reform in all parts of the nation and obtained complete suffrage pledges from 16,000 persons. Encouraged by this response, the Birmingham Union then proposed a National Conference of delegates representing all Complete Suffrage Unions. The proposed conference was approved by the Council of the League and endorsed by a special conference of more than 200 Dissenting ministers.[29]

In April 1842 more than 100 delegates assembled at Birmingham for the first National Complete Suffrage Conference. Lovett, Vincent, and other Chartists represented the working classes; John Bright, Lawrence Heyworth, and Archibald Prentice represented the middle classes. Fifteen Dissenting ministers were among the delegates. Though the working classes were represented by the Chartists, it was clear that the Complete Suffrage Conference was primarily a middle-class organization.[30]

At the opening of the Birmingham Conference, Chairman Sturge invoked a Christian spirit of peace and good will. After reading a quotation from *The Northern Star* that threatened the use of the sword, Sturge declared his pacifist conviction: "He would not take the life of another to save his own." In behalf of the working class John Collins stood for reform by "Christian and peaceable means." Miall and Vincent, who never tired of making speeches, showed at great length how complete suffrage was based on the Golden Rule.[31]

The declarations of peace and Christianity, however, did not prevent a controversy from arising that sharply divided the two classes. The Chartists insisted that the Charter should be the banner of the National Complete Suffrage Union. Lovett expressed their views when he said, "the name of the Charter has been widely recognized by millions as an epitome of their political rights. They have been persecuted and they have suffered for that name, and I think it would be doing outrage to the feelings of many were we contemptuously to spurn it." [32] Sturge presented the opposing view that "there was a great and almost universal alarm in the minds of the middle class at the name of Chartist on account of improper conduct of some who had borne this name. . . ." [33]

The chasm between the two classes could not be bridged without concessions by both sides. Willing to compromise, John Collins said he cared nothing for the name but only for the principles of the Charter. Though the representatives of the middle classes did not favor all the points of the Charter, they were willing to endorse its principles if they did not have to take its name. Unable to overcome this difficulty, the representatives agreed to hold a second conference to consider further the documents embodying "just principles of representation." [34] Before adjourning, however, they petitioned Parliament for Radical reform.[35]

A few days after the Conference had adjourned, Sharman Crawford presented its petition in the House of Commons and proposed a motion to consider the system of representation.[36] During the debates on the motion Crawford argued that the Reform Act had failed in its purpose, for it had kept power in the hands of the aristocracy and the middle classes.[37] Opposing Crawford's motion, the Conservatives assumed the attitude that complete suffrage was too extreme for serious attention. With the Conservatives and Whigs united against him, Crawford obtained a minority of only 67 Members; even so, this small minority was the best reception given to the Charter in the House of Commons.

To strengthen Radical reform in Parliament, the Complete Suffrage Union sponsored several candidates at the by-elections of 1842, only to be decisively beaten at the polls. Henry Vincent was defeated at Ipswich even though "Nonconformists flocked cheerfully to the standard. . . ." [38] Lord Nugent and George Thompson likewise failed at Southampton though endorsed by both the Union and the League.[39] Sturge also campaigned unsuccessfully at Nottingham for the ballot, complete suffrage, and shorter Parliament.[40]

During the last half of 1842 the National Complete Suffrage Union continued its agitation for Radical reform, sending missionaries on speaking tours in the same fashion in which the League sent out its lecturers. Henry Vincent, the most popular advocate of complete suffrage, entered warmly into the work; and though the physical-force Chartists sneered at him, he remained "firmly attached to that movement." [41] Two Dissenting preachers, Henry Solly and Howard Hinton, also served the Union as missionaries. As a result of the devoted work of these missionaries, the Complete Suffrage Unions greatly increased their membership.[42]

The attempt to reconcile the two classes, like other phases of moral-force Chartism, eventually met with O'Connor's opposition. O'Connor turned his wrath against the first Birmingham Conference early in 1842 and continued to denounce it in the pages of *The Northern Star*. During the summer of 1842 he seized the opportunity to take over the Complete Suffrage Unions by electing his followers to the second Birmingham Conference.[43] In the campaign to elect delegates to the Conference, intense rivalry prevailed between the Sturgites and the O'Connorites.[44] When the delegates arrived in Birmingham in December 1842 it was evident that

O'Connor had succeeded in electing a majority of physical-force Chartists.[45]

At the beginning of the Conference, therefore, Sturge resolved to keep the National Complete Suffrage Union out of O'Connor's hands. Although the Conference had convened to consider the Charter among other documents as the basis of the suffrage movement, Sturge recommended only the middle-class document, "The Bill of Rights."[46] But Lovett and other Chartists could not forsake the Charter; therefore Lovett moved that the Charter be the standard of the Complete Suffrage Unions. When he carried this motion with O'Connor's help, Sturge and his followers withdrew from the Conference. Miall, Crawford, Bright, and two Christian Chartists, Parry and Vincent, led the middle-class delegates from the Conference. As they reluctantly departed, Sturge explained why it was necessary for them to withdraw: "We cannot knowingly sit in union with any who recommend or countenance violence for the attainment of their object; or who, instead of cordially uniting with all honest men to obtain the rights of the people, waste their time in abusing those who do not exactly tread in their steps."[47]

Henceforth the middle- and the working-class delegates sat in separate conferences. But Lovett soon withdrew his followers from a meeting which O'Connor dominated. The working-class conference soon rapidly dwindled from 300 to 37 members and then disbanded, exhausted by O'Connor's long harangues.[48] In a separate meeting the middle-class leaders planned to carry on the campaign for complete suffrage but concluded that it was futile to try to reconcile the Chartists and the League. Thus came to an end what has been deemed "the noblest phase of Chartism."[49]

During the complete suffrage campaign of 1843 the Chartists, Thomas Beggs, Henry Vincent, Patrick Brewster, and John Collins, as well as several Dissenting preachers, served the Union as missionaries.[50] In the by-elections of this year the Complete Suffrage Union cooperated with the Anti-Corn-Law League and supported the same candidates. In the midst of the elections a friendly critic said that Miall was proclaiming a "new trinity" of suffrage, free trade, and religious liberty. The devotees of this "new trinity" elected James Pattison at London, John Bright at Durham, and Thomas Gisborne at Nottingham.[51] Joseph Sturge, however, was repudiated a second time by the electors of Nottingham; and when rejected the following year at Birmingham, he concluded that the time had not come for further reform, and consequently abandoned the agitation for complete suffrage.[52]

Though apparently a failure, the complete suffrage movement broadened the agitation against the Corn Laws by identifying the League with Parliamentary reform. It enabled Cobden and Bright to meet O'Connor on the same platform, where the League won "one of its largest victories." [53] The complete suffrage movement, moreover, enabled the Radicals to regain some of the esteem which they had lost when the anti-Poor Law agitators adopted the principles of the Charter. Finally, the movement improved class relationships. Henry Vincent paid it this tribute: "It brought a better feeling between the middle and working classes, and allayed the fiercer exasperation of the people by proving that men of Christian character were willing to risk popularity with the wealthy and powerful in their desire to serve them." [54]

# 9 *The Beginning of National Education*

The exponents of public education, who had been silent since the failure of Lord Brougham's bill in 1820, found their voices in the first reformed Parliament. On behalf of the Benthamite Radicals, Roebuck introduced in 1833 the following resolution: "That this House . . . will during the next session of Parliament proceed to devise a plan for the universal and national education of the whole people." [1] He justified his motion on grounds of the rapid growth of democracy among the lower classes. "They will have power," he said; "in a very short time they will be paramount. I wish them to be enlightened in order that they may use well the power which they will inevitably obtain." [2] When submitting his plan, Roebuck recognized the problem of control as the greatest obstacle to its adoption; it was "the most delicate point of all," he said, "that on which differences of opinion are most likely to arise, and heats and animosities to have place." He wanted neither Churchmen nor Dissenters to manage the schools. Instead of placing control in the hands of the church vestry, as Lord Brougham had recommended earlier, he proposed that democratically elected committees should manage the local schools and that a national minister of education should supervise the training of teachers.[3]

Only the Radicals, rejoicing in the boldness of their innovation, supported Roebuck's motion. The Whigs and Tories united quickly to overwhelm them. On behalf of the Tories, Sir Robert Peel said he was opposed to any system that trenched upon religious toleration and interfered with religious opinion.[4] Lord Althorp, speaking for the Whig Government, favored continuance of the voluntary system.[5]

In keeping with Lord Althorp's opinion the Whigs adopted a

Notes to this chapter begin on page 199.

policy of supplementing voluntary efforts. Late in the first session of the reformed Parliament Althorp, when requesting supplies, recommended that £20,000 be granted equally to the two societies for building new schools. Designed to avoid debating the question of education, his motion passed a small House of Commons by a vote of 50 to 26; but among the minority were the strongest friends of education, including Churchmen, Radicals, and Dissenters.[6] Sir Robert Inglis said he could not support any plan not based upon the principle of the Established Church. The Radicals opposed the Parliamentary grant as a halfway measure. Expressing the Dissenters' views, Richard Potter wished to postpone the grant until the Government had more efficiently employed the existing endowments.

The Dissenters outside Parliament, nevertheless, at first supported the Whig policy, believing the grant would be divided equally between the two voluntary societies. William Allen, who had previously urged a Parliamentary grant to assist the building of schools, gladly accepted the British Society's share.[7] At its annual meeting in 1834 the British Society expressed its gratitude to the Government for assisting the building of new schoolhouses and ventured to hope "that this will be extended further, and that schools on just and comprehensive principles may soon be open to every child in the British Empire." [8]

The Lords of the Treasury, who had responsibility for administering funds, apportioned the first Parliamentary grant equally between the two societies.[9] But thereafter they showed their solicitude for the Established Church by giving the larger portion to the National Society.[10] Instead of aiding the most needy places, as Lord Althorp had proposed, the Lords acted upon the rule of giving "priority to those applications where, by a small expenditure, they can forward the education of the largest number of scholars." [11] This rule obviously aided those communities most able to help themselves and virtually guaranteed more schools for Churchmen than for Dissenters. Very soon the richer National Society outran its poorer rival; at the end of five years it had received £70,000 while the British Society had received only £30,000.

The method of distributing the grant soon became a subject of acrimonious debate and sharply divided the Whigs and Radicals. Roebuck castigated the Whigs for dividing the grant so unequally between the two voluntary societies.[12] To remove this injustice he proposed a select committee to inquire into the means of establishing a national system, compulsory, tax-supported, and supervised by the state. While the Whigs accepted the motion for an inquiry, they rejected the recommendation for a secular system of education.[13]

In 1835 the Select Committee, headed by Lord Kerry, conducted its inquiry into education and reported its findings. Its returns showed that though the number of schools and scholars had more than doubled since 1818, a grave deficiency still existed. Only one person in eleven received instruction, whereas one in nine came within the school ages of seven to twelve. From this evidence Lord Brougham estimated that 300,000 children of school age lacked means of education.[14]

Spurred on by these revelations, the Dissenters increased their efforts for voluntary education. ". . . So long as there can be found one individual to whom the Bible is from necessity a sealed book," the British Society declared in its annual report, "so long as the progress of the missionary is injured by popular ignorance . . . and religious liberty cherished as the dearest privilege of man, so long it will be necessary to maintain the principles, the operation, and the testimony of the British and Foreign School Society." [15] Although the Dissenters increased their contributions to voluntary education, they did not adequately meet the needs of the growing industrial population.[16]

In 1836 the advocates of comprehensive education, therefore, organized the Manchester Society for Promoting National Education and began to agitate for government aid.[17] The Manchester reformers, Dr. James Kay, Richard Cobden, and others, wished to train all children, aged two to ten, "in morality, against improvidence, intemperance, and the want of cleanliness"; and they wished to provide for them "a life of virtue, usefulness, and honor." [18] The Manchester Society further recommended "education for all, free to all, without money and without price." [19]

In London the advocates of comprehensive education, including members of the British Society, formed the Central Society of Education and chose Thomas Wyse as chairman of its permanent committee.[20] In 1838 Wyse introduced a motion in the House of Commons requesting the Queen "to appoint a board of commissioners of education with the view especially of providing for the equitable, and efficient application of sums granted for the advancement of education. . . ." [21] He also recommended that the allocation of Parliamentary grants be taken from the Lords of the Treasury, who had shown so much preference for the Church, and placed in the hands of a board "composed of fair proportions of the representatives of the different parties and feelings. . . ." [22] With the aid of the Radicals and the Dissenters, Wyse got enough votes for his scheme to encourage Lord John Russell to take a bolder stand on education.

In 1839, when submitting the Government's plans for education, Russell recommended the appointment of a central board, not representing the various religious parties, as Wyse had suggested previously, but appointed by the Crown.[23] To this Committee of the Privy Council he delegated the responsibility of distributing the Parliamentary grant and of inspecting the schools that received it. Finally, he proposed the building of one normal school to train teachers for both voluntary societies.[24] His proposals, however, immediately antagonized the Tories and increased the Church's apprehension. Setting forth the main line of Tory opposition, Sir Robert Peel insisted upon the Church's right to establish its own schools and teach its own catechism.[25] But in spite of opposition, the Whigs proceeded with their plan and appointed the Committee of Privy Council on Education.[26]

The Committee on Education, reverting to the original purpose of Parliament, recommended that government funds be allocated according to the need of the community rather than in proportion to the amount raised locally. It prepared also to establish a normal school open to all religious groups.[27] According to the Committee's plans, Dissenters, Churchmen, and even Roman Catholics would be trained together in nonreligious subjects, leaving each party free to supply its own teachers and select its own version of the Bible.

The plan for a comprehensive normal school again aroused the Established Church to strong opposition.[28] Leading the opposition, Lord Stanley attacked the Committee in the House of Commons; and the Bishop of London denounced it in the House of Lords. "If a system of national religious education were to be based on the principle of giving every different sect the same advantages as were enjoyed by those in connection with the Established Church," the Bishop said, "then the Established Church might as well at once abdicate its functions." [29] He objected strongly to the appointment of Dissenters as chaplains and to the reading of the Roman Catholic version of the Scriptures. Finally, he opposed "any system which was not connected with the Established Church and which by implication was calculated to throw some discredit on the Church or at all events to raise Dissenting sects to a level with it in the estimation of the people." [30]

While the Established Church was denouncing the Whig policy, the Dissenters hastened to defend it. The Dissenting Ministers of the Three Denominations endorsed the new policy on the grounds that "if any portion of public money be granted . . . , it should be used for the advancement of secular education, concerning which all are agreed, and not for education in religion, on which we are so much divided." [31]

On this occasion the Wesleyan Methodists differed with the Dissenters on education. Fearful lest purely secular education should "weaken the sense of obligation on the part of parents to instruct their children and domestics in the religion of the Bible," the Wesleyan Conference resolved in 1837 "to establish and maintain in the larger circuits of the connection schools which shall embrace a purely scriptural and Wesleyan system of education." [32] A year later the Conference formed a United Committee to resist the adoption of a national system and to promote denominational education.[33] In 1839 the Conference objected to the Whig plan for a normal school because it permitted the use of the Roman Catholic version of the Scriptures.[34]

The combined opposition of the Wesleyan Methodists and the Anglican clergy compelled the Whig Ministers, hardly able to keep themselves in office, to abandon their plan for a normal school. But they salvaged other parts of their policy.[35] They retained the Committee on Education and distributed government grants on the basis of need. They also recommended that £10,000 already appropriated for a normal school be given equally to the two voluntary societies for separate normal schools. Their policy of aiding the "very poor and populous districts where subscriptions to a sufficient amount cannot be obtained" placed Dissenters on equality with Churchmen and prepared the way for government aid to Roman Catholics and Wesleyan Methodists.[36]

The Whig recommendations favoring the Dissenters' scheme of education produced a full-scale debate in the House of Commons, from which the Tories made much political capital.[37] Lord Stanley, for example, opposed placing the control of education in a government board so obviously political in character.[38] Lord Ashley denounced the scheme as "hostile to the Constitution, to the Church, and to revealed religion," and accused the Whigs of building up Dissent at the expense of the Church.[39] The debates, long and bitter, revealed how fully education, because of religious controversy, had become an issue of partisan politics.[40]

Alarmed by the debates on education, the Anglican clergy started a campaign against the Committee of Council. Under the direction of Archbishop Howley, the National Society clarified its own position by insisting that "instruction be under the superintendency of the clergy and in conformity with the doctrines of the Church . . . as the recognized teacher of religion."[41] The Archbishop then pushed through the House of Lords a motion recommending to the Queen "that no steps be taken with respect to the establishment or foundation of any plan of education for the general education of the people of this country without giving to this House . . . an opportunity of fully considering a measure of such deep importance to the highest interests of the Community."[42] After the Upper House had passed the resolution by a large majority, the Lords went in a body, led by the Archbishop, to present the request to the Queen. She graciously received them but firmly refused to comply with their request.[43] The Church's opposition, therefore, did not destroy the Committee of Council on Education or prevent it from assuming some of the functions exercised in other countries by the ministers of public instruction.[44]

In August 1839 the Committee of Council appointed as its secretary Dr. James Phillips Kay (later known as Sir James Kay-Shuttleworth), who held the office for ten years and became the moving spirit of the Committee.[45] By training and conviction he was admirably suited for the difficult task of placating the hostility between Churchmen and Dissenters.

James Kay was born in 1804, the son of a Lancashire cotton manufacturer. During his early youth Kay lived in Salford and received a grammar-school education that reinforced his virile Dissenting heritage. At the age of fifteen he went to Rochdale to be an apprentice in the banking business. While thus employed he lived at Bamford and served in a Dissenting chapel, first as a teacher and then as superintendent of a Sunday school. These early religious experiences were the formative influences of his life.[46]

At the age of twenty Kay entered the University of Edinburgh to take up the study of medicine. While engrossed in these studies he was continually nurtured by letters from his pious mother, who kept alive his benevolent impulses and deepened his compassion for the poor. Her letters repeatedly warned him against sloth and arrogance, against the enticement of temporal success, and urged him to dedicate himself more fully to Christian service.[47]

After finishing his course of study, Dr. Kay began to practice medicine in Manchester. This occupation, which he pursued for seven years, gave him many opportunities to observe the deplorable conditions of the factory workers. His desire to ameliorate their sufferings turned him from strictly professional duties to undertake those social and political reforms which struck at the roots of wretchedness.

Unfortunately, his arduous labors broke his health and forced him to leave Manchester. Still seeking to strike at the cause of misery and to heal the afflictions of the poor, he accepted a government appointment as Assistant Poor Law Commissioner for Norfolk and Suffolk. This change in his career, which so astonished his friends, he explained thus: "The purely scientific spirit was even at length overmastered by sympathy. I could not refrain from wishing to be in some degree, however humble, the instrument of a beneficial change." [48] Efficient administration of the Poor Law, sanitation, and education were the measures which he deemed most likely to remove the causes of misery and to effect a beneficial change.

Accompanied by another Assistant Poor Law Commissioner, E. C. Tufnell, Kay toured Scotland in 1837 to study its superior system of schools and to gather information on improved methods. Convinced that education accounted for the better social conditions of the working classes of Scotland, he consecrated himself anew to the task of improving the English system. His enthusiastic reports on education to the Poor Law Commissioners brought him at length to the attention of the Committee of Council, and they appointed him their secretary.

It was ironical that religion should have stood in the way of Kay's devout and benevolent undertaking. The High Church party, particularly, lacked confidence in him; and one of its leaders, in a letter to Lord Lansdowne, tried to discredit him by accusing him of Unitarianism.[49] Although unable to prevent the appointment of Kay as secretary, the Church did succeed in preventing state inspection of its schools. The Committee on Education had resolved to inspect all schools receiving state aid but excluding religious instruction.[50] The Church, however, rejected these principles of inspection. Both the clergy and the managers of the National Society were "decidedly averse" to inspection by a state officer "on grounds not only of expediency, but of principle."[51] The Society also rejected unequivocally the plan providing religious instruction limited to historical facts and general doctrines on which all sects agreed. It would accept nothing less than full religious instruction "in the school as in the sanctuary, in her catechism as in articles and liturgy, perfect and entire, without compromise or mutation, after the Apostolic model."[52] To dramatize its objections to the Whig plan the National Society refused to accept the Parliamentary grant.

The Church's firm opposition, consequently, forced the Whig Government to abandon its plan of state inspection. After a conference with the Archbishop of Canterbury and the Bishop of London, Lord John Russell agreed to their demands that the inspectors of the schools of the National Society send their reports to the bishops as well as to the Committee of Privy Council.[53] In August 1840 an order in Council made the inspectors virtual adjuncts to the parochial system by giving the archbishops power to approve the appointment of inspectors and by requiring the inspectors to report on religious as well as secular teaching. "In cases of schools connected with the National Church," the order read, "the inspectors will inquire with special care how far the doctrines and principles of the Church are instilled into the minds of the children."[54]

The Established Church, furthermore, succeeded in modifying the Committee of Council's policy of allocating Parliamentary grants. Following Russell's concordat with the bishops, the Committee reverted to the old policy, pursued previously by the Lords of the Treasury, of apportioning the grant according to the amount of private contributions. This bit of political favoritism enabled the richer National Society to establish more schools for Churchmen than the British Society could establish for Dissenters.[55] In 1841 the Committee of Council, refusing for one reason or another to act upon the Dissenters' applications for aid, granted only £1,377 to their schools. It was now the Dissenters' turn to refuse to cooperate with the government; of eighty-six schools established by the British Society during the next two years, only one applied to the Committee for government aid.[56]

The virulent controversy over education brought the Dissenters to the polls in 1841, and, as in previous campaigns, they cast their votes for the Whigs and Radicals. "A Tory Dissenter is one of the most anomalous creatures in existence," Thomas Price said, "and is as rare as he is strange and unnatural."[57] But the Dissenters, having become lukewarm toward the Whigs, did not match the political zeal of the Churchmen, whose cry of "Church in danger" brought the Conservatives to the polls in even greater numbers; and as a result the friends of comprehensive education failed to gain re-election.[58]

The Conservative victory in 1841 assured the adoption of an educational policy even more friendly to the Established Church.[59] Sir James Graham, who replaced Russell as Home Secretary, willingly carried out the concordat with the bishops. Closely cooperating with the Church, Graham resolved to increase the aid to education and to enlarge the powers of school inspectors.[60] In a letter to Sir Robert Peel he delineated a policy friendly to the Church: "By judicious measures we may gradually propagate the saving knowledge of Christian truth; we may diffuse the blessing of a Scriptural education; we may render the property of the Church more available for the sacred use of the Church . . . but all of this must be done gently, and from time to time public aid may be obtained."[61]

In February 1843 Sir James Graham explained in Parliament the details of his Factories Education Bill.[62] He planned to establish schools in the urban areas for the training of factory children and to further restrict child labor. "No children under eight," according to his plan, "are allowed to work in a factory; children between the ages of eight and thirteen may work in factories for eight hours a day; but it is a condition of their working that they shall attend school for at least two hours each day."[63] When introducing the bill, Graham frankly recognized the difficulty arising from the religious controversy over education. "This is the real difficulty," he said, "for . . . we agree in this, that religious education is, after all, the only true and safe one—the great Christian principle we admit, but unfortunately we differ as to the mode in which this Christian principle may be safely imparted."

Graham's remedy for "the real difficulty," however, did not allay the suspicions of the Dissenters, for he proposed that the new factory schools should teach religion under the supervision of the Anglican clergy. Moreover, he delegated the management of the schools to seven trustees, of whom one was the resident Anglican clergyman, two were churchwardens appointed by the clergyman, and four were appointed by the magistrate. Finally, he required the schoolmaster to be a member of the Church and his appointment approved by the bishop. "By the education clauses, as they now stand," Graham assured Gladstone, "the Church has ample security that every master in the new schools will be a Churchman, and that the teaching of the Holy Scriptures, as far as the limited exposition may be carried, will necessarily be in conformity with his creed." [64]

The Dissenters did not wait for Sir James Graham to proceed formally with his bill, but they arose at once with loud voices to denounce his measure. Their opposition spread from city to city. They sent thousands of petitions to Parliament—in the largest quantities ever received—urging members to vote against the bill. Their friends in Parliament responded to their pleas and when the bill reached its second reading, they attempted to amend it by separating the factory clauses from the educational clauses. As a representative of the Dissenters at Salford, Joseph Brotherton favored regulating child labor in the factories but opposed placing schools under clerical supervision.[65] Benjamin Hawes objected to Graham's bill because it "placed the people wholly at the mercy of the Church." [66] Mark Philips testified that the great body of Dissenters at Manchester, whom he represented, and a large portion of the Roman Catholics completely rejected the educational clauses.[67] Charles Hindley thought the bill did not sufficiently protect the interests of Dissenters who formed at Ashton under Lyne "a most important portion of society . . . and their schools were more than double those of the Church." [68]

Whig leaders now arose to defend the Dissenters. Led by Sir George Grey, they objected to the appointment of teachers subject to the approval of the bishops, and they advocated a comprehensive system not to interfere with the rights of conscience.[69] Lord John Russell especially opposed the church management of schools in manufacturing districts where a majority of the residents were Dissenters.[70]

The opponents of the Factories Education Bill chose Richard Cobden as the man most likely to cope with Lord Ashley and the factory reformers. Cobden insisted that the Dissenters were already providing efficient education and accused the Church of failing to educate the lower classes.[71]

Throughout the country the Dissenters denounced Graham's Factories Education Bill as the most illiberal measure since Lord Sidmouth's bill of 1812 and as a more odious badge of inferiority than the Test Act. The Dissenting newspaper, *The Patriot,* sounding the alarm of religious liberty, declared that the education bill combined the worst features of a church-extension bill, a test act, and a church rate for the purpose of wresting education out of the hands of Dissenters.[72] Following *The Patriot's* lead, other newspapers took up the hue and cry against Graham's bill.[73] In the *Leeds Mercury* the younger Baines assailed the bill for giving the Church control of education and for interfering with the management of factories.[74] He also expressed the fear that if children under thirteen years worked only four hours a day they would grow up without industrious habits.[75]

At Manchester the Anti-Corn-Law League considered Graham's bill to be a retaliation against manufacturers for having supported the repeal of the Corn Laws.[76] At a mass meeting of eight or ten thousand, who had assembled in Free Trade Hall to renew their vows of religious liberty, Colonel Thompson explained the significance of the bill: "The League had been formed to oppose a tyranny; and that tyranny, as a wise tyranny ought, had moved on them in turn." [77]

Denominational bodies and other national Dissenting groups, which had been organized to defend religious liberty, adopted resolutions against the Factories Education Bill. In March the London Ministers of the Three Denominations sent a deputation to remonstrate with Sir James Graham.[78] In April the Baptist Union declared that this "essentially ecclesiastical exaction" is "utterly inconsistent with the rights of conscience." [79] The Wesleyan Methodists also took action to prevent the Church from gaining control over education.[80] The Congregational Union at its annual meeting deprecated the teaching of the church catechism "in which the doctrine of sacramental religion and salvation is so clearly taught," and demanded complete equality for all Christians to teach their particular doctrines.[81]

The noisy opposition of Methodists and Dissenters finally compelled the Conservative Government to modify its educational policy. When Sir James Graham introduced his amended Factories Education Bill, he acknowledged that the petitions against his previous bill had been "numerous almost without parallel." [82] To mitigate the wrath of the Dissenters Graham made minor concessions to them, but on the critical issue of who should teach there was no compromise, for the appointment of the master was still subject to the veto of the bishops. So long as this provision remained in the bill, the Dissenters would have no part of it.

Throughout the country the opposition to the amended Factories Education Bill waxed stronger than the agitation against the original bill. At the annual meeting of the British and Foreign School Society, Andrew Reed, who made the major address, accused the Established Church of trying to gain control of education in those areas where the Dissenters were in a majority. He further urged the Dissenting preachers to unite with the Anti-Corn-Law League to defend the principle of freedom in both religion and trade: "We ask then that we shall be free; in labor, free; in trade, free; in speech, free; in religion, free: perfectly free." [83]

In response to this and many other eloquent pleas for freedom, the Dissenters sent thousands of petitions to Parliament against Graham's bill; by May 5 they had sent 13,060 petitions bearing 2,000,000 signatures, and by June 15 they had increased this number to 24,000 with 4,000,000 names.[84] Such overwhelming opposition compelled Sir James Graham to give up his measure altogether. He had hoped, he said, that the amendments would obviate the objections urged by the Dissenting body: "I am bound to say that in that hope I have been entirely disappointed; the objections to the measure have not been removed or even mitigated by the modifications and the opposition to my plan continues unabated." [85]

Acknowledging the force of the Dissenters' opposition, Sir Robert Peel wrote to Lord Ashley: "It is but a sorry and lamentable triumph that Dissent has achieved." [86] And the next day Ashley replied: "Let this last trial be taken as sufficient proof that united education is an impossibility. It ought never again be attempted. The Dissenters and the Church have each laid down their limits which they will not pass; and there is no power that can either force, persuade, or delude them." [87]

The Conservatives thus failed to establish a national system of education under Church control, just as the Whigs had previously failed to establish a comprehensive system broad enough to include all religious denominations. The compromise resulting from this impasse was a mixed system whereby the government financed and inspected schools belonging to voluntary societies. This cumbersome and expensive system undoubtedly impeded the progress of general education. That England failed to establish a national system at a time when Prussia and the United States were moving rapidly ahead was in part the consequence of the disorganized state of both major political parties. The Whigs could not satisfy the Dissenters when opposed by the Established Church; and the Conservatives could not please the Church when confronted by the union of hostile Methodists and Dissenters. In addition to education, other great national movements, factory reform and free trade, divided the nation along religious lines. The leaders of Church and Dissent consequently moved into the arena of economic reform, Churchmen taking up the question of factory legislation and Dissenters adopting the question of free trade.

# 10. *The Repeal of the Corn Laws*

It was no coincidence that Archibald Prentice dedicated his famous *History of the Anti-Corn-Law League* "to John Childs, Esq., of Bungay in Suffolk, a zealous supporter from early manhood of civil, religious, and commercial liberty . . . , the successful abater of the monopoly which tripled or quadrupled the price of the Bible." The monopoly in religion was socially and politically associated with the monopoly in grain.

In 1815 the Tory landlords, fortified with political power gained by successfully waging the war against France, enacted a new Corn Law to maintain the high wartime price of grain. Seeking to peg the price of wheat at 80*s*. a quarter, they prohibited the importation of wheat when the market price fell below this level. But the plan to legislate high prices had failed by 1822, and the landlords had to accept lower prices for their grain. Although the outbursts of public hostility to the Corn Laws were only sporadic, it became increasingly clear that some amendment was necessary. In 1828 a new Corn Law provided a sliding scale which permitted the duty on imported grain to vary inversely with the market price; that is, as the price of wheat fell below 73*s*. a quarter, the duties were increased proportionately. Under the Corn Law of 1828, which continued to protect the landlords, a national free-trade agitation arose.[1]

The campaign against the Corn Laws, although it began in 1815, failed to gain national significance until the liberal politicians of Manchester, financed by the manufacturers, adopted it as a humanitarian reform. The Anti-Corn-Law League originated in Manchester and received from its citizens a large portion of the wealth which made possible the agitation on a national scale.[2]

The Anti-Corn-Law League owed its success largely to the leadership of Richard Cobden, who devised its policies and determined

Notes to this chapter begin on page 205.

the character of its propaganda. Cobden so excelled as a Parliamentary speaker that his advocacy of free trade made him the symbol of the middle classes in the reformed House of Commons. The Reform Bill had admitted representatives of the factory towns, but Cobden made such representation a reality. The conflict over the Corn Laws, it has been wisely said, "was not merely a battle about a customs duty; it was a struggle for political influence and social equality between the landed aristocracy and the great industrialists." [3]

Owing to the prevalence of Evangelical Christianity, Cobden was able to understand and gain the support of different religious factions. The Evangelicals had confidence in him from the moment they heard him speak phrases full of emotion and moral idealism. This aspect of his success Cobden explained in a letter to his friend, George Combe:

> It is fortunate for me that whilst possessing a strong logical faculty which keeps me in the path of rationalism, I have religious sympathy which enables me to cooperate with men of exclusively religious sentiment. I mean it is fortunate for my powers of usefulness in this my day and generation. To this circumstance I am greatly indebted for the success of the free trade struggle which has been more indebted to the organ of veneration for its success than is generally known.[4]

A member of the Established Church, Cobden's interest in Evangelical causes and his espousal of religious freedom endeared him to the Dissenters. He shared their enthusiasm for temperance, world peace, and the abolition of colonial slavery.[5] On the questions of education and municipal reform, Cobden allied himself with the Radical-Dissenting party in Manchester rather than with the Tory-Church party. That he had brought the Dissenters into the League as a body Cobden frankly acknowledged:

> We have, I believe, the majority of every religious denomination with us—I mean the Dissenting denominations; we have them almost *en masse,* both ministers and laymen; and I believe the only body against us, as a body, are the members of the Church of England. The clergy of the Church of England have been placed in a most invidious position by the mode in which their tithe commutation was fixed . . . fluctuating according to the price of corn.[6]

Cobden understood better than most of his contemporaries that the monopoly in food was closely related to the monopoly in religion, for the commutation of tithes fluctuated with the price of wheat, thus giving the Anglican clergy interest in maintaining the high price of grain. Therefore he went to the Dissenters with this appeal: "We advocate the abolition of the Corn Law, because we believe that to be the foster parent of all other monopolies. . . ." [7] His success in linking free trade and religious liberty Cobden explained in a summary of the League's agitation:

> We have carried it on by those means by which the middle class usually carries on its movements. We have had our meeting of Dissenting ministers; we have obtained the cooperation of the ladies, we have resorted to parties, and taken those pacific means for carrying out our views which mark us as a middle-class set of agitators.[8]

After a careful study of propaganda techniques, Cobden concluded that successful agitators had followed the precedents established by John Wesley. Mass movements, such as the abolition of slavery and the Reform Bill, he thought, "had copied intentionally or unintentionally the Wesleyan model." [9] He consciously followed Methodist precedents, therefore, when organizing and promoting the League. At the beginning of the agitation against the Corn Laws he was clear as to the course he should follow. "It appears to me that a moral and even a religious spirit may be infused into the topic," he said, "and if agitated in the same manner that the question of slavery has been, it will be irresistible." [10]

The lecturers of the League, the chief agitators against the Corn Laws, went out like Methodist preachers on circuit, from town to town, to anathematize the wicked landlords. "Missionaries were found and did good service," Henry Ashworth said in describing the work of the League. "They were instructed to impress the people with the iniquity involved in the action of the laws and to cheer their auditors with evidence of progress from time to time, and certainty of eventual repeal. . . ." [11]

The League's lecturers went first to the chapels of northern England and Scotland, where they found a warm welcome awaiting them. As a result of this reception, they sent an enthusiastic report to the League Council: "We confidently trust that ere long those religious bodies who granted the use of their chapels . . . to Mr. George Thompson and others who advocated the cause of the Negro slave, will afford our lecturers a similar opportunity of appealing to their Christian sympathies in behalf of the industrious laborers of their own country, who are oppressed by a corn law." [12]

Although the theory of free trade was in the well of the lecturer's thinking, economic theories seldom came up in the bucket of his speaking.[13] Only occasionally did he invoke Adam Smith's *Wealth of Nations* to bless his campaign. Economic though the question was, a discussion on the level of abstract theory could not gain popularity. A. W. Paulton, the editor of the League's journals, as well as its first lecturer, was able to overcome the dryness of his subject by making it a class issue. He concluded more than one of his addresses by quoting from Lord Byron's *Age of Bronze:*

> For what were all the landed patriots born?
> To hunt, and vote, and raise the price of corn.
> Safe in the barns, these Sabine tillers sent
> Their brethren out to battle—Why? for rent!
> Year after year they voted, cent per cent,
> Blood, sweat, tear-wrung millions; Why? for rent! [14]

The League lecturers frequently appealed to religious sentiment. Shearman, for example, delivered one lecture on "The Immorality and Irreligion of the Corn Laws," in order to interest the "religious part of the community and the gentler sex especially." [15] After lecturing to a crowd of 2,000 in the streets of Boston on the religious aspects of free trade, Sydney Smith reported to the League that the "religious people were pondering the matter very seriously, and many confessed that the Corn Law is opposed to Christianity." [16]

Early in the campaign against the Corn Laws the League enlisted the Dissenting ministers as advocates of free trade. To achieve this purpose it employed George Thompson and John Bright. Both were well-known leaders of the Dissenters, Thompson as an abolitionist and Bright as an opponent of church rates.

Thompson began his work for the League by organizing a tea party for the Dissenters. He invited the political exponents of religious liberty, Joseph Brotherton, Mark Philips, John Bowring, and Lawrence Heyworth, to address the Dissenters on behalf of free trade. Having previously appealed to them for the abolition of slavery, Thompson placed the cause of free trade "not on the narrow ground of political expediency, or temporary necessity, but upon the high, impregnable foundations of immutable truth and justice." [17]

While Thompson was bringing the antislavery forces into the League, John Bright was seeking the advocates of religious freedom. This he did readily, for he had become a symbol of the Dissenters' opposition to church rates.[18] Bright thus brought to the League the Dissenters' growing resentment of both the aristocracy and the Established Church.[19]

Together Bright and Thompson early gained the full support of the Dissenting preachers. At a meeting of the League in April 1841 two Manchester preachers, S. Beardsall and W. M. Mountford, proposed and passed a resolution challenging all religious denominations to oppose the Corn Laws in the name of Christ and humanity.[20] Responding to the League's challenge, the General Body of the Protestant Dissenting Ministers of the Three Denominations met on June 4, 1841, and adopted the following resolutions:

> While abstaining from party politics, they claim the right to utter their deliberate opinion on such great and general measures, as plainly and deeply involve the weal and woe of the entire community.
>
> That they regard all interference with trade and commerce as unwise and injurious, whether on the principle of bounty or prohibition; that freedom is the natural and necessary element of commerce; and that the less any government shall legislate for it, the more it will prosper.
>
> That of all such restrictions those affecting the necessities of life are the most unwise and unrighteous, as they favor the few at the expense of the many, as they reduce the means of the poor to increase the means of the rich. . . .
>
> Our industrious poor are threatened with low wages and dear food; the craving children in myriads of families look up and are not fed, the parent asks to purchase bread in the cheapest market, and he is denied, and he resents the denial.
>
> Especially this body, as composed of Christian ministers, do deprecate and deplore the immoral and irreligious tendency of the restrictions complained of. . . .[21]

After the London Ministers had endorsed the League's agitation against the Corn Laws, George Thompson took steps to promote a national meeting of all Dissenting preachers. He first invited the preachers of Manchester to act as a provisional committee.[22] In response to his invitation, twenty-eight Dissenting preachers met on July 11, endorsed his proposals, and sent to the preachers of all denominations the following address:

> Receive the present address as if from the friends of the suffering poor, and the lovers of peace and righteousness. For a while let us lay aside our sectarian and partisan differences, and on the hallowed ground of Christian charity, assemble for the purpose of bettering the

condition of famishing multitudes. As friends of humanity let us plead the cause of the poor. As expounders and defenders of the principle of immutable justice, let us protest against laws, under whatever form, which deny to our necessitous fellow countrymen a share in the bounties which the Creator has provided for the wants of his creatures.[23]

More than 1,500 preachers replied to the free-trade letter and only six opposed the repeal of the Corn Laws. On August 17, 645 ministers convened in Manchester. They represented the various denominations as follows: Independent, 276; Baptist, 182; Presbyterian (Scotch and English), 52; Methodist (all varieties, mainly New Connection), 59; Unitarians, 23; Roman Catholic, 10; Church of England, 2; Church of Scotland, 2; and minor sects, 39. Only two principal denominations, the Wesleyan Methodists and the Church of England, were not officially represented.[24]

The ministers who assembled at Manchester felt that they were doing the will of God. That their action might be deemed partisan was denied at once by the venerable John Pye Smith: "Our object is to teach the politics which flow from piety, the politics of equitable benevolence, the politics of the Gospel, and the politics of Jesus our Lord and Saviour." [25]

On the closing day of the Conference the League Council deputed Richard Cobden with a message thanking the preachers for their cooperation. Cobden addressed them as follows:

> There wanted but the mighty impulse this conference could give, the greatest impulse that could affect the human mind in any country, and infinitely the greatest that can move a religious country such as this; there was wanted but this conference . . . to declare that the law was opposed to the law of God, was anti-scriptural and anti-Christian, and the Corn Laws would be from that moment virtually abolished.[26]

The Conference on free trade sent the *Report of the Conference of Ministers of All Denominations on the Corn Laws* to those chapels that had not been represented. In the preface of this *Report* the ministers claimed "No event in modern times has so excited general interest in the country as the convention of ministers of religion, from all parts of the empire, to consider the operation of laws restricting the food of the people." For several months after the preachers had returned home they sent to the League Council reports of free-trade meetings and of sermons preached against the

Corn Laws. Thus Cobden, with the aid of Bright and Thompson, had gained respectability for the League.

Owing to the success of the Manchester Ministers' Conference, similar conferences were promoted in Wales and Scotland. At Carnarvon 40 preachers gathered to denounce the Corn Laws.[27] More important was the meeting in Edinburgh in January 1842 when 580 ministers from all parts of the kingdom pronounced their anathemas upon the Corn Laws.[28] The ministers of Scotland, like those of England, opposed the Corn Laws on religious grounds, declaring it an injustice "to legislate for the benefit of the few to the detriment of the many." On the positive side they sanguinely hoped that "free trade would diffuse civilization, perpetuate peace, and make possible the spread of the Gospel and the final triumph of Christianity." [29]

When the Free Trade Hall was first opened in Manchester in 1843, the League invited political and religious leaders to help celebrate the occasion. The leaders of both political parties having declined the invitation, the League displayed religious celebrities to demonstrate its respectability. One hundred thirty-three Dissenting preachers, representing constituencies in all parts of the country, attended the grand opening of the Free Trade Hall. The meeting might have been mistaken for one to promote religious freedom, for Mark Philips presided while John Bright and George Thompson addressed the free-trade delegates.[30]

Following this triumph at Manchester, the League decided to invade London, which had heretofore stifled free trade under a heavy blanket of apathy. During March 1843 the League carefully prepared the ground for its public campaign by sending R. H. Greg, William Evans, Hamer Stansfield, and Henry Ashworth to establish an office and solicit funds. These men, all Dissenters, were chosen for the purpose of reaching the full purses of wealthy Dissenters; and Ashworth, in particular, was sent to solicit the Society of Friends, for, as Cobden wrote to him: "They have a good deal of influence over the city moneyed interest, which has the ear of the Government." [31]

The principal lecturer in the London campaign was the Unitarian preacher, William Johnson Fox, who soon won distinction as the League's most stirring orator.[32] Although Cobden and Bright spoke from the same platform, they did not excel Fox's eloquence. After Cobden and Bright had made their cogent pleas for free trade,

Fox swept the audience along with a highly emotional appeal for action.[33]

The first result of the London campaign was the election of James Pattison, an exponent of free trade, to succeed Sir Matthew Wood, who had long represented the London Dissenters in Parliament. This campaign linked religious liberty with free trade. In an address to the London electors, *The League* berated Lord Baring, the Tory candidate for upholding church rates and the Factories Education Bill.[34] With the endorsement of the advocates of both free trade and religious liberty, Pattison won the election by a large majority.

The London agitation for free trade, which lasted two years, was concluded with a grand bazaar, the purpose of which was to demonstrate the League's strength and respectability. Prominent Dissenting preachers, John Pye Smith, James Massie, Thomas Price, F. A. Cox, and Richard Fletcher, as representatives of the major denominations, gladly lent their moral influence to the occasion.[35] Sanctioned by religion and endowed with moral fervor, the Anti-Corn-Law League was able to make a lasting impression upon the metropolis and Parliament. The metropolitan press thereafter became less hostile. "How different is the tone of this same press now!" exclaimed a writer of *The League,* "not one scurrilous paragraph; not one unmanly jest." [36]

Meanwhile, in other parts of the country the campaign against the Corn Laws had lost some of its popular appeal. The abundant harvest of 1843 and the return of prosperity lessened the response to free trade. The League Council, therefore, changed its policy. Great agitator that he was, Richard Cobden recognized the changing economic conditions and abandoned the original plan of using the League chiefly as a propaganda agency.[37] In a speech at Covent Garden in September 1843 he requested that no more petitions be sent to Parliament; and he proposed, instead, to aid the registration of small borough electors. Since this new plan was distinctly political, Cobden assured the pious Dissenters that "there is not a man amongst us who aims at making a political life his profession." [38]

During 1844 Cobden, Bright, and Ashworth invaded the rural areas to help register voters. The three speakers, the A. B. C.'s of the League, conducted a broad and intensive campaign.[39] Ashworth estimated that 150 public meetings were held in the small Parliamentary boroughs, that 600 lectures were delivered, that 2,000,000 tracts were distributed, and that 20,000 copies of *The League* were circulated weekly.[40] Such costly campaigning was made possible by the generous financial support of several wealthy Dissenters. Edward Baines used the *Mercury* at Leeds to assist in raising funds and persuaded John Marshall to give generously to support the campaign.[41] The wealthy Dissenters, Robert H. Greg and Edward Strutt, were also among those who contributed to the League's funds. Their gifts, added to the contributions of others, enabled the League to spend £86,000 in the campaign of 1844.

Dissenting preachers, meanwhile, continued to aid the League with sermons and lectures. In rural areas, where free trade was unpopular, their chapels were frequently the only public places open to the League's lecturers. Moreover, the Dissenting preachers, John Brooks, James Martineau, and John Burnet, served the League as lecturers.[42]

Neither the registration of voters nor the national agitation against the Corn Laws increased the number of free traders in Parliament; consequently, the motion to repeal the Corn Laws on March 13, 1845, obtained no greater support than in the two preceding sessions of Parliament.[43] More progress had been made, however, than appeared in the Parliamentary divisions. Cobden's speeches were heavy blows at the doctrine of protection. Few tried to refute his arguments; and no one arose to challenge his exhaustive array of statistics. Unable to answer Cobden's arguments, Sir Robert Peel remained silent and increased the alarm of the landlords.[44] Lord John Russell also virtually capitulated to Cobden at the opening of Parliament when he said: "I am convinced that protection is not the support but the bane of agriculture." [45]

During 1845 the League kept on its course with an eye single to one objective—the total repeal of the Corn Laws. Confronted with the charge of cant and hypocrisy, the free traders never denied their religious motivation nor hesitated to sanction their cause with quotation from Holy Writ. They persistently proclaimed free trade as a religious issue. One writer of *The League,* for example, expressed his pious faith thus: "A monopoly in food is an audacious interference with the Divine government of Providence . . . it is a setting up of the stunted intellect of selfishness as a rival to omniscience." [46]

During 1845 William J. Fox, the principal writer for *The League,* addressed free-trade letters to important persons and groups. In a letter addressed to Sir Robert Inglis, he admonished the Anglican Church for its defense of the Corn Laws.[47] In another addressed to the Evangelical societies he earnestly pleaded for their support: "The warfare against monopoly, waged by the Anti-Corn-Law League, is no mean, sordid struggle for pecuniary advantage. Their agitation is . . . of the holiest principle. Their motives are in their Bibles. Their warrant is contained in divine law and their desire is expressed in Christian prayer." [48]

In the summer of 1845 bad weather came to the aid of the League's agitation. Prospects for an abundant harvest were bright in the early summer, but then rains began to fall and kept on falling. The price of wheat rose from 47s. a quarter in June to 53s. in August. Woe increased with the potato blight in Ireland. These economic conditions gave the League an opportunity to conduct another national campaign against the Corn Laws. In face of these conditions the leaders of both political parties finally abandoned protection. Lord John Russell first conceded victory to the League in a speech at Edinburgh on November 22 when he declared: "It is no longer worth while to contend for a fixed duty." A few days later Lord Morpeth, the Whig leader of Yorkshire, wrote to Edward Baines, "I wish to record in the most emphatic way I can my conviction that the time has come for a final repeal of the Corn Laws. . . ." [49] Even more momentous was the announcement of *The Times* on December 4, 1845, that Sir Robert Peel had been converted to free trade.

Upon making this radical change in policy, Peel resigned from office but was compelled to resume because the Whigs refused to form a ministry. When Parliament convened in January 1846 Sir Robert Peel proposed a bill admitting Indian corn and buckwheat free of duty and placing a small scale of duties on other grains, even these to be abolished within three years. The great triumph of free trade came at last on May 15, 1846, when Peel's bill passed its third reading in the House of Commons.[50]

After the passing of Peel's bill the Anti-Corn-Law League dissolved itself. Active to the last, the younger Edward Baines exhorted the members to continue their vigilance on behalf of religious freedom.[51] Fox and Bright participated in these last rites, regretting somewhat that such a fellowship was coming to an end. Cobden brought to a close these long years of heavy responsibility with a feeling of spiritual victory: "I shall never despair of this moral power to conduct this good ship [the Government] through whatever storm may arise, which will save us from anarchy at one end or tyranny at the other end of society." Free trade was a victory, he thought, "like that of religious liberty, one which the people should not let go." [52]

The triumph of free trade, a middle-class victory second only to the Reform Bill, was the result of the growing wealth and power of commerce and industry. This power was manifested by the larger political influence of the Dissenting chapels and by the affluence of the philanthropists who gave generously to the support of the League.

Free trade was never solely a commercial philosophy of self-interest. It would never have become a national movement if its appeal had been merely that of increased trade. For many people it was an expression of religious idealism and humanitarianism.[53] Those interested in feeding the hungry, in saving souls, and in gaining religious equality adopted free trade as their own and supported the League to its final triumph. While the Evangelical Dissenters were promoting free trade as a means of lifting the people from their destitution, the Wesleyan Methodists and the Evangelicals of the Church of England were promoting factory reform as the proper method of improving the conditions of the people.

# 11. *The Ten Hours Bill*

During the 1820's, while the Tories continued to block further factory legislation, a few Christian manufacturers of Lancashire kept alive the cause of the factory children and perpetuated the reforming zeal of the elder Peel. Foremost among these was Joseph Brotherton, a manufacturer who devoted his life to the reform of the factory system. As a boy he entered his father's cotton factory in Manchester and at the age of nineteen became a partner in the business. A few years later he experienced a religious conversion which led him to unite with the Bible Christians. Accepting their strict sectarian views, he became a vegetarian and a total abstainer from alcoholic beverages. At the age of thirty-five, already successful in business, he accepted the call to be the pastor of one of the chapels of this denomination. Neither religious convictions nor business pursuits kept him from local politics. He campaigned for the abolition of slavery, free trade, and improvement of factory conditions. After helping to organize Short Time Committees in Lancashire, he contributed generously to their support. He was elected by Salford to the first Reformed Parliament and from that time to the passage of the ten hours bill, he never ceased advocating factory legislation.[1]

John Fielden, a member of the Methodist-Unitarians, was as resolute an opponent of the factory system as Brotherton and was even more influential than he as a reformer of the factory system. At an early age he began working in his father's mills at Todmorden where he experienced, with other children, suffering which endowed him with life-long sympathy for factory children. When he became the operator of his own mills at Todmorden, he continued to seek reduction in the hours of labor. A Radical in political thought, he never permitted the Radicals' economic doctrines to

Notes to this chapter begin on page 208.

blind him to the need for factory legislation.[2] After the passing of the Reform Bill, he was elected to represent Oldham. "When I consented to become a member of Parliament," Fielden wrote, "it was not with a view of joining party men or aiding in party movements; but in order to assist by my vote in doing such things as I thought would benefit the labouring people. . . ." [3]

The humanitarian zeal for factory reform spread from Lancashire to the West Riding of Yorkshire, where a small group of Christian manufacturers took up the cause of the children and carried it on for twenty years. The most important leader of this group was John Wood, the owner of a spinning mill at Bradford.[4] By 1830 his factory, which employed 500 hands, was among the largest and most prosperous of the country. He was obviously successful. Yet a sensitive, religious conscience would not let him find contentment in success. "He knew he was rich," a close friend wrote, "but his enjoyment of wealth was tainted by the impression that many had endured grievous wrongs during its acquisition. . . ." [5] Motivated by neither commercial nor political considerations, Wood undertook the cause of the factory children and never deviated from this calling until he had liberated them from their long hours of labor. By his counsel and wealth this devout Evangelical Churchman guided and sustained the Yorkshire Short Time Committees during their long and hectic campaign for a ten-hour day.[6]

John Wood made his largest contribution to the ten hours movement when he persuaded Richard Oastler, a man as pious as himself, that the factory system was as cruel and as unjust as West Indian slavery.[7] Reared a Methodist, Oastler went to a Moravian boarding school at Fulneck where he received instruction that in no way conflicted with his religious upbringing. After eight years at Fulneck, he turned to the study of law but soon gave up this career in deference to his father's moral scruples against it. He then studied architecture, only to quit that, too, after four years, owing to poor eyesight. At the age of twenty-one he began the trade of a cloth merchant and this he carried on for nine years, until he succeeded his father as the steward on an estate near Huddersfield. His career followed his father's in other respects. He, too, was a Methodist local preacher, a visitor for the Bible Society, and an Abolitionist. When he became a member of the Established Church, he did not abandon the Methodism in which he had been so thoroughly trained.

The first fruit of Richard Oastler's conversion to factory reform was a letter in the *Leeds Mercury* addressed to the Abolitionists of Yorkshire.[8] "It is the pride of Britain," he said, "that a slave cannot exist on her soil; and if I read the genius of her constitution, I find that slavery is most abhorrent to it. . . ." After this introduction, Oastler delivered a shock to the religious consciences of the Yorkshire Abolitionists by boldly declaring: "Thousands of our fellow-creatures and fellow-subjects, both male and female, the miserable inhabitants of a Yorkshire town . . . are this very moment existing in a state of slavery, more horrid than are the victims of that hellish system of colonial slavery." He concluded his letter, a Pauline epistle to Yorkshire, with an urgent plea, "Why should not children working in them [the worsted mills] be protected by legislative enactments, as well as those who work in cotton mills? Christians should feel and act for those whom Christ so eminently loved, and declared that 'of such is the Kingdom of Heaven.'"

Richard Oastler tried to do what other factory reformers had done before him, what William Smith and Wilberforce had done in Parliament. He sought to enlist the cooperation of the antislavery forces and the Evangelical preachers on the side of the factory children; in short, to make factory legislation a righteous cause. The earlier factory reformers had never succeeded in arousing a national sentiment against the factory system, but Oastler with a torrential flow of words and bursts of passion—almost madness at times—was able to arouse the West Riding of Yorkshire and to transform a timid movement into a vociferous and militant crusade.[9]

When Oastler began to preach against the factory system, the factory workers, though bitterly dissatisfied, lacked the ability to channel their discontent into a national reform movement. In Lancashire the Short Time Committees, according to Philip Grant, "were broken down and disheartened for the lack of support." The agitation in Yorkshire and the controversy over Oastler's letter brought new hope to the Lancashire Committees, who began to feel "that in God's providence new allies had sprung up from whom succor and support might be expected." [10] In Yorkshire the Short Time Committees of workingmen, gaining new strength, turned to Oastler for leadership.

On a Sunday morning in June 1831 six factory workers from the Short Time Committee of Huddersfield called at Oastler's home to discuss his letters on "Yorkshire Slavery." At first Oastler refused to talk with them because it seemed like a desecration of the Sabbath, but when they reminded him that they could not come on any other day, he sent his family to church, while he remained behind to do an act of charity. The workers urged him to adopt the ten hours bill as the only remedy for the abuses of the factory system and requested him to be the advocate of this reform. At first Oastler hesitated to accept their invitation since they were Radical in politics and Dissenters in religion, while he was a Tory Churchman. But after a lengthy discussion they agreed "to work together with the understanding that parties in politics and sects in religion should not be allowed to interfere between us." [11]

When Oastler addressed his letter to the Leeds Abolitionists, he expected all Dissenters to unite in a crusade to liberate the children from their factory slavery. But in this expectation he was keenly disappointed, for the Dissenters were then fully occupied with political reform. Moreover, their doctrine of religious freedom predisposed them to favor the individualism of free trade and to oppose the paternalism of factory reform. Resolved to abolish all monopolies in politics, religion, and trade, they feared legislative interference with factory workers as an extension of Tory control.

Shortly after the publication of Oastler's letter, John Wood and several other manufacturers of the West Riding petitioned Parliament to reduce the hours of labor. But John C. Hobhouse, who had previously sponsored legislation, was unwilling to introduce a ten hours bill.[12] Consequently, Oastler and the Short Time Committees turned to Michael Thomas Sadler as their Parliamentary representative.

Sadler, who was born in 1780 at Snelston, Derbyshire, grew up in the midst of a controversy over Methodism. One of his earliest literary efforts was a defense of the Methodists against the attacks of the local vicar.[13] Early in life he attended a school at Doveridge, where he acquired a knowledge of Latin and Greek. Left to his own inclination for a year or so thereafter, he spent his time reading religious literature and studying classical languages. He then tried his hand at versifying the Psalms, but refrained from publishing his work when he discovered that Robert Southey had already done such a book. At the age of twenty he went to Leeds to join his brother in business as an importer of Irish linens. But being poorly suited by temperament for such an occupation, he left the tedium of business to his brother and turned his attention to religion and politics. As a member of the Stranger's Friend Society, he visited the poor and sick of Leeds. He served also as the superintendent of a Sunday school for several hundred children.

As treasurer of the local Poor-Rates Board, he acquired a lasting sympathy for the poor and an intimate knowledge of working-class problems.

On the simple moral grounds of obeying Christ's commands to clothe the naked, feed the poor, and minister to the sick, Sadler accepted Oastler's invitation to become the Parliamentary advocate of factory legislation. He had previously objected to Hobhouse's bill because it provided inadequate protection. This objection he wrote to Oastler on November 20, 1831, "I am persuaded . . . that ten hours can never be receded from by those who love children, or wish to obtain the approbation of Him who was indeed their friend and lover." [14]

In December 1831 Sadler obtained permission to introduce a factory bill, but the Whig Ministers delayed its passage by appointing a Committee of Inquiry.[15] Under Sadler's direction the Committee conducted an extensive inquiry and compiled volumes of information on factory conditions. Although some opponents of factory legislation sat on the Committee, Sadler carefully selected those witnesses whose testimony would substantiate the claims of the reformers. Oastler, for example, testified that only a ten hours bill would be a satisfactory remedy for factory conditions.[16] The Rev. George S. Bull gave evidence showing that the long hours of factory labor hindered the progress of the Sunday schools. In supporting this claim Bull submitted a statement signed by 68 Sunday-school teachers of the several denominations in the township of Bowling. The teachers unanimously agreed that the factory system hindered religious instruction and caused moral degradation.[17] In addition to Sunday-school teachers and clergymen, surgeons and physicians testified to the deleterious effects upon health and longevity. John Richard Farre, who had only recently returned from the practice of medicine in the West Indies, testified that the slaves there were better off than the factory children of England.

While Sadler's Committee was conducting its investigation, the Reform Bill became law; and in the election that followed Sadler had to seek another constituency. He decided to stand as a Tory candidate for Leeds. But the Whigs, still riding on the crest of Reform Bill sentiment, carried Leeds and elected Macaulay and Marshall. This defeat marked the end of Sadler's political career. In poor health, exhausted by his strenuous work on the Committee of Inquiry, he moved to Belfast. He died there in 1835.

After the defeat of Sadler, it was necessary for the factory reformers to find another Parliamentary leader. The delegates of the Short Time Committees, unable to agree upon anyone, decided to send the Anglican clergyman George S. Bull to confer with the friends of factory reform in Parliament. By selecting Bull as their envoy they expressed their preference for a Christian humanitarian like Sadler to a political Radical like Hobhouse.[18]

Upon arriving in London, Bull conferred with Sir Andrew Agnew, the leader of the Scottish Sabbatarians, who recommended Lord Ashley.[19] The Sabbatarians, as well as other Evangelicals, would gladly accept Lord Ashley as leader for he had already distinguished himself in the work of the religious societies and in the reform of the asylums for the insane. The question that troubled both Bull and Agnew was, Would Ashley accept the cause of the factory children? For him to do so meant a parting of ways. It meant cutting himself off from the Duke of Wellington whose confidence he had already won. Hesitating to accept so gratuitous a burden, Ashley refused to give Bull an answer until he had prayed about it and talked with pious friends. When they urged him to accept, he reluctantly agreed to do so. His reply to the Short Time Committees was a religious dedication of his life to the factory children: "It seems no one else will undertake it," he wrote, "so I will; and without cant or hypocrisy, which I hate, I assure you that I dare not refuse the request you have so earnestly pressed. I believe it is my duty to God and to the poor, and I trust He will support me." [20]

Lord Ashley's humanitarianism stemmed from his early Evangelical training and from a youthful conversion experience. Known in public life first as Lord Ashley and later as the Earl of Shaftesbury, Anthony Ashley-Cooper was born in 1801, the son of Cropley Ashley Cooper, the sixth Earl of Shaftesbury. His mother was the daughter of the fourth Duke of Marlborough. Both parents, unfortunately, were so occupied with the duties of public life that they failed to attend to the needs of their sensitive son.[21] Neglected by his parents and mistreated by the boys at school, Anthony's early childhood was miserable except for the love and sympathy of Moria Millis. This faithful household servant, by her example of constant devotion, imparted to him her simple creed and religious attitudes. Since she was the only person completely devoted to him, her death brought great sorrow to his early youth and left a lasting impression on him. After her death he turned for consolation to the Bible, which she had taught him to read, and persevered in the habit of daily prayer despite the ridicule of his fellow students. At the age of fourteen or fifteen, while still in school at Harrow, he had a deep emotional experience which was a turning point in his life. By chance he witnessed a crude funeral procession of drunken workingmen bearing one of their fellows to his grave. This sad spectacle, which he felt was the disparagement of everything worth living for, so overwhelmed him with emotion that he vowed to God he would devote his life to improving the condition of the poor. Thus religiously committed from his youth, Lord Ashley could not, with a good conscience, refuse to be the Parliamentary spokesman for factory legislation.

In February 1833 Lord Ashley announced in the House of Commons that he intended to reintroduce Sadler's ten hours bill.[22] The Whig Ministers, however, took the question in hand and enacted their own law. The Whig Act of 1833, which applied to all textile factories except silk, prohibited the employment of children under nine, limited to eight hours a day the work of children nine to twelve, and reduced to sixty-nine hours a week the work of young persons thirteen to eighteen. It also prevented night work for all persons under eighteen. Other important provisions of the Act were the compulsory education of children under thirteen, the appointment of inspectors to enforce the law, and the relay system for children to prevent interference with adult labor.[23]

The Act of 1833, however, did not please the manufacturers. Growing increasingly hostile to the law during 1835 and 1836, they resolved to strike out those clauses which restricted the hours of children twelve and thirteen years of age. The leader of the opposition in Yorkshire was the younger Edward Baines. "Some of the provisions of the Act," he said, "have proved to be quite impractical." It had already compelled the masters to discharge the children nine to eleven years old. "If the Act should continue in force, all children under twelve years of age would be discharged in 1835, and this," he thought, "would make it impossible in many cases to carry on the mills. . . ."[24] A Whig and a Dissenter, Baines feared factory legislation as a new kind of restriction on trade and individual liberty. "All restrictions on industry," he thought, "should be imposed with a delicate and cautious hand. England has manufacturing rivals; and if Parliament were, from a false humanity, to limit . . . our workmen, one of our principal advantages over other nations would be sacrificed, and the labourers themselves would be the greatest sufferers."[25]

Baines persuaded many Dissenters, especially among the Baptists and Congregationalists, to accept the doctrines of free trade and noninterference as a part of their creed. At Manchester, Unitarians had also become foes of factory legislation. An influential Unitarian, Harriet Martineau, was a popularizer of political economy. At the time when the factory acts were claiming the attention of Parliament she published nine small volumes, *Illustrations of Political Economy,* to propagate what she deemed to be a new science. "In an enlightened nation like our own," she wrote in the preface of one of the volumes, "there are followers of every science. . . . And yet political economy has been less studied than perhaps any other science whatever—and not at all by those whom it most concerns, the mass of the people." [26] The "new science" had convinced her that "all interference of Government with the direction and the rewards of industry is a violation of its duty towards its subjects." [27]

Owing to the manufacturers' mounting hostility to the Act of 1833, the Whig Ministers decided to amend those clauses restricting children twelve and thirteen years of age. As soon as the Whig bill had passed its first reading, the Short Time Committees began sending petitions in support of the existing law. They sent one from Manchester with 35,000 signatures; one from Glasgow with 15,000; one from Leeds with 9,000; one from Stockport with 8,000; one from Ashton with 4,000; and one from Warrington with 3,000.[28] This popular agitation among the workers of the factory towns prevented the Whigs from repealing any part of the Act of 1833. As they could not undo the legislation which they had passed while reforming zeal was at its peak, the Whigs were compelled to find new means of enforcing the law and to provide more facilities for education. Since the manufacturers could not comply with the educational requirements, the Whigs assumed greater responsibility for education by appointing in 1839 a Committee in Council on Education and by voting larger financial aid. This phase of the factory legislation, however, got snarled in the barbed wire of sectarianism. While Dissenters eagerly supported the Whig policies for public education, the Church stood as a stone wall against them. Consequently, as long as the Whigs remained in office, they were unable to enforce the educational provisions of the factory laws.

During the years 1837 to 1841, while the Whigs were in power, a severe trade depression stopped the wheels of industry and threw people on the streets without jobs or bread. Hungry and resentful, the workingmen listened to the Chartist threats of revolutionary violence. The ten hours bill could not compete with Chartism, for the ten-hour day meant nothing to people out of work.[29] At about the same time, the Anti-Corn-Law League won many followers among the working classes by advocating the repeal of the Corn Laws in order to reduce the cost of bread.[30] Consequently, the factory question, because of Chartism and free trade, languished throughout the country until after the return of prosperity.

When the Tories came into office in 1841, Lord Ashley compelled them to face the factory question. To silence the clamor for a ten hours bill and to satisfy the Church's demand for more religious education, Sir James Graham introduced a factories education bill in 1843. He proposed to raise the minimum age of employment from eight to nine years, and to limit to six and a half hours the labor of children under thirteen. His bill also required a half day of school for all factory children. The education provisions of this bill, however, were unsatisfactory to the Dissenters and they defeated it. Lord Ashley then insisted that the Conservatives proceed with a factory bill minus the educational clauses. In February 1844 Sir James Graham introduced another factory bill.[31]

While this bill was being considered, the Short Time Committees carried on an agitation in the northern industrial towns to line up the Anglican clergy for factory legislation. At Leeds they won the endorsement of the influential Dr. Hook as well as the support of other Churchmen. In Manchester the clergymen of the Church took the lead in organizing a huge demonstration in favor of legislation. During the agitation in these and other cities the Short Time Committees, with the help of the Anglican clergy, sent scores of petitions to Parliament requesting a ten hours bill.[32]

During the Parliamentary debates of 1844 John Bright arose as the new champion of the factory system. Curtly rejecting the indictment brought against the manufacturers, he asserted that the industrial population of Lancashire was superior in health and morals to the rural population. As a Quaker he stoutly defended the benevolence of the Dissenters, their chapels and schools, their voluntary system in religion and education. Heretofore, politicians had cowered before Lord Ashley's moral and religious sentiments; but now John Bright, equally pious and moralistic, challenged Ashley on moral grounds. "It appears to me . . . ," Bright said after listening to Ashley for two hours, "that he has taken a one-sided view, a most unjust and unfair view of the question; it may not be intentionally, but still a view which cannot be borne out by the facts. . . ." [33] He went on at length to show that Ashley had relied upon faulty sources of information and upon agents who were peccable. He even cast doubt on Ashley's integrity by accusing him of being more concerned for the poor industrial workers of Lancashire than for the poor agricultural laborers of his own country. "The noble Lord is the representative of the sugar monopolists of Liverpool," Bright said scornfully, "and after voting to deprive the people of sugar, he is perfectly consistent in denying them the liberty even to work. The people ask for freedom for their industry, for the removal of shackles on their trade; you deny it to them, and then forbid them to labour, as if working less would give them more food, whilst your monopoly laws make food scarce and dear." [34]

In spite of Bright's opposition and the opposition of the Conservative Ministers, Lord Ashley and his friends patiently waited for an opportunity to introduce another ten hours bill. Possessing a clear majority in the House of Commons in favor of a shorter working day, Ashley was confident of the ultimate passage of his bill. Early in 1846 he introduced his last ten hours bill. But before the bill came to its second reading, the debates on the Corn Laws intervened. The catastrophe of the Irish potato famine convinced Ashley, if he had not been convinced before, that the time had come to repeal the import duties on grain, and as a representative of an agricultural constituency favoring protection, he felt bound to resign from the House of Commons.[35] This he did two days after he had introduced his last ten hours bill but with the assurance that his measure was in the safe hands of John Fielden.

Fielden's Christian benevolence led him to seek the repeal of the Corn Laws as well as to advocate factory legislation.[36] "There is no natural cause for our distresses," he said; "we have fertile land, the first herds and flocks in the world, and the most skillful husbandmen. . . . I think that these interests are all conducive to the prosperity of the nation; that they must go together and that the ruin of either will leave the others comparatively insecure." Providence had bestowed blessings on all workers, he thought, but men had willfully violated the design of Heaven.[37]

During May 1846 Fielden introduced Lord Ashley's ten hours bill, but the Conservatives again blocked its passage. On a motion to postpone it for six months, Peel won a majority of 10 in a House of 396 members.[38] But this was a costly victory. Having already lost many Conservative followers, owing to the repeal of the Corn

Laws, Peel was forced to resign when defeated on the Irish Coercion Bill. With the return of the Whigs the passage of a ten hours bill was virtually assured.

The change of governments brought new courage and enthusiasm to the Short Time Committees. Lord Ashley toured the principal towns of Lancashire where he gained many new friends for factory legislation.[39] Nearly everywhere the Anglican clergy came forward to greet him and to endorse the ten hours bill. At a large meeting in Manchester, C. D. Wray presided and other Anglican clergymen spoke in favor of Ashley's bill. At the same time Dr. Hook, the vicar of Leeds, was winning the support of the clergy in the West Riding. Oastler again took up the agitation and carried it into Scotland, where his religious zeal did much to overcome the sentiment against interference.[40] He won a major victory for factory legislation by persuading Thomas Chalmers to allow Christian charity to take precedence over economic principles. After converting Chalmers, Oastler gained a hearing from those influential Presbyterians who had opposed slavery. At Edinburgh he appealed to the abolitionists by expressing the hope "that as abolition of West Indian Negro slavery was . . . to be attributed pre-eminently to the influence of Christian principle, so the abolition of home slavery, of factory slavery, would be won by application of the same principle." [41]

With great popular support behind him, John Fielden introduced a ten hours bill that differed only slightly from the measure brought by Lord Ashley the year before. It limited the hours of young people, aged thirteen to eighteen, to eleven hours a day during the first year and to ten hours thereafter.[42] Fielden reminded the House that his bill contained about the same provisions as the one proposed by the elder Sir Robert Peel. Unable to invent any new argument after three decades of debate and controversy, he relied chiefly on the larger humanitarianism of the House of Commons. Rejecting the principle of noninterference, he recommended as a sounder principle the state's "care of the lives, the health, and the morals of the people."

In spite of the Conservative opposition, the ten hours bill passed its third reading in May 1847.[43] The Radicals Joseph Hume and John A. Roebuck used every tactic of obstruction to prevent its passage. Standing with this recalcitrant minority were the Dissenters John Bright, Mark Philips, and John Bowring. In the Upper House the exponent of political economy, Lord Brougham, berated the bishops for letting their emotions pervert their judgment. Undaunted by his sharp tongue, the bishops gave their moral reasons favoring the ten hours bill; with their endorsement it passed the second reading by a vote of 53 to 11 and then went rapidly through further stages to become law.[44] Although the war for a shorter working day continued, the decisive battles had been fought and won.

During the last stages of the bill Lord Ashley frequently resorted to prayer to thank God for the blessings of victory. When news came that it had passed its third reading in the House of Lords, he prayed: "God in His mercy grant that these operatives may receive the cup of salvation. . . ."[45] The following day he met with the Parliamentary leaders and the delegates of the Short Time Committees to celebrate their victory. As reported by Philip Grant, the celebration was as sober and serious as a prayer meeting. Their first resolution was "That we are deeply thankful to Almighty God for the success which has attended our efforts in this sacred cause. . . ."[46]

So the factory question ended as it had begun, a religious crusade to free little children from the long hours of labor and to give them an opportunity for education and a chance to enjoy the bliss of home life. The greatest reformers, Sadler, Oastler, and Ashley, were devout Evangelicals. The benevolent factory owners, whose wealth and influence had counted for so much, Wood, Fielden, Hindley, and Brotherton, were likewise devout men motivated by Christian teaching. As Christians, they acted independently of political parties and strove to keep their cause above partisan politics. They led the crusade for the factory children in much the same manner as they had conducted the campaign against slavery. They visited churches and chapels and spoke in language that sounded like sermons. They petitioned Parliament, and when their petitions went unanswered, they waited in patience, for they felt God was on their side and would in His own time bring victory.

# 12. *The Origin of the Liberal Party*

During the decade from 1837 to 1847 the Dissenters grew increasingly hostile to all religious establishments. Their militancy expressed itself in three separate movements, one to abolish church rates, another to block the government grant to the Roman Catholic College of Maynooth, and a third to prevent the Church from dominating elementary education. The voluntaryists in religion and education openly repudiated the Whigs and attempted to elect Radicals and Liberals to Parliament.

The election of 1837—it has been seen previously—was the great turning point in politics, for it dissolved the alliance between the Whigs and Dissenters that had rested for a century and a half upon the principle of religious toleration. The spirit of reform having spent itself, the Whigs refused to redress religious grievances and permitted an Irish tithe bill to pass without appropriating the revenues of the Church of Ireland.[1] Inasmuch as the Whigs did nothing about church rates, the Dissenters turned to the Radicals.[2] They expressed their preference for the Radicals by voting for George Grote's annual motion for the ballot.[3] After uniting with the Radicals, they laid plans in 1839 for a campaign against the Whigs, and this campaign was supported by the same magazines and newspapers which had heretofore sponsored Whig men and measures.[4] The *Eclectic Review,* which was now edited by Thomas Price, firmly upheld the Radicals. In Price's preface to a new series he proposed "to bring about the happy consummation which Dissenters so devoutly desire—the dissolution of the disgraceful connection between church and state." [5] Josiah Conder, the editor of *The Patriot,* who had cooperated with the Whigs for many years, reluctantly joined the ranks of the Radicals.[6]

As the Dissenters quit the Whigs, they formed new organizations

Notes to this chapter begin on page 211.

to align themselves with the Radicals. In November 1838 the advocates of religious freedom, including both Price and Conder, met with the London Radicals to form an organization designed to abolish church rates and separate church and state. Unlike the older Dissenting organizations which had chosen Whigs for their presiding officers, the new Religious Freedom Society selected the Radical Charles Lushington.[7] Distinctly political in character, the Society resolved to elect to Parliament only those candidates who professed full religious equality. As the Radicals had previously used the Church Rates Abolition Society to compel the Whigs to take a more liberal course, so they now intended to use the Religious Freedom Society to arouse a movement in the country against the Whigs.[8]

Many Evangelical Dissenters, however, were not content to use political pressure against the Church, for they still aspired to reform it from within and to convert its clergy to the voluntary principle. In 1836 the Evangelicals of Birmingham formed the Voluntary Church Society with the object, not of injuring the Episcopal Church, nor of sharing in its wealth, but of separating it from the state.[9] Evangelicals of other cities soon formed similar societies, and these federated in 1839 to establish the Evangelical Voluntary Church Association.[10] A few years later the Association, headed by the Evangelical Sir Culling Eardley Smith, was reorganized as the Evangelical Alliance.

As the new organizations won followers and increased their prestige, the older Dissenting bodies, seeking merely the redress of grievances, declined. The Protestant Society, still seeking moderate reform, attempted in 1839 to exempt chapels from the poor rates and to achieve freedom of worship in the workhouses.[11] More than any other Dissenting organization, the Protestant Society had been the achievement of one man, and as John Wilks' strength diminished with old age, his Society proportionately lost its influence. Furthermore, the Society suffered the loss of two of its distinguished friends in the deaths of Lord Holland and the Duke of Sussex. Little was heard of the Society after 1843; a few years later it was disbanded and its funds were transferred to the Dissenting Deputies.[12]

During the late 1830's the Dissenting Deputies, who had cooperated with the Whigs over a long period of time, also underwent transformation. In 1836 the Evangelicals, by invoking a creedal test, drove the Unitarians out of the organization, and they continued the attack until Parliament, by the Chapels Act of 1844, assured the Unitarians of the right to hold their property. This internecine warfare destroyed the leadership of the Unitarians, and the Dissenting Deputies consequently lost some of the political influence which they had previously exercised.

The abolition of church rates was the first phase of the Dissenters' campaign to disestablish the Church. During the late 1830's they passively resisted paying the rates, and in towns where they controlled the church vestries they would not levy rates.[13] At Manchester great crowds assembled to vote down the collection of a church rate.[14] At Rochdale an anti-church rates mob threatened such violence in 1840 that troops were called out to prevent rioting.[15] At Sheffield a similar mob did riot in 1824 and thereafter for twenty years the Dissenters levied no rate. At Leeds the Dissenters under Edward Baines controlled the vestry of 75,000 people and supervised scrupulously the levy of rates.[16] At Birmingham George F. Muntz, who led the anti-church rates party, was prosecuted and convicted in 1837 for nonpayment of rates, only to have the decision reversed the next year.[17] The fires of religious resentments were thus kept burning in the chapels like candles on the altar and passed from city to city. During 1842 the Dissenters levied no rates in fifty-three towns and in many other places they refused to pay rates which had been legally levied.[18]

The prosecution and imprisonment of Dissenters for nonpayment of rates brought several cases into national prominence. The first of the "Church rates martyrs," John Childs, was sent to jail for not paying a rate of 17s. 6d.[19] Early in 1839 John Thorogood, "the martyr of Chelmsford," was imprisoned for nonpayment of a small sum; while he languished in prison for more than a year, the Dissenters exulted in their sense of persecution. Eventually, Edward Baines brought his case before the House of Commons and denounced the Whigs for doing nothing about church rates or ecclesiastical courts.[20] Since the Whigs refused to release Thorogood, Thomas Duncombe again brought his case before the House of Commons in February of the next year and then introduced a motion to exempt Dissenters from paying the rates. Supported in the debates by only Dissenters and Radicals, Duncombe obtained 62 votes against the payment of church rates.[21]

The Whig Government eventually released Thorogood, but while his case was being settled, another arose to national attention. In November 1840 William Baines was incarcerated in the county jail at Leicester for the nonpayment of a rate, and while he was there, 36 other persons of his parish, who had been cited for the same offense, were awaiting trial. In the midst of great excitement the Dissenters of Leicester conducted a campaign for his release; they sent petitions to Parliament, one signed by 6,000 prominent residents and another, signed by women only, bearing 7,000 signatures. Responding to these petitions Sir John Easthope in March 1841 again censured the Whig Ministers by moving that Baines' imprisonment for the nonpayment of church rates was "a violation of the principle of religious liberty." [22] On a motion censuring the Whigs, the Radicals and Dissenters again mustered only a small minority against the combination of Whigs and Conservatives.

The bitterness over the imprisonment of Dissenters was aggravated by the indecision of the courts. In 1837 a majority of the church vestry at Braintree voted against a church rate, but in spite of the majority the churchwardens decided to levy it. Subsequently a church court, under the jurisdiction of the Bishop of London, held that such a rate was legal; but when the case was appealed to the Court of the Queen's Bench in 1840, Lord Denman ruled the rate illegal. The case then went to the Court of Exchequer and Judge Tindal reopened the whole question by suggesting that the churchwardens and a minority of the vestry might levy a rate if the majority failed to do so. Acting on this suggestion, the churchwardens of Braintree, supported by a minority of the vestry, promptly levied a rate; and this time the Court of the Queen's Bench held the rate valid. The decision was oil on the fires of religious resentment which continued to burn until the House of Lords finally ruled in 1853 that a church rate levied by the churchwardens and a minority of the vestry was illegal.[23]

The national controversy over rates induced Edward Miall, a Congregational minister at Leicester, to take up the warfare against religious establishments. When William Baines was sent to prison for not paying rates, Miall led the agitation for his release.[24] He visited Voluntary Church Associations in several places to solicit financial help from leading Dissenters. As a result of this campaign, Miall decided to start a new magazine with the single purpose of separating church and state.

In April 1841 Edward Miall published the *Nonconformist,* the first issue carrying on its title page the militant inscription, "The Dissidence of Dissent and the Protestantism of the Protestant Religion." In his "Address to the Readers" Miall said, "The primary object is to show that a national establishment of religion is essentially vicious . . . politically and religiously. . . ." It soon appeared that Miall was also motivated by a resentment of aristocrats; "let them claim what they will," he said, "but suffer them no longer to be lords in the Church of Jesus Christ."[25] Expecting no relief from the aristocratic House of Commons, Miall made the *Nonconformist* the organ of the complete suffrage movement and lined up the Dissenters at the polls behind the Radicals.

Under Miall's leadership many Dissenters turned from the Whigs in the general election of 1841 and gave their votes to the Radicals. At the May meeting of the Religious Freedom Society, Sir John Easthope, who had sponsored anti-church rate legislation, urged the Dissenters "to make common cause with the enemies of monopoly."[26] In response to this appeal, several Voluntary Church Associations formed political clubs and supported those Radicals who had voted against church rates. At Leeds the elder Baines, upon retiring from Parliament, nominated Joseph Hume as a constant friend of religious liberty and free trade. But even with Baines' support, the venerable leader of the Radicals failed to win the election.[27] Other elections also went against the Radicals, for the Established Church and its influential body of clergy were decidedly against them at the polls.[28] The Conservatives having emerged from the elections with a majority of 70 or 80 members, the Dissenters could only lament that "the electors have been coerced like serfs and slaves."[29] In this dour mood they were prepared to receive Herbert Spencer's harsh and thoroughgoing liberalism.

In a series of ten essays on "The Proper Sphere of Government," which were published in the *Nonconformist* during 1842 and 1843, Spencer constructed a new political platform to combine economists, Radicals, and Dissenters. Beginning with the doctrine of *laissez faire* as a law of nature, he reduced the functions of government to very narrow limits.[30] He preferred voluntary charity to the new Poor Law; he rejected the Corn Law as a violation of natural law. He feared public education. The citizen, he thought, had no more right to ask the government to educate his children than to expect it to feed and clothe them; and if the state should undertake education, it would inevitably violate freedom of conscience and lead to "static mediocrity." In these essays Spencer went beyond most Dissenters in regarding the Established Church as a heavy tax on the people and a hindrance to progress.[31]

The political events of 1843, seeming to confirm Spencer's conclusions, impelled the Dissenters toward a more extreme voluntaryism. In this fateful year the intrusion of Parliament into the religious affairs of Scotland disrupted the Scottish Church and led to the formation of the new Free Church of Scotland. The heroic example of those 474 Scottish ministers, who resigned their homes and livings, as a protest against state interference, gave the English Dissenters a stronger faith in voluntaryism. At the same time, Sir James Graham's Factories Education Bill filled them with alarm lest the Church gain complete control of education.

After the Dissenters had reached a peak of excitement in their agitation against the Factories Education Bill, Miall decided to organize them in a militant campaign against all religious endowments. He began by getting the endorsement of a dozen Radical newspapers as well as the cooperation of *The Patriot* and the *Eclectic Review*.[32] He then enlisted the Religious Freedom Societies of Leicester, Newcastle, and London, and with their aid he set up a provisional committee of 200 members to whom he delegated the task of promoting the Anti-State Church Convention.[33] Preparing for the Convention, the provisional committee met in February 1844, and set forth their objectives as follows: to watch with vigilance the proceedings of Parliament, to prevent the imposition of church rates, to assist those persecuted for the nonpayment of rates, and to separate the church from the state. To achieve these aims, the Committee invited the Dissenting chapels and denominational organizations to send delegates to a proposed Anti-State Church Convention.[34]

On April 30, 1844, 740 delegates convened in London to protest the union of church and state and to form a new association with the purpose of dissolving that "unholy alliance." The new Anti-State Church Association was the most comprehensive and imposing of the several Dissenting bodies which had been organized to promote religious freedom. It had a council of 500 and a permanent executive committee of 50 members. It also had a Parliamentary committee to elect Dissenters to Parliament and to pledge other candidates against state churches.[35]

Not all Dissenters, however, could conscientiously participate in a body so distinctly political in character. Those pious men, who had originally formed the Evangelical Voluntary Church Association, continued to cherish the hope that "true Christian principles" would triumph within the Established Church. Led by John Angell James and other ministers of the Congregational Union, they proposed the formation of an interdenominational union that would incorporate such Evangelical bodies as the Baptists, Congregationalists, Wesleyan Methodists, and the Secession Church of Scotland. At the end of the May meetings in 1843 these leaders agreed to form an alliance in commemoration of the fiftieth anniversary of the London Missionary Society. Finally, in October 1845, 200 delegates from seventeen denominations met in Liverpool to establish the Evangelical Alliance.[36] Although the Evangelicals professed to disdain political action, they revealed how political they were by their vehement opposition to the endowment of the Roman Catholic College of Maynooth.

The vexatious religious problems that had caused the fall of Sir Robert Peel's first Conservative Ministry threatened to disrupt his second. When Peel first suggested increasing the grant to Maynooth College, which trained the Roman Catholic priests of Ireland, William E. Gladstone resigned as president of the Board of Trade.[37] On April 3, 1845, Peel nevertheless introduced his motion in the House of Commons to increase the annual grant from £9,000 to £26,000 and, in addition, to allot £30,000 for buildings.[38] He defended this action, which he knew would excite great discord among Conservatives, as a measure of relief to needy priests and as a means of pacifying Ireland.

The Parliamentary opposition to the Maynooth grant was even more violent than Peel had expected. Sir Robert Inglis, the acknowledged defender of the Anglican Church in the House of Commons, denounced it as the initial endowment of the Irish Catholic priests. In spite of the opposition of Churchmen and Dissenters, Peel carried his motion by 216 ayes to 114 noes.[39] But it was ominous for the future of his Ministry that the majority embraced 100 Whigs and Radicals, while the minority comprised many of his Conservative followers.[40]

During six nights of debates in the House of Commons on the second reading of the Maynooth College bill, the Dissenters had ample opportunity to expound their principles of voluntaryism. Thomas S. Duncombe, their acknowledged spokesman, said that while they had sympathy for the suffering of the Irish clergy, they "stood on the broad ground of no endowment. . . ." [41] In a more belligerent mood, John Bright ridiculed the grant as hush money to quiet the priests' agitation.[42] On behalf of the Scottish Dissenters, Fox Maule cited the rapid growth of the Free Church of Scotland as proof of the feasibility of the voluntary principle. The sharpest controversy arose over Henry G. Ward's motion that the Maynooth grant be paid from "funds already applicable to ecclesiastical purposes in Ireland." On this amendment the Radicals and Dissenters mustered a minority of 148 members against 322 Whigs and Conservatives.[43]

While Parliament was debating the Maynooth grant, Dissenters and Churchmen toured the country beating their war drums against it. As a result of their noisy demonstration, 8,758 petitions, with more than 1,000,000 signatures, were sent to Parliament.[44] In addition to public demonstrations, the denominational bodies organized pressure groups to deal with members of Parliament. On March 18 these groups unified their forces by forming the Central Anti-Maynooth Committee. With Sir Culling Eardley Smith as chairman, the Committee met every day while Parliament was debating the Maynooth bill and directed the "no popery" campaign against it. Though Macaulay derided this agitation as "the bray of Exeter Hall," his ridicule hardly lessened the zeal of men who felt they were fighting "the second battle of the Reformation."[45]

Those Dissenters, however, who had formed the Anti-State Church Association to promote voluntaryism were not content merely to raise the "no popery" cry against Roman Catholicism. Under the leadership of Price, Conder, and Miall, they formed a separate conference to oppose the third reading of the Maynooth College bill.[46] They then addressed a letter to the Irish Catholics offering to help them obtain full civil liberty and assuring them that as Dissenters they were opposed not merely to Catholic endowments but to all religious endowments. Their campaign for religious liberty, however, had no more effect on Parliament than the "no popery" cry of the Anglican Church. The Maynooth bill, despite the opposition of both Churchmen and Dissenters, passed the House of Commons by a large majority; and it then went quickly through the House of Lords, notwithstanding the opposition of a majority of the bishops.[47]

Though badly defeated in their battle against the Maynooth grant, the Dissenters continued to wage war against religious establishments. They redoubled their efforts to organize their denominational schools in order to free themselves from the intermeddling of the state. The Congregationalists were first to start the movement for voluntaryism in education. They established a Central Committee to raise £100,000 for new schools, and then decided to make their schools denominational rather than comprehensive.[48] Shortly thereafter the Baptist Union also began to build its denominational schools and, like the Congregational Union, it, too, separated from the British and Foreign School Society.

While the Dissenters were establishing voluntary schools, the Established Church was enjoying the increased patronage of a friendly Conservative Government. From 1839 to 1850 the Government granted a total of £500,000 for new buildings, of which £405,000 went to schools connected with the Church of England, £8,000 to the Wesleyan Methodist schools, £1,049 to the Roman Catholic schools, £51,000 to the British and Foreign Society's schools, and £37,000 to workhouse schools.[49] This inequitable distribution of public funds increased the Dissenters' fears that public aid meant the domination of education by the Established Church.

When Lord John Russell, who had just returned to office, proposed in 1846 to increase the annual Parliamentary grant to education, the Dissenters rallied their forces to oppose him. The younger Edward Baines began the attack on Russell in the pages of the *Leeds Mercury*. In other places the Anti-State Church Association took up the agitation against the Whig program and produced 4,000 petitions with 500,000 signatures against increased aid to education.[50]

The Dissenters' opposition did not prevent Russell from proceeding with his program. He first obtained the cooperation of the Wesleyan Methodists by assuring them that no aid would be given to Roman Catholic schools, and then requested Parliament to grant £100,000 annually to education.[51] The Conservatives readily complied with his request, only Radicals and Dissenters refusing it.[52] On behalf of the Dissenters, John Bright objected to the Whig policy because "its object, tendency, and result will be to give enormous and increased power to the clergy of the Established Church." He frankly preferred the voluntary principle in education as he preferred *laissez faire* in business. "If there be one principle more certain than another," he said, "I suppose it is this, what a people is able to do for itself, their Government should not attempt to do for it." [53] Thomas Duncombe then moved that a select committee be appointed "to inquire into the justice and expediency" of an additional grant. After three nights of debate on the general question of public aid to education, the Whigs and Conservatives united to defeat the Radicals and Dissenters by 342 votes to 47.[54]

While Parliament debated the question of public aid to education, the Dissenters descended on London to oppose the legislation in the name of religious liberty. This time they came not merely to make speeches and sign petitions but to take direct political action against the Whigs in the forthcoming elections. Under the direction of the Anti-State Church Association 500 delegates representing congregations in all parts of the country met in London in April 1847 to launch the new movement.[55] Resolved to support only those candidates "who hold sacred the claims of religious liberty," they formed the Parliamentary Committee and delegated to it the task of finding voluntaryist candidates. With Samuel Morley as chairman, the Committee drew up a list of 53 candidates and recommended them as worthy of representing the Dissenters.[56] The Committee urged the Dissenters, on the other hand, not to support Lord John Russell or any other candidate who held his views of the Church. Further preparing for the elections, the Committee solicited £50,000 to register freehold voters and to bear the campaign expenses of their chosen candidates.[57]

During the elections of 1847 the Dissenters openly campaigned against the Whigs in several important constituencies. At Edinburgh they formed an election committee with the purpose of defeating Macaulay. They chose Charles Cowan, "an avowed voluntaryist," as their candidate, and had great satisfaction not only in defeating the most eloquent defender of Whig policies but also in returning two candidates pledged to voluntaryism.[58]

In London the Dissenting Deputies, who had at last come to accept the principle of disestablishment, took charge of the voluntaryist campaign. The Deputies sent "An Address to the Nonconformist Electors of Great Britain" instructing them to pledge candidates on five different issues of religious liberty and requesting them specifically to reject Lord John Russell.[59] During the London campaign, the Dissenting Deputies endorsed and helped to elect James Pattison, Sir George Larpent, and Baron Rothschild, though the last, a Jew, could not take his seat because of religious disabilities. That Russell was ultimately returned victoriously was the result, so the Deputies thought, of his having been supported by the Conservatives as well as the Whigs.[60] If the return of Russell was disappointing, the Dissenters rejoiced in the defeat of Benjamin Hawes at Lambeth and in the return of George Thompson for Tower Hamlet. As a result of the metropolitan voluntaryist campaign, the Dissenting Deputies boasted that they elected 14 of the 15 candidates whom they had pledged to full religious liberty.[61]

In Lancashire a committee of the Anti-State Church Association assisted in electing John Bright and T. M. Gibson for Manchester.[62] In addition, they worked for the election of Richard Cobden for Stockport and Charles Villiers for South Lancashire. It was clear from these campaigns that a new political organization, comprising men who believed in free trade, complete suffrage, and voluntaryism, had arisen in Lancashire to challenge the Whigs.

The younger Edward Baines, who headed the voluntaryist movement in Yorkshire, was not so successful as John Bright had been in electing voluntaryist candidates. Baines sponsored Joseph Sturge at Leeds; and although Sturge received 1,976 votes he failed to win the election.[63] Edward Miall was defeated at Halifax. In several contests of the West Riding, however, candidates, famous as advocates of free trade and religious liberty, were elected without the expense or effort of a campaign. Most important was the election of Richard Cobden for the West Riding.[64] It was as evident in Yorkshire, as in Lancashire, that a political party, made of new men and new issues, had arisen to challenge the old Whig leadership.

In other manufacturing and commercial cities, where Dissenters had formerly supported the Whigs, they now turned to the Radicals or to their own voluntaryist candidates. From Leicester they returned Joshua Walmsley; and at Norwich they elected Samuel M. Peto. At Birmingham both successful candidates, William Scholefield and Frederick G. Muntz, belonged to the anti-church rate faction. As a result of the voluntaryist campaign in these and other cities, the Anti-State Church Association claimed victory for 26 Dissenting candidates and for a total of 60 Members of Parliament pledged against the state endowment of religion.[65]

From this survey of the political activities of militant Dissent during the election of 1847 one may conclude that voluntaryism was an essential part of the new liberalism. Free traders and voluntaryists were the same people and their object was one—to abolish exclusive aristocratic privileges in church and state. To achieve this end they desired a thorough reform of Parliament. The Liberal party consisted of free traders, Benthamite Radicals, and Dissenters; and their faith in religious liberty, *laissez faire,* and democracy were the ingredients of the new liberalism.

# *13. Conclusion*

The reform movements during the three decades after the Napoleonic Wars carried England far along the road from aristocracy to democracy. When the Revolution of 1848 convulsed the countries on the Continent, England avoided bloodshed because harsh social conditions had been partly ameliorated and political power had already been redistributed so that a majority of people confidently expected further reform and firmly believed they had in hand the means to effect a peaceful change in society.

England escaped from revolution, moreover, because middle-class reformers had faithfully taught their countrymen to use constitutional means to achieve their ends. Such reformers felt a heavy moral responsibility that often showed through their sober faces. They did more than save England from revolution. They brought a new social consciousness of men's needs at home and abroad, a new consciousness of the pathetic factory children, the abused prisoners, the unpitied insane, and, beyond sight, the colored man in Africa and the wretched slaves of the West Indies.

It would be too simple to say that the Wesleyan revival alone saved England from revolution. Yet one must recognize the significant role of the Evangelical reformers. Deeply committed to righteous causes, they so closely identified themselves with a single measure that to see the man was to know his cause. Too rigid and stern for polite society and too uncompromising for practical politics, their devotion to their panacea endeared them to their followers and fitted them for the leadership of mass movements. Although they failed to understand the economic causes of wretchedness, their faith held their followers together in a close fellowship and inspired them with the confidence that their petitions would be heeded and their grievances redressed.

After acknowledging the importance of the Evangelicals, one must also recognize the Benthamite Radicals as important middle-class reformers. They surely were not motivated by religion, and they rarely stopped scheming to take counsel of their hearts. With the audacity of men of a new science, they dared to call to judgment inherited traditions and institutions. In one important respect they resembled the Clapham Sect. As the latter supplied a national leadership for the humanitarian reformers of the north, so the London Radicals gave guidance to the liberal reformers of Leeds, Birmingham, and Manchester. Too doctrinaire to be popular, the Radicals depended upon the northern propagandists to translate their ideas into national movements. Although doctrinaire, they gained the support of businessmen by advocating free trade; although irreligious, they won a following among the Dissenters by advocating religious liberty.

The Unitarians, themselves stern rationalists, helped to bridge the gulf between the Dissenters and the Radicals. Until the passing of the Reform Bill, William Smith and the London Unitarians were the national political leaders of Dissent. When Smith retired from Parliament, John Wilks, the Radical member for Boston, became the Dissenters' national spokesman. The coincidence of rationalism and romanticism among the Dissenters explains, in part, their effectiveness as reformers. They enthusiastically campaigned for the repeal of the Corn Laws, but they failed to help the factory workers gain a shorter working day. John Bright and William Johnson Fox devoted themselves to free trade in the name of religious liberty, but the same idealism prevented them from crusading for the factory children.

Since there was no contradiction in the question of slavery, the Dissenters freely participated in the crusades to abolish the slave trade and to emancipate the West Indian slaves. Benevolent Quakers and the Clapham Evangelicals, the leaders of these mass movements, were also the founders of missionary societies. It was no coincidence that Wilberforce, the greatest of the Abolitionists, opened the door of India to the missionaries. Nor was it a coincidence that missionaries were also Abolitionists. Emotionally identified with the slaves, they wrote volumes of letters explaining the conditions of the slaves, and when they returned home, they toured the countryside to arouse sympathy for the slaves and resentment of the slaveholders.

As antislavery was a phase of Christian foreign missions to save the soul of the colored man, so elementary education, at first, was a phase of home missions to uplift underprivileged people. The London Quakers and the Clapham Evangelicals, the leading exponents of education, thought of the National School Society and the British and Foreign School Society as agencies to spread Christianity.

However great as humanitarian reformers, the Evangelical Churchmen and Wesleyan Methodists were not liberal reformers. But the Evangelical Dissenters did not abandon their tradition of religious liberty when they adopted Wesley's faith and practice. Like other Evangelicals, the Dissenters' paramount concern was the abolition of slavery; at the same time, however, they were deeply committed to the reform of Parliament. Their doctrine of religious liberty was the essence of political liberalism. They were almost unanimous in believing that the state should not interfere with religion nor bar anyone from public office on account of religion. True to this doctrine, the Dissenters sought civil equality for the Irish Catholics as well as for themselves, and thus raised the Irish question to a national level in English politics.

The persistent desire for religious equality brought the Dissenters into politics on the side of the Whigs, an alliance which lasted for more than a century. But after the passing of the Reform Bill, the Dissenters increasingly demanded the disestablishment of the Irish and English Churches. To this extreme the Whigs would not go; hence, the Dissenters turned to the Benthamite Radicals. In the election of 1847 they supported those candidates who had advocated free trade, complete suffrage, and voluntaryism in education, and thus helped to form a Liberal party in opposition to the Whigs.

While the Dissenters were participating in Liberal politics, the Anglicans were contending as strenuously for Conservative candidates. Identified with the old agrarian social order, the Established Church upheld the interests of country gentlemen and the privileges of the aristocracy. The bishops and the clergy constantly opposed Radical reform as well as the Reform Bill. That the Church was conservative is not surprising, for a long history had imposed upon it this social function. Its towering sanctuaries called men to reverence their inheritance. Its hierarchy raised the bishops to the pinnacle of leadership and invested them with the authority that held society together. Its sacraments made men depend upon established institutions for salvation. The Church was, indeed, a conservator in an age of social conflict and economic transformation.

Liberal and humanitarian reforms have been treated here in their religious aspects. These movements have been explained previously in the statistics of bread, shoes, and employment. It is no simple task to measure the material possessions of a people; it is more difficult to plumb their faith. But as long as life is more than bread, the attempt should be made, however forbidding, to penetrate the mysteries of a people's hopes and fears and to unlock the treasures by which they live.

# *Notes*

## Chapter 1

### SOCIAL AND POLITICAL ALIGNMENTS

1. James Bennett, *History of the Dissenters, 1808–1838* (London, 1839), p. 240.

2. Elie Halévy, *England in 1815* (New York, Peter Smith, 1949), p. 424.

3. All of these groups, whether Dissenters, Churchmen, or Methodists, are best understood from 1800 to 1815 in terms of the Evangelical or Wesleyan revival.

4. David Bogue and James Bennett, *History of Dissenters* (London, 1808), III, 333.

5. *Parliamentary Debates,* 1st series, XX, 888. Lord Stanhope, the constant friend of religious liberty, thought these statistics proved that a majority of the people were Dissenters.

6. For the weakness of the Church in the industrial and urban areas, see the debates in 1818 on the bill to appropriate funds for building new churches. *Parliamentary Debates,* 1st series, XXXVII, 1118. The Church was especially weak in the dioceses of York and Chester. The first religious census, taken in 1851, showed the nation equally divided between Church and Dissent with about three million each. It also showed the Dissenters strongest in the manufacturing towns and counties.

7. The terms Nonconformist and Free Church were rarely used during the first half of the century.

8. 1 Will. and Mary, sess. 1, cap. 18.

9. Earl Morse Wilbur, *Our Unitarian Heritage* (Boston: Beacon Press, 1925), p. 289.

10. Humphry Sandwith, "Methodism and Its Relation to the Church and the Nation," a series of articles in *Wesleyan Methodist Magazine*, 3rd series, VIII (1829).

11. *Ibid.*, 314.

12. Herbert S. Skeats and Charles S. Miall, *History of the Free Churches of England* (revised edition; London, 1894), p. 507.

13. Henry W. Clark, *History of English Non-conformity* (London, 1913), II, 329–31.

14. Francis W. Cornish, *The English Church in the Nineteenth Century* (London: Macmillan, 1910), Part I, p. 6.

15. Ernest M. Howse, *Saints in Politics* (Toronto: University of Toronto Press, 1952), p. 25.

16. For Elie Halévy's statement that Evangelicalism saved England from revolution, see his *England in 1815*, p. 387.

17. Robert Torbet, *A History of the Baptists* (Philadelphia: The Judson Press, 1950), p. 106.

18. *Evangelical Magazine*, VIII (1799), 256.

19. For example, the income of 1825 was £474,960. See *Christian Observer*, XXIV (1825), 843.

20. G. R. Balleine, *A History of the Evangelical Party in the Church of England* (London, 1909), p. 155.

21. The principal Evangelicals in Parliament from 1800 to 1830 were Thomas Fowell Buxton (who succeeded Wilberforce as the leader of the Abolitionists), Charles and Robert Grant, Stephen Lushington, Sir George H. Rose, Dudley Ryder (Lord Harrowby after 1798), John Shore (Lord Teignmouth after 1797), Henry Thornton, Nicholas Vansittart (Lord Bexley after 1823), and William Wilberforce. These were Evangelical Churchmen, although Buxton was as closely associated with the Quakers as with Churchmen. In close cooperation with

these "Saints" of the Church were the Dissenters, Joseph Butterworth, Thomas Thompson, and William Smith.

22. *A Sketch of the History and Proceedings of the Deputies Appointed to Protect the Civil Rights of Protestant Dissenters* (London, 1813), pp. 1–4.

23. Bernard Lord Manning, *The Protestant Dissenting Deputies* (Cambridge: University Press, 1952), p. 37.

24. Howse, *Saints in Politics,* p. 17.

25. *Baptist Magazine,* III (1811), 342; Clark, *op. cit.,* II, 301.

## Chapter 2

### The Growth of Religious Liberty

1. Thomas E. May, *The Constitutional History of England, 1760–1860* (3rd ed.; New York: Armstrong and Son, 1886), II, 392.

2. 13 Car. II, Stat. II, cap. 1.

3. 25 Car. II, cap. 2.

4. Earl M. Wilbur, *Our Unitarian Heritage* (Boston: Beacon Press, 1925), p. 371.

5. Thomas Belsham, *The Rights of Conscience Asserted and Defined* (London, 1812), p. 13.

6. Robert Hall, "Apology for the Freedom of the Press," in the *Works of Robert Hall,* ed. by Olinthus Gregory (12th edition; London, 1861), III, 142.

7. Josiah Conder, *On Protestant Nonconformity* (London, 1818), II, 489.

8. *Parliamentary History,* 1st series, XXVI, 830–32.

9. *Ibid.*, XXVIII, 40.

10. *Ibid.*, XXVIII, 450.

11. Burke wrote his *Reflections on the Revolution in France* as a reply to a sermon preached by Richard Price, *A Discourse on the Love of Our Country.*

12. *Sketch of the History of the Protestant Dissenting Deputies* (London, 1813), p. 55.

13. *Loc. cit.*

14. Conrad Gill, *History of Birmingham* (London; Oxford University Press, 1952), I, 143.

15. Arthur Redford and Ina S. Russell, *The History of Local Government in Manchester* (London, 1939), II, 195.

16. Archibald Prentice, *Recollections of Manchester* (2nd edition, Manchester, 1851), p. 3.

17. *Ibid.*, p. 11.

18. R. W. Greaves, *The Corporation of Leicester* (London: Oxford University Press, 1939), p. 111.

19. H. McLachlan, *English Education under the Test Acts, 1662–1820* (Manchester, 1932), p. 252.

20. *Sketch of the Dissenting Deputies,* p. 138.

21. Parliamentary Debates, 1st series, XV, 854.

22. *Ibid.*, XV, 633.

23. *Sketch of the Dissenting Deputies,* p. 85.

24. *Parliamentary Debates,* 1st series, XIX, 1132.

25. Henry Richard Lord Holland, *Further Memoirs of the Whig*

*Party, 1807–1821,* ed. by Lord Stavordale (London, 1905), p. 101.

26. *Parliamentary Debates,* 1st series, XX, 234.

27. *Ibid.,* XX, 250.

28. *Ibid.,* XXIII, 149–50.

29. *Evangelical Magazine,* XX (1812), 114.

30. *Parliamentary Debates,* 1st series, XXIII, 890.

31. 52 Geo. III, cap. 155.

32. *Parliamentary Debates,* 1st series, XXIII, 1105.

33. 55 Geo. III, cap. 160, also, *Sketch of Dissenting Deputies,* p. 117.

34. Ernest M. Howse, *Saints in Politics* (Toronto: University of Toronto Press, 1952), pp. 68–72.

35. Robert G. Torbet, *A History of the Baptists* (Philadelphia: The Judson Press, 1950), p. 106.

36. Francis Warre Cornish, *The English Church in the Nineteenth Century* (London: Macmillan, 1910), Part I, p. 46.

37. William Wilberforce, *The Life of William Wilberforce,* ed. by Robert and Samuel Wilberforce (London, 1838), IV, 11–12.

38. *Ibid.,* IV, 125.

39. *Parliamentary Debates,* 1st series, XXIV, 735.

40. *Ibid.,* XXV, 745.

41. *Ibid.,* XXVI, 361.

42. "Report of the Protestant Society," *Baptist Magazine,* XI (1819), 253.

43. *Parliamentary Debates,* 1st series, XL, 1515.

44. See below, p. 44.

45. *Parliamentary Debates,* 2nd series, II, 423.

46. 3 Geo. IV, cap. 126.

47. "Report of the Protestant Society," *Baptist Magazine,* XVIII (1826), 331.

48. Bernard Lord Manning, *The Protestant Dissenting Deputies* (Cambridge, The University Press, 1952), p. 228.

49. Henry W. Clark, *History of English Nonconformity* (London: Chapman and Hall, 1913), II, 305.

50. Manning, *Dissenting Deputies,* p. 229.

51. "Report of the Protestant Society," *Baptist Magazine,* XIX (1827), 281.

52. *Parliamentary Debates,* 2nd series, XVIII, 759.

53. *Ibid.,* XVIII, 1457.

54. *Ibid.,* XIX, 130.

55. *Ibid.,* XVIII, 715.

56. Manning, *Dissenting Deputies,* p. 235.

57. *Parliamentary Debates,* 2nd series, XVIII, 694.

58. *Ibid.,* 690.

59. *Ibid.,* 772.

60. *Ibid.,* 782.

61. *Ibid.,* 1202.

62. *Ibid.*, 1207.

63. *Ibid.*, 1605.

64. Horace Twiss, *The Public and Private Life of Lord Chancellor Eldon* (2nd edition, London, 1844), III, 45.

65. *Baptist Magazine,* XX (1828), 122.

66. *Christian Observer,* XXVII (1828), 206.

67. *Ibid.*, 279.

68. *Report of the Speeches and Proceedings of a Dinner to Commemorate the Abolition of the Sacramental Test* (London, 1828).

69. Manning, *Dissenting Deputies,* p. 252.

70. Joseph Priestley, "A Free Address to Those Who Have Petitioned for the Repeal of the Late Act of Parliament in Favour of Roman Catholics," in *Theological and Miscellaneous Works,* ed. by J. T. Rutt (London, 1823), XX, 499–515.

71. Robert Hall, "On the Love of Freedom," *Works,* III, 47.

72. Hall, "Zeal without Innovation," *Works,* III, 98.

73. *Monthly Repository,* XXIV (1829), 147.

74. *Baptist Magazine,* XXI (1829), 122.

75. *Christian Observer,* XXIX, 129. Michael T. Sadler, an exception to this rule, opposed Emancipation.

76. *Parliamentary Debates,* 2nd series, XXI, 394–97

77. John W. Croker, *Correspondence and Diaries* (New York: Scribner's Sons, 1884), I, 416.

78. Charles C. F. Greville, *A Journal of the Reigns of King George*

*IV and King William IV*, ed. by Henry Reeve (London, 1875), I, 198.

79. *Monthly Repository*, XXIV (1829), 446.

80. "Report of the Protestant Society," *Baptist Magazine*, XX (1828), 294.

## Chapter 3

### The Rise of Popular Education

1. John William Adamson, *English Education, 1789–1902* (Cambridge, 1930), p. 18.

2. Committee of Council on Education, *On the School in Its Relations to the State, the Church, and the Community* (London, 1847), p. 6.

3. *Ibid.*, p. 3.

4. Henry B. Binns, *A Century of Education, Being the Centenary History of the British and Foreign School Society, 1808–1908* (London, 1908), p. 7.

5. Francis Adams, *History of the Elementary School Contest in England* (London, 1882), p. 51.

6. Lord Brougham's Committee on Education, *Report of Minutes of Evidence . . .* , 1816, II, 188.

7. Binns, *British and Foreign School Society*, p. 18.

8. *Ibid.*, p. 87.

9. British and Foreign School Society, *Manual*, 1844, p. 116.

10. Binns, *op. cit.*, p. 171.

11. Spencer Walpole, *A History of England* (London, 1890), I, 329.

12. *Parliamentary Debates,* 1st series, VIII, 802.

13. *Ibid.,* 883.

14. Sir Samuel Romilly, *Memoirs of His Life, Written by Himself* (London, 1840), II, 209.

15. *Parliamentary Debates,* 1st series, IX, 1177.

16. *Ibid.,* 1179.

17. Sarah Trimmer, *A Comparative View of the New Plan of Education* (London, 1805), p. 46 ff.

18. *The Education of the Poor . . . A Digest of the Reports for Bettering the Condition of the Poor* (London, 1809), p. 39.

19. *Ibid.,* p. 40.

20. *Ibid.,* p. 97.

21. Francis W. Cornish, *The English Church in the Nineteenth Century* (London, 1910), Part I, 96.

22. National Society for Promotion of the Education of the Poor in the Principles of the Established Church, *First Annual Report of . . . with an Account of the Proceedings for the Formation of the Society . . .* (London, 1812), p. 27.

23. *Ibid.,* p. 23.

24. Lord Brougham's Committee on Education, *Report of Minutes of Evidence,* 1816, II, 190.

25. Binns, *History of British and Foreign School Society,* p. 82.

26. *Quarterly Review,* XV (1816), 225.

27. Adamson, *English Education,* p. 47.

28. Parliamentary Debates, 2nd series, II, 62.

29. Lord Brougham's Committee, *Third Report from the Select Committee*, p. 61.

30. *Ibid.*, p. 63.

31. Adamson, *English Education*, p. 10. See Priestley, *Essay on the First Principle of Government and on the Nature of Civil and Religious Liberty* (1768).

32. Binns, *History of the British and Foreign School Society*, p. 38.

33. Elie Halévy, *The Growth of Philosophical Radicalism* (London, 1928), p. 286.

34. *Ibid.*, p. 430.

35. *Edinburgh Review*, XXXIV, 220.

36. *Parliamentary Debates*, 2nd series, II, 73.

37. *Ibid.*, 365.

38. *Edinburgh Review*, XXXIV, 215.

39. *Ibid.*, 247.

40. *Parliamentary Debates*, 3rd series, L, 592.

41. Halévy, *A History of the English People* (New York: Peter Smith, 1949), II, 213.

42. *Parliamentary Debates*, 3rd series, XXIV, 1299.

43. *Ibid.*, 1300.

## Chapter 4

### The Abolition of Colonial Slavery

1. Thomas Clarkson, *The History of the Abolition of the African Slave Trade* (2 vols., London, 1808), I, 113.

2. *Ibid.*, I, 256.

3. Ernest M. Howse, *Saints in Politics* (Toronto, 1952), p. 31.

4. Reginald Coupland, *Wilberforce, A Narrative* (Oxford, 1923), p. 141.

5. Clarkson, *op. cit.*, I, 209.

6. *Ibid.*, I, 229–30.

7. Coupland, *Wilberforce,* p. 32.

8. *Ibid.*, p. 91.

9. *Parliamentary History,* XXVIII, 1207–10.

10. Howse, *Saints in Politics,* p. 37

11. Clarkson, *op. cit.*, II, 359.

12. Coupland, *Wilberforce,* pp. 248–52.

13. Howse, *Saints in Politics,* p. 57.

14. Clarkson, *op. cit.*, II, 502.

15. *Parliamentary Debates,* 1st series, VIII, 257, 717.

16. *Ibid.*, VIII, 995.

17. Coupland, *Wilberforce,* p. 454.

18. Charles Buxton, *Memoirs of Sir Thomas Fowell Buxton* (London, 1849), p. 16.

19. Joseph B. Braithwaite, *Memoirs of Joseph John Gurney* (London, 1854), pp. 124–31.

20. Buxton, *Memoirs,* p. 48.

21. *Ibid.*, p. 94.

22. Coupland, *Wilberforce,* p. 472.

23. Anti-Slavery Society, *Report,* 1824, pp. 1–6.

24. William Allen, *Life of William Allen* (3 vols., London, 1846), I, 326.

25. *Parliamentary Debates,* 2nd series, VIII, 630.

26. *Ibid.,* IX, 275.

27. *Ibid.,* IX, 311.

28. *Ibid.,* IX, 315.

29. Anti-Slavery Society, *Report,* August 1823.

30. *Annual Register* (History), 1824, pp. 176–87. Also, Anti-Slavery Society, *Report,* 1824, pp. 6–16.

31. Frank J. Klingberg, *The Anti-Slavery Movement in England* (New Haven, 1926), p. 220.

32. *Parliamentary Debates,* 2nd series, XI, 963, 1315.

33. Anti-Slavery Society, *Proceedings,* 1824, pp. 70–79.

34. *Minutes of the Methodist Conference,* VI, 51.

35. *Parliamentary Debates,* 2nd series, XIII, 1311.

36. Buxton, *Memoirs,* p. 211.

37. Anti-Slavery Society, *Account of the Receipts and Disbursements for the Years 1829 & 1830,* p. 2.

38. William L. Mathieson, *British Slavery and Its Abolition* (London, 1926), p. 196.

39. *Parliamentary Debates,* 2nd series, XXV, 1172–92.

40. Anti-Slavery Society, *Address to the Electors and People of the United Kingdom,* 1830, p. 1.

41. *Baptist Magazine,* XXII (1830), 343.

42. *Report of the Agency Committee of the Anti-Slavery Society,* 1831, pp. 6–7.

43. *Parliamentary Debates,* 3rd series, XIII, 1230–31.

44. *Baptist Magazine,* XXV (1833), 80.

45. *Anti-Slavery Monthly Reporter,* V, 32.

46. Klingberg, *The Anti-Slavery Movement,* p. 273.

47. Charles C. F. Greville, *A Journal of the Reigns of King George IV and King William IV* (London, 1875), II, 347.

48. *Wesleyan Methodist Magazine,* XIII (1834), 229.

49. *Parliamentary Debates,* 3rd series, XVI, 283.

50. Henry Whiteley, *Three Months in Jamaica* (London, 1833), p. 22.

51. *Baptist Magazine,* XXV (1833), 282.

52. *Wesleyan Methodist Magazine,* XII (1833), 366.

53. *Parliamentary Debates,* 3rd series, XVII, 1230–31.

54. *Ibid.,* XIX, 1238–39.

55. 3 and 4 Will. IV, cap. 73.

56. Francis W. Cornish, *The English Church in the Nineteenth Century* (London, 1910), Part I, p. 28.

57. Henry Richard, *Memoirs of Joseph Sturge* (London, 1864), pp. 123–32.

58. *Eclectic Review,* 4th series, IV, 55.

59. *Ibid.,* 54.

60. Mathieson, *op. cit.,* p. 293.

61. *Parliamentary Debates,* 3rd series, XL, 1356.

62. *Ibid.,* XLIII, 123–26.

63. Henry Richard, *Memoirs of Joseph Sturge,* p. 171.

## Chapter 5

### THE REFORM BILL OF 1832

1. James Bennett, *Memoirs of the Life of the Rev. David Bogue* (London, 1827), p. 427.

2. Robert Robinson, *A Plan of Lectures on the Principles of Nonconformity for the Instruction of Catechumen* (5th edition; London, 1778), p. 49.

3. Joseph Priestley, *Theological and Miscellaneous Works* (London, 1823), XXII, 484.

4. *Ibid.,* 392.

5. Robert Hall, *Christianity Consistent with the Love of Freedom* in *The Miscellaneous Works of Robert Hall* (12th edition; London, 1861), III, 24.

6. Hall, *An Apology for the Freedom of the Press,* in his *Works,* III, 152.

7. G. S. Veitch, *The Genesis of Parliamentary Reform* (London, 1913), p. 160.

8. Anthony Lincoln, *Some Political and Social Ideas of English Dissent* (Cambridge: The University Press, 1938), p. 133.

9. *A Sketch of the History and Proceedings of the Deputies* (London, 1813), p. 55.

10. J. R. M. Butler, *The Passing of the Great Reform Bill* (London: Longmans, Green, 1914), p. 14.

11. The Dissenters considered Fox "an oracle of political wisdom." See, for example, Robert Aspland's sermon at the time of Fox's death in the *Monthly Repository*, 1806, p. 607.

12. Hall, *Miscellaneous Works*, III, 81.

13. *Ibid.*, p. 190.

14. Robert Vaughan, *Thoughts on the Past and Present State of Religious Parties in England* (London, 1838), p. xii.

15. *Congregational Magazine*, III (1827), *Supplement.*

16. J. L. and Barbara Hammond, *The Age of the Chartists* (London: Longmans, Green, 1930), p. 223.

17. *Parliamentary Debates*, 3rd series, XXXVI, 1278.

18. *Ibid.*, XX, 436.

19. *Ibid.*, XXII, 509.

20. *Ibid.*, XXXIV, 79.

21. John Wade, *The Extraordinary Black Book* (London, 1832), p. 83.

22. *Parliamentary Debates*, 2nd series, XVIII, 697.

23. Sidney and Beatrice Webb, *English Local Government* (London, 1922), II, 702.

24. R. W. Greaves, *The Corporation of Leicester, 1689–1836* (London: Oxford University Press, 1939), p. 97.

25. S. and B. Webb, *op. cit.*, II, 441.

26. As related by Thomas Spring Rice in a debate on church rates in 1837, *Parliamentary Debates,* 3rd series, XXXVI, 1212.

27. S. and B. Webb, *op. cit.,* II, 475.

28. *Ibid.,* I, 94–95.

29. Jessie K. Buckley, *Joseph Parkes of Birmingham* (London: Methuen, 1926), p. 22.

30. *Ibid.,* p. 52.

31. John A. Langford, *A Century of Birmingham Life* (Birmingham, 1868), II, 454.

32. Arthur Redford and I. S. Russell, *The History of Local Government in Manchester* (London, 1939), I, 303.

33. S. and B. Webb, *op. cit.,* I, 102.

34. David Bogue and James Bennett, *History of the Dissenters* (London, 1808), IV, 550.

35. Quoted by Richard Garnett in *The Life of William Johnson Fox* (London, 1910), p. 94.

36. *Ibid.,* pp. 96–97.

37. *Ibid.,* p. 112.

38. Edward Baines, Jr., *The Life of Edward Baines* (London, 1859), p. 18.

39. William H. Mills, *The Manchester Guardian* (London: Chatto, 1921), p. 33.

40. Archibald Prentice, *Historical Sketches of Manchester* (Manchester, 1851), p. 247.

41. Mills, *op. cit.,* p. 29.

42. Prentice, *Historical Sketches,* p. 68.

43. Redford and Russell, *op. cit.,* I, 256.

44. Archibald Prentice, *History of the Anti-Corn Law League* (London, 1853), I, 2.

45. Asa Briggs, *The Press and Public Opinion in Early Nineteenth Century Birmingham* (Oxford: Dugdale Society, Occasional Paper #8, 1949), p. 24.

46. Conrad Gill, *History of Birmingham* (London: Oxford University Press, 1952), I, 202.

47. C. M. Wakefield, *Life of Thomas Attwood* (London, 1885), p. 122.

48. *Ibid.,* p. 205.

49. *Ibid.,* p. 414.

50. *Ibid.,* p. 382.

51. Langford, *A Century of Birmingham Life,* II, 472.

52. Rollo Russell, *Early Correspondence of Lord John Russell* (London, 1913), I, 199.

53. "Report of the Protestant Society" in *The Monthly Repository,* 1821, p. 378.

54. "Report of the Protestant Society" in *Baptist Magazine,* XXVI (1834), 243.

55. "Report of the Dissenting Deputies" in *Baptist Magazine,* XIX (1827), June issue. Members of the Committee from the House of Lords were Lord Holland and Lord King; from the House of Commons: Lord Milton, Lord Ebrington, Lord Althorp, Lord Nugent, George Byng, Alexander Dawson, John Wood, J. B. Monck, John Easthope, John Smith, John Maberly, W. L. Maberly, George Philips, W. W. Whitmore, John Calcraft,

Henry Brougham, Sir Robert Wilson, Sir George Robinson, N. Calvert, C. F. Palmer, M. Fitzgerald, George R. Philips, W. B. Baring, and Lord John Russell.

56. "Report of the Dissenting Deputies" in *Baptist Magazine,* 1831, p. 79.

57. *Baptist Magazine,* XXII (1830), 343.

58. *Minutes of the Conference,* VI, 613; also, see *Methodist Magazine,* 1830, p. 609.

59. *Anti-Slavery Monthly Reporter,* III, 220.

60. *Annual Register,* 1830 (History), p. 59.

61. Henry Lord Brougham, *Life and Times of Lord Brougham* (New York, 1872), II, 31.

62. *Ibid.,* II, 34.

63. *Anti-Slavery Reporter,* III, 361–68.

64. *Annual Register,* 1830 (History), p. 149.

65. John Croker estimated that the Tories had 203 of the rotten borough seats and that the Whigs had 73. See the *Croker Papers* (New York, 1884), I, 342.

66. *Parliamentary Debates,* 3rd series, I, 53.

67. *Ibid.,* II, 994.

68. *Ibid.,* II, 1082.

69. *Ibid.,* II, 1157.

70. *Christian Observer,* XXIX (1830), 245.

71. *Baptist Magazine,* XXIII (1831), 155.

72. Charles C. F. Greville, *A Journal of the Reigns of King George IV and King William IV* (London: Longmans, Green, 1874), II, 79.

73. "Report of the Dissenting Deputies" in *Baptist Magazine,* XXIII (1831), 116.

74. *The Times* (of London), May 7, 1831.

75. *Anti-Slavery Reporter,* VI, 66.

76. *Eclectic Review,* 3rd series, V, 448.

77. *The Times* (of London), June 1, 1831.

78. Wellington, *Despatches, Correspondence, and Memoranda of the Duke of Wellington* (London, 1880), VIII, 39.

79. *Christian Observer,* XXX (1831), 348.

80. *Parliamentary Debates,* 3rd series, VII, 464.

81. *Ibid.,* 943.

82. *Ibid.,* 968.

83. *Ibid.,* 920–28.

84. Wakefield, *Life of Thomas Attwood,* p. 176.

85. *Parliamentary Debates,* 3rd series, VII, 1317.

86. *Ibid.,* VIII, 304.

87. *Ibid.,* VIII, 470.

88. Wellington, *Despatches,* VII, 35.

89. *Annual Register,* 1831 (Chronology), p. 161.

90. *Ibid.,* pp. 171–75.

91. Wakefield, *Life of Thomas Attwood,* p. 179.

92. Gill, *History of Birmingham,* I, 208.

93. Wakefield, *Life of Thomas Attwood,* p. 212.

94. *Parliamentary Debates,* 3rd series, XIII, 374; 2 and 3 Will. IV, cap. 45.

95. *Croker Papers,* I, 571.

96. *Patriot,* June 6, 1832.

97. *Methodist Magazine,* 3rd series, XI, 532.

98. *Christian Observer,* XXXI (1832), 498.

## Chapter 6

### The Redress of Religious Grievances

1. *Evangelical Magazine,* XL (1832), 308.

2. *Baptist Magazine,* XXIV (1832), 581.

3. *The Times* (London), November 7, 1832.

4. For full accounts of the elections see *The Times* during December 1832.

5. Charles S. Parker, *Sir Robert Peel,* II, 209.

6. Wellington to Croker, March 6, 1833, in *Croker's Correspondence and Diaries,* II, 9. See also Parker, *Sir Robert Peel,* II, 223.

7. *Parliamentary Debates,* 3rd series, XV, 639.

8. 3 and 4 Will. IV, cap. 82.

9. *Parliamentary Debates,* 3rd series, XV, 310.

10. *Ibid.,* XVII, 221.

11. *Ibid.,* XX, 249.

12. *Claims of the Protestant Dissenters* (London, 1833), p. 3.

13. *Ibid.,* p. 32.

14. "Report of the United Committee," *Baptist Magazine,* XXV (1833), 279–80.

15. *Parliamentary Debates,* 3rd series, XVII, 194.

16. Charles C. F. Greville, *A Journal of the Reigns of George IV and William IV,* II, 309–10.

17. *Parliamentary Debates,* 3rd series, XVI, 405, 1283.

18. *Ibid.,* XV, 507.

19. *Ibid.,* XVI, 477.

20. *Ibid.,* XVII, 1386.

21. *Edinburgh Review,* LVIII, 199–226, 457–68.

22. *Eclectic Review,* 3rd series, X (1833), 303.

23. Both *The Times* and the *Morning Chronicle* of London carried accounts of this agitation.

24. *Report of Speeches Delivered at Manchester* (Manchester, 1834), p. 4.

25. *Annual Register,* 1834 (Chronicle), p. 7.

26. *Parliamentary Debates,* 3rd series, XXV, 886.

27. *Ibid.,* XX, 779.

28. *Ibid.*, XXII, 1015.

29. *Ibid.*, XXIII, 606.

30. Charles S. Parker, *Life and Letters of Sir James Graham,* I, 187.

31. *Lord Melbourne Papers,* p. 205.

32. *Ibid.*, p. 209.

33. Parker, *Sir Robert Peel,* II, 265.

34. *Ibid.*, 284.

35. *Eclectic Review,* 3rd series, XIII (1835), 53.

36. *Baptist Magazine,* XXVII (1835), 30.

37. James, *Life and Letters,* p. 349. James lamented that political activities of the Dissenters hindered their growth in piety.

38. *The Times* (London), January 12 and February 3, 1835.

39. Greville, *George IV and William IV,* III, 191–92.

40. *Ibid.*, 198.

41. Parker, *Sir Robert Peel,* II, 287.

42. M. M. Torrens, *Memoirs of Lord Melbourne,* II, 71.

43. *Parliamentary Debates,* 3rd series, XXVI, 1090.

44. *Ibid.*, XXVII, 772.

45. For a summary of his ministry see Peel to Croker, April 14, 1835, *Croker Papers,* II, 72.

46. *Lord Melbourne Papers,* p. 239.

47. *The Patriot,* May 20, 1835, and *Voluntary Church Magazine,* III, 331.

48. *Parliamentary Debates,* 3rd series, XXVIII, 78.

49. *Ibid.,* XXXVIII, 1126.

50. S. and B. Webb, *Local Government,* II, 391. Russell estimated that nine tenths of the Dissenters were excluded from the corporations.

51. *Parliamentary Debates,* 3rd series, XXVIII, 557.

52. *Ibid.,* XXIX, 1112.

53. *Eclectic Review,* 4th series, V, 23.

54. Bernard Lord Manning, *The Protestant Dissenting Deputies,* p. 276.

55. "Report of Dissenting Deputies," December 23, 1835, in *Baptist Magazine,* 1836.

56. *Parliamentary Debates,* 3rd series, XXXI, 378.

57. *Ibid.,* XXXIV, 1011.

58. Manning, *Dissenting Deputies,* p. 277.

59. *Congregational Magazine,* 1836, p. 332.

60. *Eclectic Review,* 4th series, VI (1839), 498.

61. Melbourne to Russell, December 15, 1836, in Walpole, *Life of Lord John Russell,* I, 260.

62. *Parliamentary Debates,* 3rd series, XXXIV, 536.

63. Skeats and Miall, *History of the Free Churches of England,* p. 484.

64. Melbourne to the King, February 5, 1837, *Lord Melbourne Papers,* p. 324.

65. *Parliamentary Debates,* 3rd series, XXXVI, 540.

66. *Ibid.,* XXXVI, 150.

67. *The Times* (London), July 1837 for accounts of the elections.

68. *Eclectic Review,* 4th series, II (1837), 209.

69. Sir Edward Baines, *Life of Edward Baines,* p. 201.

70. Parker, *Sir Robert Peel,* II, 349.

71. Walpole, *Life of Lord John Russell,* I, 285.

## Chapter 7

### The Radical Reform of Parliament

1. Mark Hovell, *The Chartist Movement* (Manchester, 1918), p. 5.

2. Jeremy Bentham to Daniel O'Connell, July 15, 1828, in Bentham's *Collected Works* (ed. by John Bowring; London, 1843), X, 595.

3. Bentham's *Collected Works,* II, 468.

4. *Ibid.,* III, 445.

5. Bentham to O'Connell, August 3, 1828, *ibid.,* X, 599.

6. Alexander Bain, *James Mill* (London, 1882), p. 266.

7. H. Grote [Mrs. George Grote], *The Personal Life of George Grote* (London, 1883), p. 73.

8. *The Times* (London), November 15, 1832.

9. *Ibid.*, December 10, 1832.

10. *Ibid.*, November 20, 21, 22, 27, 1832.

11. *Ibid.*, December 13, 1832.

12. *Ibid.*, December 15, 1832.

13. James Grant, *Random Recollections of the House of Commons* (London, 1837), p. 7.

14. Grote, *Life of George Grote,* p. 75.

15. *Parliamentary Debates,* 3rd series, XVII, 638.

16. *Ibid.*, XVII, 657.

17. *Ibid.*, XIX, 1107.

18. *Ibid.*, XIX, 1144.

19. *Ibid.*, XVIII, 961.

20. *Ibid.*, XXIII, 1086.

21. *Ibid.*, XXVIII, 369.

22. Grote, *Life of George Grote,* p. 110.

23. Archibald Prentice, *History of the Anti-Corn Law League* (London, 1853), I, 49.

24. Herbert S. Skeats and Charles S. Miall, *History of the Free Churches of England* (London, 1894), p. 485.

25. *Parliamentary Debates,* 3rd series, XXXIV, 663.

26. William Lovett, *The Life and Struggles of William Lovett* (London, 1876), p. 94.

27. S. Maccoby, *English Radicalism, 1832–1852* (London, 1935), p. 161.

28. R. G. Gammage, *History of the Chartist Movement, 1837–1854* (London, 1894), p. 10.

29. Lovett, *Life and Struggles,* p. 22.

30. *Ibid.,* p. 30.

31. *Morning Chronicle* (London), February 16, 1837.

32. Radical M.P.'s present were Hume, O'Connell, Roebuck, Leader, Perronet Thompson, Hindley, Crawford, and Bowring. These Radicals favored religious freedom and free trade as well as reform.

33. Gammage, *The Chartist Movement,* Appendix B.

34. Herbert McLachlan, *The Methodist Unitarian Movement* (Manchester, 1919), p. 118.

35. C. M. Wakefield, *Life of Thomas Attwood* (London, 1885), pp. 298–99.

36. Lovett, *Life and Struggles,* p. 68.

37. Gammage, *The Chartist Movement,* p. 27.

38. Thomas Carlyle, *Chartism* (Boston, 1840), p. 24.

39. Hovell, *The Chartist Movement,* p. 86.

40. *Methodist Conference Minutes,* VII, 417.

41. George J. Holyoake, *Life of Joseph Rayner Stephens* (London, 1881), p. 129.

42. Gammage, *The Chartist Movement,* p. 59.

43. Hovell, *The Chartist Movement,* p. 92.

44. *Parliamentary Debates,* 3rd series, XL, 1222.

45. Holyoake, *Life of Joseph Rayner Stephens,* p. 146.

46. Wakefield, *Life of Thomas Attwood,* pp. 345–47.

47. For the text of the National Petition see, Frank F. Rosenblatt, *The Chartist Movement in Its Economic and Social Aspects* (New York, 1916), Appendix C.

48. *Parliamentary Debates,* 3rd series, XLIX, 234.

49. Gammage, *The Chartist Movement,* p. 21.

50. Wakefield, *Life of Thomas Attwood,* p. 339.

51. Lovett, *Life and Struggles,* p. 181.

52. Quoted by Julius West, *A History of the Chartist Movement* (London, 1920), p. 94.

53. Lovett, *Life and Struggles,* p. 171.

54. *Ibid.,* p. 204.

55. Harold U. Faulkner, *Chartism and the Churches* (New York, 1916), p. 18.

56. *Parliamentary Debates,* 3rd series, XLVIII, 222.

57. *Ibid.,* 3rd series, XLIX, 236.

58. Rosenblatt, *The Chartist Movement,* p. 171.

59. David Williams, *John Frost, A Study in Chartism* (Cardiff, 1939), p. 98.

60. Lovett, *Life and Struggles,* p. 233. *The English Chartist,* I, 6, gives 380 prisoners in England and 63 in Ireland.

61. West, *The Chartist Movement,* p. 146.

## Chapter 8

### Christian Chartists and Complete Suffrage

1. *Chartist Circular,* I, Preface.

2. *Ibid.,* No. 1, September 28, 1839.

3. *Ibid.,* I, 23.

4. *Ibid.,* II, 601.

5. *Ibid.,* I, 72.

6. *Ibid.,* II, 558.

7. *Ibid.,* I, 162.

8. *Ibid.,* I, 110.

9. See Harold U. Faulkner, *Chartism and the Churches* (New York, 1916), pp. 18, 28.

10. *English Chartist and Temperance Record,* I, 134, 139.

11. *Northern Star,* April 3, 1841.

12. J. L. and Barbara Hammond, *The Age of the Chartists* (London, 1930), p. 252.

13. Henry Solly, *These Eighty Years, or the Story of an Unfinished Life* (London, 1893), p. 346.

14. Lovett and Collins, *Chartism,* p. 11.

15. Lovett, *Life and Struggles,* p. 195.

16. Hovell, *The Chartist Movement,* p. 204.

17. William Dorling, *Henry Vincent* (London, 1879), p. 55.

18. *English Chartist and Temperance Record,* I, 42.

19. Samuel Smiles, *Autobiography,* ed. by Thomas MacKay (New York, 1905), pp. 85–87. Smiles was brought to Leeds as the editor of *The Times* to regain the ground lost to O'Connor. He offered Lovett, upon his release from prison, a place with the paper but he refused to accept it.

20. *Ibid.,* pp. 90–92. It made its first appeal to the middle class August 10, 1840, and held its first public meeting during the same month.

21. *Ibid.,* p. 96.

22. *English Chartist,* I, 13.

23. Stephen Hobhouse, *Joseph Sturge: His Life and Work* (London, 1919), pp. 7–11.

24. *Ibid.,* p. 13.

25. Hobhouse, *Joseph Sturge,* p. 57.

26. Henry Richard, *Memoirs of Joseph Sturge* (London, 1919), p. 292.

27. Richard, *Joseph Sturge,* p. 301.

28. Lovett, *Life and Struggles,* p. 273.

29. Henry Ashworth, *Recollections of Richard Cobden, M.P., and the Anti-Corn-Law League* (London, 1876), p. 37. The Methodists did not participate in this ministerial meeting; the Wesleyan Conference did not support either the League or Radical political reform.

30. Cf. *Nonconformist,* II (1842), 215, 234.

31. *Report of Proceedings,* pp. 8–14.

32. *Nonconformist,* II (1842), 242.

33. *Report of Proceedings,* p. 59.

34. *Ibid.,* p. 67.

35. *Ibid.,* p. 71.

36. *Parliamentary Debates,* 3rd series, LXIII, 907.

37. *Ibid.,* 919.

38. Dorling, *Henry Vincent,* p. 36.

39. *Nonconformist,* II (1842), 549.

40. Richard, *Joseph Sturge,* p. 310.

41. Dorling, *Henry Vincent,* p. 36.

42. *Nonconformist,* III (1843), 356–57.

43. *English Chartist,* II, 129.

44. Henry Solly, *These Eighty Years,* I, 406.

45. Lovett, *Life and Struggles,* p. 275.

46. R. G. Gammage, *History of the Chartist Movement,* p. 243.

47. Richard, *Joseph Sturge,* p. 317.

48. Gammage, *op. cit.,* p. 242.

49. Julius West, *A History of the Chartist Movement* (London, 1920), p. 287.

50. *Nonconformist,* III (1843), 330. Such preachers were Edward Miall, J. E. Giles, Thomas Scales, John Cummins, J. P. Mursell, W. J. Fox, and W. Linwood.

51. Concerning the elections the *Manchester Times,* April 22, 1843, made the following editorial comment:

> And this is strongly suggestive of cordial cooperation amongst three powerful bodies which have each some degree of organization. Each has its own object to carry out by its own organization. The League is constituted solely to carry the total repeal of the Corn Laws, and it very properly refuses to mix in any other agitation; it is the especial business of the Complete Suffrage Union to promote further parliamentary reform; and the Dissenters in their combination have in view no other than the achievement of religious liberty. . . . But while these separate bodies may best pursue their distinct objects by separate organization and separate agitation, there is no reason why the members of each may not unite when they have the opportunity of securing the election of a candidate whose tried and well-known principles are a guarantee that he will support the objects of all. Gisborne and Bright had the support of those three classes of reformers, and the success of one and the moral triumph of the other give strong assurance that a similar cordiality of union would give to the leaguers, the suffragists, and the dissenters the power of turning the scale in most of the boroughs and in many of the counties.

52. Richard, *Joseph Sturge,* p. 321.

53. Gammage, *The Chartist Movement,* p. 255.

54. Dorling, *Henry Vincent,* p. 81.

## Chapter 9

### The Beginning of National Education

1. *Parliamentary Debates,* 3rd series, XX, 196.

2. *Ibid.,* 159.

3. *Ibid.*, 163.

4. *Ibid.*, 173.

5. *Ibid.*, 168.

6. *Ibid.*, 733.

7. William Allen, *The Life of William Allen with Selections from His Correspondence* (London, 1848), II, 154.

8. British and Foreign School Society, *Twenty-Ninth Annual Report,* 1834, p. xi.

9. In the first year the British Society received £9,536. *Ibid.*, p. 34.

10. British and Foreign School Society, *Thirty-First Annual Report,* 1836, p. 10.

11. *Thirtieth Annual Report,* 1835, p. 16.

12. *Parliamentary Debates,* 3rd series, XXIV, 129.

13. *Ibid.*, 139.

14. *Ibid.*, XXVII, 1299.

15. British and Foreign School Society, *Thirtieth Annual Report,* 1835, p. 46.

16. Manchester Friends of Education, *Report of the Speeches Delivered at a Dinner Given to James Simpson, Esq., by the Friends of Education in Manchester* (Manchester, 1836), p. 14.

17. *Ibid.*, p. iv.

18. *Ibid.*, p. 6.

19. *Ibid.*, p. 11.

20. Central Society of Education, *Second Annual Report,* p. x.

21. *Parliamentary Debates,* 3rd series, XL, 710.

22. *Ibid.*, 716.

23. *Parliamentary Debates,* 3rd series, XLV, 280.

24. Sir James Kay-Shuttleworth, *Four Periods of Public Education* (London, 1862), pp. 179–81.

25. *Parliamentary Debates,* 3rd series, XLIX, 302.

26. Usually referred to as Committee of Council. This was the only government board of education until 1899. See John W. Adamson, *English Education 1789–1902* (Cambridge, 1930), p. 14.

27. *Minutes of the Committee of Council, 1839–40,* I, vi.

28. *Parliamentary Debates,* 3rd series, XLVII, 680.

29. *Ibid.*, 757.

30. *Ibid.*, 759.

31. *Congregational Magazine,* 2nd series, IV (1840), 265.

32. *Minutes of the Methodist Conference,* VIII, 233.

33. *Ibid.*, IX, 354.

34. Elie Halévy in *The Triumph of Reform, 1830–1841* (New York: Peter Smith, 1950), p. 224, asserts that the Methodists were acting solely against the Catholics. I think they were also interested in establishing their own denominational schools.

35. John Earl Russell, *Recollections and Suggestions, 1813–1837* (London, 1875), p. 375.

36. *Minutes of the Committee of Council, 1839–40,* I, vii.

37. *Parliamentary Debates,* 3rd series, XLVIII, 245.

38. *Ibid.*, 270.

39. *Ibid.*, 275.

40. *Ibid.*, 670–81.

41. Francis W. Cornish, *The English Church in the Nineteenth Century* (London, 1910), I, 204.

42. *Parliamentary Debates*, 3rd series, XLVIII, 1255.

43. *Annual Register*, 1839 (History), p. 171.

44. Frank Smith, *The Life and Work of Sir James Kay-Shuttleworth* (London, 1923), p. 82.

45. Adamson, *Public Education*, p. 124.

46. His son, Lord Shuttleworth, wrote his recollections of his father's religion: "My father's parents had brought him up as a member of the congregation of the Independent Chapel at Bamford. . . . Deep religious faith, a thorough knowledge of the Bible, and extensive reading in biblical literature were common to both my parents and constituted a strong bond between them." Quoted by Smith, *op. cit.*, p. 331.

47. *Ibid.*, pp. 7–10.

48. *Ibid.*, p. 30.

49. *Ibid.*, p. 76.

50. *Minutes of the Committee of Council, 1842–43*, p. 403.

51. National Society, *Twenty-Ninth Annual Report*, 1840, p. 4.

52. *Ibid.*, p. 2.

53. Russell, *Recollections and Suggestions*, p. 376.

54. *Minutes of the Committee of Council, 1844*, I, 23.

55. *Ibid.*, 21.

56. *Ibid.*, 27.

57. *Eclectic Review,* 1841, p. 111.

58. *Congregational Magazine,* 2nd series, V (1841), 595.

59. This change in ministries during August 1841 caused Secretary Kay much anxiety. See Smith, *op. cit.,* p. 137.

60. Charles S. Parker, *Life and Letters of Sir James Graham* (London, 1907), I, 337. Expecting the Tories to pursue a policy more friendly to the Church, Lord Brougham on October 21, 1841, wrote to Graham to assure him that he would support additional financial aid to education "notwithstanding such a drawback."

61. Charles S. Parker, *Sir Robert Peel* (3 vols., London: 1891–99), II, 548.

62. *Parliamentary Debates,* 3rd series, LXVII, 75.

63. *Ibid.,* 84.

64. Parker, *Sir James Graham,* I, 344.

65. *Parliamentary Debates,* 3rd series, LXVII, 1418.

66. *Ibid.,* 1417.

67. *Ibid.,* 1419.

68. *Ibid.,* 1420.

69. *Ibid.,* 1442.

70. *Ibid.,* 1474.

71. *Ibid.,* 1471.

72. *The Patriot,* March 13, 1843, p. 164.

73. The newspapers favoring the Dissenters were the *Bradford Observer, Leeds Times, Manchester Times, Nottingham Mer-*

*cury, Globe,* and *Morning Advertiser.* George Hadfield at a meeting of the friends of Dissenters' education thanked these papers for their help and rebuked the *Manchester Guardian* for not going along with them. See *Nonconformist,* III, 467.

74. Edward Baines, Jr., *Two Letters to Lord Wharncliffe on the Government Education Bill* (London, 1843), p. 4.

75. *Leeds Mercury,* April 22, 1843.

76. *The Patriot,* March 30, 1843.

77. *Nonconformist,* III (1843), 319. Similar meetings were held at Rochdale, Bolton, Hull, Bradford, Ipswich, and Bristol.

78. *Baptist Magazine,* XXXV (1843), 214.

79. *Ibid.,* 312.

80. *Minutes of the Methodist Conference,* IX, 543.

81. *Congregational Magazine,* 2nd series, VII (1843), 369–70.

82. *Parliamentary Debates,* 3rd series, LXVIII, 1104.

83. Andrew Reed, *Factories Education Bill: A Speech upon the Subject of the Altered Bill,* p. 12.

84. *Nonconformist,* III, 577. See also *Life of Edward Miall,* p. 91. In the House of Commons on July 25, 1843, Joseph Hume said that 25,535 petitions with 4,064,832 signatures had been sent in against the bill; and 170 petitions with 312,669 signatures for it.

85. *Parliamentary Debates,* 3rd series, LXIX, 1568.

86. C. S. Parker, *Sir Robert Peel,* II, 560.

87. *Ibid.,* 562.

## Chapter 10

### The Repeal of the Corn Laws

1. For an evaluation of the various Corn Laws see Donald G. Barnes, *A History of the English Corn Laws* (London, 1930), pp. 285–87.

2. At Manchester political parties continued to be divided along religious lines. See Archibald Prentice, *History of the Anti-Corn Law League* (London, 1853), I, 1.

3. John Morley, *The Life of Richard Cobden* (London, 1881), I, 187.

4. *Ibid.*, 199.

5. *Ibid.*, 130.

6. Cobden, *Speeches on Questions of Public Policy*, edited by John Bright and J. E. T. Rogers (London, 1870), p. 183.

7. *Ibid.*, p. 40.

8. Morley, *The Life of Richard Cobden*, I, 249.

9. Cobden, "England, Ireland, and America," in his *Political Writings* (London, 1867), I, 35.

10. Morley, *The Life of Richard Cobden*, I, 126.

11. Henry Ashworth, *Recollections of Richard Cobden, M.P., and the Anti-Corn Law League* (London, 1876), p. 37.

12. *Anti-Corn Law Circular*, No. 6, June 25, 1839.

13. C. R. Fay, *The Corn Laws and Social England* (Cambridge: The University Press, 1932), p. 140. Fay says: "Cobden and Bright, of course, were too shrewd to try such mysteries [eco-

nomic theories] upon their public. They talked their simpler statistical moralities. But the endorsement of political economy was at their service; and they assumed it when calling down the wrath of heaven upon landlords and landlords' monopoly."

14. Ashworth, *Recollections,* p. 38.

15. *Anti-Corn Law Circular,* No. 6, June 25, 1839.

16. *Ibid.,* No. 3, April 28, 1839.

17. Archibald Prentice, *History of the Anti-Corn Law League* (London, 1853), I, 232.

18. George M. Trevelyan, *Life of John Bright* (London, 1925), p. 36.

19. John Bright, *Speeches on Questions of Public Policy,* edited by James E. T. Rogers (London, 1869), pp. 419–20.

20. Prentice, I, 202.

21. "Report of the Dissenting Ministers . . . ," *Congregational Magazine,* 2nd series, V (1841), 354.

22. *Report of the Conference of Ministers of all Denominations on the Corn Laws* (London, 1841), p. 281.

23. *Ibid.,* p. 283.

24. *The Patriot,* August 22, 1841, gives the list of ministers.

25. *Report of the Conference . . . on the Corn Laws,* p. 238.

26. Prentice, I, 240.

27. *Congregational Magazine,* 2nd series, VI (1842), 143.

28. *The Corn Laws Condemned on Account of Their Injustice and Immoral Tendency by Upwards of Five Hundred Ministers* (Edinburgh, 1842), p. 68.

29. *Ibid.*, p. 83.

30. Prentice, II, 114.

31. Morley, *The Life of Richard Cobden,* I, 331.

32. Richard and Edward Garnett, *The Life of W. J. Fox* (London, 1929), p. 269.

33. For an estimate of the leading personalities of the League compare: C. R. Fay, *op. cit.*, p. 100.

34. *The League,* No. 3, October 14, 1843.

35. *The League,* No. 88, May 31, 1845.

36. *Ibid.*, No. 87, May 24, 1845.

37. For the effects of the abundant harvests during 1842–1844 see Barnes, *A History of the English Corn Laws,* pp. 259–61.

38. Cobden, *Speeches on Questions of Public Policy,* p. 40.

39. The avowed purpose of the League was the registration of voters qualified by the Reform Bill of 1832 but who had not exercised their right to vote. In following this course of action, the League made the law a political reality by attacking the apathy of the voters and in aiding them to overcome the vexatious objectors to new voters. For an exposition of this problem and the politics which it involved, see Charles Seymour, *Electoral Problems in England and Wales* (New Haven: Yale University Press, 1915), pp. 104–32.

40. Ashworth, *Recollections,* p. 282. Ashworth, like Bright, was a Quaker.

41. *The League,* No. 90, June 14, 1845; see also No. 17, January 20, 1844.

42. *The League,* No. 17, January 20, 1844.

43. *Parliamentary Debates,* 3rd series, LXXVIII, 882–84.

44. *The League*, No. 80, April 5, 1845.

45. *Ibid.*, No. 72, February 8, 1845.

46. *Ibid.*, No. 82, April 19, 1845.

47. *Ibid.*, No. 68, January 11, 1845.

48. *Ibid.*, No. 84, May 3, 1845.

49. For Lord John Russell's explanation of his conduct on the Corn Laws and his refusal to accept office see *Parliamentary Debates*, 3rd series, LXXXIII, 96–111.

50. *Parliamentary Debates*, 3rd series, LXXXVI, 327–29. On January 22 Peel, in the debates on the address to the Queen, indicated his intention of repealing the Corn Laws. Volume LXXXIII, 67. On February 27 his bill passed its second reading by a vote of 337 to 240. Volume LXXXIV, 340–54.

51. Prentice, II, 443.

52. John Morley, *Life of Richard Cobden*, I, 202.

53. "Was the system [free trade] no more than a philosophy of businessmen? the ethics of commercial travellers? We shall wrong the Manchester School if we fail to recognize the humanitarian element in its propaganda." Elie Halévy, *History of the English People, 1830–1841*, p. 339.

## Chapter 11

### The Ten Hours Bill

1. Philip Grant, *The Ten Hours Bill, the History of Factory Legislation* (Manchester, 1866), p. 147.

2. Alfred (pseudonym of Samuel Kydd), *History of the Factory Movement* (London, 1856), I, 326.

3. John Fielden, *Curse of the Factory System,* p. iii.

4. Cecil Driver, *Tory Radical, the Life of Richard Oastler* (New York, 1946), p. 39.

5. Alfred, I, 279.

6. Grant, *The Ten Hours Bill,* p. 67. Grant, who was secretary of the Lancashire Central Short Time Committee, estimated that Wood spent £40,000 to promote the agitation for factory legislation.

7. Driver, *Tory Radical,* p. 44, gives an account of this episode which was like a religious conversion.

8. *Leeds Mercury,* October 16, 1830. Driver quotes the letter in his *Tory Radical,* pp. 42–44.

9. Alfred, I, 104; Driver, pp. 49–57.

10. Grant, *The Ten Hours Bill,* p. 21.

11. Alfred, I, 124.

12. *Parliamentary Debates,* 3rd series, IV, 1447.

13. Michael Thomas Sadler, *Memoirs of the Life and Writings of Michael Thomas Sadler* (London, 1842), p. ii.

14. Alfred, I, 131.

15. *Parliamentary Debates,* 3rd series, IX, 255.

16. *Report from the Select Committee on the Bill to Regulate the Labour of Children in the Mills and Factories of the United Kingdom* (House of Commons, 1832), p. 454.

17. *Ibid.,* p. 417.

18. Alfred, I, 324.

19. J. L. and Barbara Hammon, *Lord Shaftesbury* (London, 1923), p. 20.

20. Edwin Hodder, *The Life and Work of the Seventh Earl of Shaftesbury* (London, 1887), I, 149.

21. *Ibid.*, I, 36.

22. *Parliamentary Debates,* 3rd series, XV, 390.

23. 3 and 4 Will. IV, cap. 103.

24. Edward Baines, *History of the Cotton Manufacture in Great Britain* (London, 1835), p, 479.

25. *Ibid.*, p. 481.

26. Harriet Martineau, *Illustrations of Political Economy* (London, 1834), IX, 12.

27. *Ibid.*, IX, 124.

28. *Parliamentary Debates,* 3rd series, XXXIII, 772.

29. Grant, *The Ten Hours Bill,* p. 63. Grant proudly claimed that not one seditious speech had been made by any member of a Short Time Committee.

30. John Morley, *Life of Richard Cobden,* I, 115.

31. *Parliamentary Debates,* 3rd series, LXXII, 277.

32. Alfred, II, 214.

33. *Parliamentary Debates,* 3rd series, LXXIII, 1132.

34. *Ibid.*, p. 1151.

35. Hammond, *Earl of Shaftesbury,* p. 112.

36. Alfred, II, 331.

37. John Fielden, *The Curse of the Factory System,* p. iii.

38. Of the 186 members voting for Lord Ashley's ten hours amendment on March 22, 1844, 117 voted for John Fielden, and only 7 against him.

39. Hammond, *Lord Shaftesbury,* p. 117.

40. Driver, *Tory Radical,* pp. 468–69.

41. Alfred, II, 250. See also Grant, *The Ten Hours Bill,* p. 76.

42. *Parliamentary Debates,* 3rd series, LXXXIX, 487.

43. *Ibid.,* XCII, 312.

44. *Ibid.,* 946.

45. Hodder, *Earl of Shaftesbury,* II, 193.

46. *Ibid.,* p. 135.

## Chapter 12

### The Origin of the Liberal Party

1. 1 and 2 Vict. cap. 109.

2. *Parliamentary Debates,* 3rd series, XL, 889.

3. *Ibid.,* 1221.

4. *Eclectic Review,* 4th series, VI, 316–17.

5. *Ibid.,* I, iv.

6. *The Patriot,* May 1, May 9, and June 10, 1839.

7. Herbert S. Skeats and Charles S. Miall, *History of the Free Churches of England* (revised edition; London, 1894), p. 491.

8. *Baptist Magazine,* XXX (1838), 548.

9. Thomas Morgan, *A Lecture on the Views and Designs of the Birmingham Voluntary Church Society* (Birmingham, 1836), pp. 5–22. Also, John Burnet, *On the Voluntary Church Society* (Birmingham, 1836), pp. 11–21.

10. *Eclectic Review,* 4th series, VII (1840), 365.

11. *The Patriot,* May 13, 1839, p. 320.

12. Bernard Lord Manning, *The Protestant Dissenting Deputies* (Cambridge. The University Press, 1952), p. 48.

13. *Parliamentary Debates,* 3rd series, LII, 103.

14. *Ibid.,* XXXVI, 1212.

15. George M. Trevelyan, *The Life of John Bright* (Boston: Houghton Mifflin, 1913), pp. 40–43. Like other Quakers, the Bright family passively resisted the rates. Because he refused to pay, John's father had suffered the distraint of his property twenty times.

16. Sidney and Beatrice Webb, *English Local Government* (London: Longmans, Green, 1906), I, 96–97.

17. John A. Langford, *A Century of Birmingham Life* (Birmingham, 1868), II, 571. In 1837 anti-church rates riots occurred at Birmingham.

18. For the controversies that raged in most industrial towns and cities, see the *Nonconformist,* II, 1842. At twenty-two different places goods were seized for nonpayment of rates.

19. Manning, *Dissenting Deputies,* p. 179.

20. Sir Edward Baines, *Life of Edward Baines* (London, 1859), p. 214.

21. *Parliamentary Debates,* 3rd series, LII, 116.

22. *Ibid.*, LVII, 390.

23. Sir Thomas E. May, *The Constitutional History of England* (New York, 1886), II, 405–7.

24. Arthur Miall, *The Life of Edward Miall* (London, 1884), p. 27.

25. *Ibid.*, p. 65.

26. *The Patriot,* May 6, 1841, p. 300.

27. Baines, *The Life of Edward Baines,* p. 233.

28. *Annual Register,* 1841 (History), p. 144.

29. *Congregational Magazine,* 2nd series, V (1841), 595.

30. *Nonconformist,* II (1842), 411.

31. *Ibid.*, III (1843), 18.

32. *Ibid.*, III, 577, 594, 690.

33. *Ibid.*, III, 818.

34. *Baptist Magazine,* XXXVI (1844), 146–47.

35. *Ibid.*, 305–9.

36. *Congregational Magazine,* 2nd series, IX (1845), 766–90; also, John Angell James, *The Life and Letters of John Angell James* (London, 1861), pp. 399–402.

37. John Morley, *The Life of William Ewart Gladstone* (London: Macmillan, 1903), I, 279.

38. *Parliamentary Debates,* 3rd series, LXXIX, 18.

39. *Ibid.*, 108.

40. Charles C. F. Greville, *A Journal of the Reign of Queen Victoria, from 1837 to 1852* (London, 1885), II, 277.

41. *Parliamentary Debates,* 3rd series, LXXIX, 1000.

42. *Ibid.,* 820.

43. *Ibid.,* 1311.

44. *The Times* (London), May 21, 1845.

45. *Congregational Magazine,* 2nd series, IX (1845), 321.

46. *Proceedings of the Protestant Dissenters' Anti-Maynooth Conference* (London: Anti-State Church Association, 1845), pp. 3–4.

47. *Parliamentary Debates,* 3rd series, LXXX, 745.

48. *Congregational Year Book,* 1849, p. 33.

49. *Educational Census of 1851.* George Graham (Registrar General), *Report,* p. 14.

50. Baines, *Life of Edward Baines,* p. 286.

51. *Parliamentary Debates,* 3rd series, XCI, 951.

52. *Ibid.,* 952.

53. *Ibid.,* 1090.

54. *Ibid.,* 1315.

55. *Eclectic Review,* 4th series, XXI (1847), 358.

56. Edwin Hodder, *Life of Mr. Samuel Morley, M.P.* (London, 1887), p. 101.

57. *Eclectic Review,* 4th series, XXI (1847), 358.

58. G. Otto Trevelyan, *The Life and Letters of Lord Macaulay* (New York, 1875), p. 166.

59. Manning, *The Dissenting Deputies,* p. 349.

60. *Eclectic Review,* 4th series, XXII (1847), 366.

61. *Ibid.,* 373.

62. George B. Smith, *The Life and Speeches of John Bright* (New York, 1881), p. 141.

63. *Leeds Mercury,* July 31, 1847.

64. *Eclectic Review,* 4th series, XXII (1847), 112.

65. Arthur Miall, *The Life of Edward Miall,* p. 128. When the new Parliament met, the voluntaryists introduced a motion censuring the Ecclesiastical Commissioners, and mustered a minority of 65 votes. See *Parliamentary Debates,* 3rd series, XCV, 1121.

The principal Dissenters elected in 1847 were the following:

Baines, Matthew T.
Bowring, Sir John
Bright, John
Brotherton, Joseph
Cowan, Charles
Craig, William G.
Fox, William J.
Heywood, James
Hindley, Charles
Kershaw, James
Marshall, James G.
Muntz, George F.
Peto, Samuel M.
Scholefield, William
Smith, John B.
Strutt, Edward
Talfourd, Sir Thomas N.
Thompson, George
Thornely, Thomas
Wilson, James
Williams, Sir John

The leading Radicals pledged to voluntaryism in 1847 were:

Aglionby, Henry A.
Buller, Charles
Clay, Sir William
Clay, James
Crawford, William S.
D'Eyncourt, C. Tennyson
Divett, Edward
Duncombe, Thomas S.
Evans, William
Ewart, William
Humphery, John
Lushington, Charles
Molesworth, Sir William
Pattison, James
Strickland, Sir George
Thompson, Thomas P.
Trelawny, Sir John
Wakley, Thomas
Walmsley, Sir Joshua
Ward, Henry G.

# *Bibliography*

These lists include the principal items in the footnotes and are designed to indicate the scope and character of the materials on which this study is based. The place of publication is London unless otherwise noted.

### *Government Publications*

Parliamentary Debates:

"Cobbett's Parliamentary History of England from 1066 to 1803." 36 vols., 1806–1828.

"Cobbett's and (after Vol. XXIII) Hansard's Parliamentary Debates." 3 series from 1803.

Parliamentary Papers:

"Report of the Minutes of Evidence Taken before the Select Committee on the State of Children Employed in the Manufactories of the United Kingdom." 1816.

"Report of the Select Committee Appointed to Inquire into the Education of the Lower Orders in the Metropolis. . . ." 1816.

"Report of the Select Committee Appointed to Inquire into the Education of the Lower Orders." 1818.

"Report from the Committee on Employment of Boys in Sweeping Chimneys. . . ." 1817.

"Minutes of Evidence Taken before the Lords' Committee to Whom Was Referred the Bill for the Preservation of the Health and Morals of Apprentices and Others Employed in the Cotton Mills and Factories." 1818.

"Report from the Committee on the Bill to Regulate the Labour of Children in the Mills and Factories of the United Kingdom." 1832.

"First Report of the Commissioners for Inquiring into the Employment of Children in Factories." 1833.

"Supplemental Report. . . ." (Same Commission). 1834.
"Annual Reports of the Inspectors of Factories." From 1834.
"Report from the Select Committee Appointed to Inquire into the Present State of Education of the People in England and Wales." 1834.
"Report of the Commissioners on the Revenues and Patronage of the Established Church in England and Wales." 1835.
"Minutes of Committee of Council on Education." From 1840.
"First Report of the Select Committee Appointed to Inquire into the Operation of the Act for the Regulation of Mills and Factories." 1840.
"Seventh Report. . . ." (Same Committee). 1841.
"Report of the Commission on the Employment of Children in Mines and Collieries." 1842.
"Census of Great Britain, 1851. Religious Worship–England and Wales." 1853.

*Reports of Societies and Meetings*

British and Foreign Bible Society. "Annual Reports." From 1805.
British and Foreign School Society. "Annual Reports." From 1811.
"Epistles from the Yearly Meeting of Friends, Held in London, to the Quarterly Meetings in Great Britain, Ireland, and Elsewhere from 1681 to 1857, Inclusive." 2 vols., 1858.
"Minutes of the General Assembly of the General Baptist Churches in England." Edited by W. T. Whitley, 2 vols., 1910.
"Minutes of the Methodist Conference from the First Held in London by the Late Rev. John Wesley, M.A., in the Year 1744." Vol. I, 1812.
The National Society for Promoting the Education of the Poor in the Principles of the Church of England throughout England and Wales. "Annual Reports." From 1812.
Religious Tract Society. "Annual Reports." From 1799.
"Report of the British and Foreign Bible Society with Extracts from the Correspondence." 3 vols., 1813.
"Report of the Conference of Ministers of All Denominations on the Corn Laws . . . with a Digest of the Documents Contributed During the Conference." 1841.
"Report of the Proceedings at a Conference of Delegates of the Middle and Working Classes. . . ." 1842.
"Report of the Proceedings of the Protestant Dissenters' Anti-Maynooth Conference, Held at Crosby Hall, London, with a Cor-

rect List of Delegates and Ministers." Anti-State-Church Association, 1845.

*Biographies, Diaries, and Memoirs*

Allen, William, "Life of William Allen, with Selections from His Correspondence." 3 vols., 1846.

Ashworth, Henry, "Recollections of Richard Cobden, M.P., and the Anti-Corn Law League." 1876.

Aspinall, Arthur, ed., "The Correspondence of Charles Arbuthnot." Royal Historical Society, 1941.

Aspland, Robert B., "Memoirs of the Rev. Robert Aspland." 1849.

Bain, Alexander, "James Mill, A Biography." 1882.

Baines, Sir Edward, "Life of Edward Baines." 1859.

Bennett, James, "Memoirs of the Life of the Rev. David Bogue." 1827.

Bowring, Sir John, "Autobiographical Recollections . . . with a Brief Memoir by L. B. Bowring." 1877.

Braithwaite, Joseph Bevan, ed., "Memoirs of Joseph John Gurney." 2 vols., 1854.

Brougham, Henry Peter Lord, "The Life and Times of Henry Lord Brougham." 3 vols., New York, 1872.

Buckley, Jessie K., "Joseph Parkes of Birmingham." 1926.

Buxton, Charles, "Memoirs of Sir Thomas Fowell Buxton, with Selections from His Correspondence." 1849.

Cecil, David, "The Young Melbourne." New York, 1939.

Conder, E. R., "Josiah Conder, a Memoir." 1857.

Coupland, Reginald, "Wilberforce." Oxford, 1923.

Dale, R. W., "The Life and Letters of John Angell James, Including an Unfinished Autobiography." New York, 1861.

Dorling, William, "Henry Vincent: A Biographical Sketch." 1879.

Fry, Elizabeth, "Memoir of the Life of Elizabeth Fry, with Extracts from Her Journal and Letters." 2 vols., 1847.

Garnett, Richard and Edward, "The Life of William Johnson Fox." 1909.

Greville, Charles C. F., "Journals of the Reigns of George IV and William IV." 3 vols., 1874.

———, "A Journal of the Reign of Queen Victoria from 1847 to 1852." 3 vols., 1885.

Gregory, Olinthus, "A Brief Memoir of the Life of Robert Hall." 1833.

Grote, Harriet (Mrs. George Grote), "The Personal Life of George Grote." 1883.

Gurney, Joseph John, "A Familiar Sketch of the Late William Wilberforce." Norwich, 1838.

Hanna, William, "Memoirs of the Life and Writings of Thomas Chalmers." 4 vols., 1849–52.

Hinton, John Howard, "Memoir of William Knibb." 1847.

Hobhouse, Stephen, "Joseph Sturge, His Life and Work." 1919.

Hodder, Edwin, "The Life and Work of the Seventh Earl of Shaftesbury." 3 vols., 1889.

———, "Life of Mr. Samuel Morley, M.P." 1887.

Holland, Henry Richard, 3rd Baron, "Memoirs of the Whig Party During My Time." 2 vols., 1852–54.

———, "Further Memoirs of the Whig Party, 1807 to 1821, with Some Miscellaneous Reminiscences." Edited by Lord Stavordale, 1905.

Holyoake, George Jacob, "The Life of Joseph Rayner Stephens." 1881.

Jennings, Louis J., ed., "The Correspondence and Diaries of John Wilson Croker." 2 vols., New York, 1884.

Leader, Robert E., ed., "Life and Letters of John Arthur Roebuck, with Chapters of Autobiography." 1897.

Le Marchant, Sir Denis, "Memoirs of John Charles Viscount Althorp, Third Earl Spencer." 1876.

Lovett, William, "Life and Struggles of William Lovett in His Pursuit of Bread, Knowledge, and Freedom." 1876.

Maxwell, Sir Herbert, ed., "The Creevey Papers, A Selection from the Correspondence and Diaries of the late Thomas Creevey, M.P." New York, 1923.

Miall, Arthur, "The Life of Edward Miall." 1884.

Mill, John Stuart, "Autobiography." New York, 1924.

Morley, John, "Life of Richard Cobden." 2 vols., 1881.

New, Chester W., "Lord Durham, A Biography of John George Lambton, First Earl Durham." Oxford, 1929.

Parker, Charles S., ed., "Sir Robert Peel, from His Private Papers." 3 vols., 1899.

———, "Life and Letters of Sir James Graham." 2 vols., 1907.

Pellew, George, "The Life and Correspondence of the Right Honourable Henry Addington, First Viscount Sidmouth." 3 vols., 1847.

Podmore, Frank, "Robert Owen." New York, 1924.

Raikes, Thomas, "A Portion of the Journal Kept by Thomas Raikes." 4 vols., 1857.

Richard, Henry, "Memoirs of Joseph Sturge." 1864.

Ritchie, James Ewing, "The Life and Times of Viscount Palmerston." 2 vols., 1867.

Robertson, William, "Life and Times of the Right Honourable John Bright." 1883.

Romilly, Sir Samuel, "The Memoirs of Sir Samuel Romilly, Written by Himself, with Selections from His Correspondence." Edited by his sons, 3 vols., 1840.

Russell, John, Earl, "Recollections and Suggestions." 1875.

Russell, Rollo, "Early Correspondence of Lord John Russell." 2 vols., 1913.

Sanders, Lloyd C., ed., "Lord Melbourne's Papers." 1889.

Seeley, Robert Benton, "Memoirs of the Life and Writings of Michael Thomas Sadler." 1842.

Smith, Frank, "The Life and Works of Sir James Kay-Shuttleworth." 1923.

Smith, George B., "The Life and Speeches of John Bright." New York, 1881.

Solly, Henry, "These Eighty Years, or the Story of an Unfinished Life." 2 vols., 1893.

Torrens, William M., "Memoirs of the Right Honourable William, Second Viscount Melbourne." 1875.

Trevelyan, George Macaulay, "Lord Grey of the Reform Bill, Being the Life of Charles, Second Earl Grey." New York, 1920.

———, "The Life of John Bright." New York, 1925.

Trevelyan, George Otto, "The Life and Letters of Lord Macaulay." 2 vols., New York, 1876.

Twiss, Horace, "The Public and Private Life of Lord Chancellor Eldon, with Selections from His Correspondence." 3 vols., 1844.

Wakefield, C. M., "Life of Thomas Attwood." 1885.

Wallas, Graham, "The Life of Francis Place." 2nd edition, New York, 1918.

Walpole, Spencer, "The Life of Lord John Russell." 2 vols., 1889.

Wellington, Arthur Wellesley, First Duke of, "Despatches, Correspondence, and Memoranda." 8 vols., 1867–80.

Wilberforce, Robert I. and Samuel, eds., "The Life of William Wilberforce." 5 vols., 1838.

———, "The Correspondence of William Wilberforce." 2 vols., 1840.

*Contemporary Books and Pamphlets*

Adshead, Joseph, "Evidence of the State of the Labouring Classes." 1842.

Alfred (Samuel Kydd), "The History of the Factory Movement, from the Year 1802 to the Enactment of the Ten Hours Bill." 2 vols., 1857.

"An Enquiry into the Principle and Tendency of the Bill now Pending Parliament for Imposing Certain Restrictions on Cotton Factories." 1818.

Arnold, Thomas, "Principles of Church Reform." 1833.

"A Refutation of the Catechism on the Corn Laws." 1829.

Aspland, Robert, "A Plea for Unitarian Dissenters." 1813.

Atkinson, William, "A Candid Inquiry into the Democratic Schemes of the Dissenters During These Troublesome Times. . . ." 1801.

Baines, Edward, Jr., "On the Moral Influence of Free Trade and Its Effects on the Prosperity of Nations." 1830.

———, "The Social, Educational, and Religious State of the Manufacturing Districts." 1843.

———, "The Amended Education Bill, a Letter to Sir James Graham." Leeds, 1843.

———, "Reasons in Favour of Free Trade in Corn and against a Fixed Duty, in Three Letters to the Right Hon. Lord John Russell." Leeds, 1844.

Baines, Edward, Jr., "Letters to Lord John Russell . . . on the State of Education. . . ." 1847.

Belsham, Thomas, "The Rights of Conscience Asserted and Defined. . . ." 1813.

Bennett, James, "A History of Dissenters, 1808–1838." 1839.

Bentham, Jeremy, "Plan of Parliamentary Reform . . . with an Introduction Showing the Necessity of Radical, and the Inadequacy of Moderate Reform." 1817.

———, "Church-of-Englandism and Its Catechism Examined . . . with Strictures on the Exclusionary System as Pursued in the National Society Schools. . . ." 1818.

———, "The Works of Jeremy Bentham." Edited by John Bowring. 11 vols., Edinburgh, 1843.

Binney, Thomas, "Conscientious Clerical Nonconformity." 1839.

Bogue, David, "Reasons for Seeking a Repeal of the Corporation and Test Acts." 1790.

———, and James Bennett, "History of Dissenters." 4 vols., 1808.

Bright, John, "The Late Church Rates Contests." 1840.
———, "Speeches on Questions of Public Policy." Edited by James E. T. Rogers, 1869.
Brougham, Henry Peter, "An Inquiry into the Colonial Policy of the European Powers." Edinburgh, 1803.
———, "Practical Observations on the Education of the People, Addressed to the Working Classes and Their Employers." 1825.
Bull, George Stringer, "An Appeal on Behalf of the Factory Children." Bradford, 1832.
Burnet, John, "On the Voluntary Church Society of Birmingham." 1836.
Buxton, Thomas Fowell, "An Inquiry Whether Crime Be Produced or Prevented by Our Present System of Prison Discipline." 1817.
———, "The African Slave Trade and Its Remedy." 1840.
Carlyle, Thomas, "Chartism." Boston, 1840.
"The Case of the Dissenters, in a Letter Addressed to the Lord Chancellor." 1833.
"Circular Letter from the Ministers and Messengers of the Lancashire and Yorkshire Association of Baptist Churches." 1833.
Cobden, Richard, "England, Ireland, and America." 1835.
Conder, Josiah, "On Protestant Nonconformity." 2 vols., 1818.
———, "Wages or the Whip, an Essay on the Comparative Cost and Productiveness of Free and Slave Labour." 1833.
Condy, George, "An Argument for Placing Factory Children within the Pale of the Law." 1833.
"The Dissenters' Appeal, a Letter to the Right Honourable, Earl Grey." 1833.
Dod, Charles R. P., "Parliamentary Companion." 1852.
———, "Electoral Facts, 1832–1852." 1853.
Dunn, Henry, "National Education, the Question of Questions." 2nd edition, 1838.
Ewart, William, "The Reform of the Reform Bill." 1837
"Facts and Documents Connected with the Late Insurrections in Jamaica and the Violations of Civil and Religious Liberty." 1832.
Fielden, John, "The Curse of the Factory System." 1836.
Finlay, Kirkman, "Letter to Lord Ashley on the Cotton Factory System and the Ten Hours Factory Bill." Glasgow, 1833.
Foster, John, "Essay on the Evils of Popular Ignorance." 1820.
———, "Letters on the Voluntary Principle." 1834.
Fox, William Johnson, "The Corn Law Question Considered in Its Moral Bearings." 1839.

Gammage, R. G., "History of the Chartist Movement, 1837–1854." 1854.
Giles, John Eustace, "Socialism as a Religious Theory, Irrational and Absurd." 1839.
———, "Speech to the Anti-Corn Law League." Manchester, 1842.
Gladstone, William E., "The State in Its Relations with the Church." 1838.
Gould, Nathaniel, "Information Concerning the State of Children Employed in the Cotton Factories." Manchester, 1818.
Graham, William, "The Advantages and Disadvantages of Ecclesiastical Establishments." 1821.
Grant, James, "Random Recollections of the House of Commons, from the Year 1830 to the Close of 1835." 1837.
Grant, Philip, "The Ten Hours Bill, the History of Factory Legislation." 1866.
Greg, Robert H., "The Factory Question and the Ten Hours Bill." 1837.
Gurney, Joseph John, "The Distinguishing Views and Practices of the Society of Friends." 1824.
———, "Speeches in Celebration of the Repeal of the Test and Corporation Acts." 1828.
Hall, Robert, "Works." Edited by Olinthus Gregory. 6 vols., 1831.
Harwood, Philip, "Six Lectures on the Corn Law Monopoly and Free Trade." 1843.
Henley, Robert Lord, "A Plan of Church Reform." 1832.
Heyworth, Lawrence, "The Corn Laws." Manchester, 1843.
Hill, Rowland, "A Serious Investigation of the Nature of and Effects of Parochial Assessments Being Charged on Places of Religious Worship." 1811.
———, "Religious Freedom in Danger; or, the Toleration Act Invaded by Parochial Assessments." 1816.
Hinton, John Howard, "A Plea for Liberty of Conscience; a Letter to the Right Hon. Sir James Graham on the Educational Clauses of the Factories Bill." 1843.
Hook, Walter Farquhar, "On Means of Rendering More Efficient the Education of the People." 1846.
Horner, Leonard, "On the Employment of Children in Factories. . . ." 1840.
Ivimey, Joseph, "A History of the English Baptists." 4 vols., 1811–30.
———, "The Utter Extinction of Slavery." 1832.

James, John Angell, "Christian Fellowship, or the Church Member's Guide." 1822.

———, "Pastoral Address." 1834.

———, "Dissent and the Church of England." 1831.

———, "Protestant Nonconformity–Its Rise and Present State in Birmingham." 1849.

"Justifiable Conformity, a Few Hints to Protestant Dissenters at the Present Crisis." 1834.

Kay-Shuttleworth, James Philips, "The Moral and Physical Conditions of the Working Classes in the Cotton Manufacture in Manchester." 1832.

———, "Public Education as Affected by the Minutes of the Committee of Privy Council, from 1846–1852." 1853.

———, "Four Periods of Public Education." 1862.

Kentish, John, "The Situation and Duty of Protestant Dissenters." 1829.

Knibb, William, "Colonial Slavery: A Defense of Baptist Missionaries from the Charge of Inciting the Late Rebellion in Jamaica." 1832.

Lovett, William, and John Collins, "Chartism, A New Organization of the People. . . ." 1840.

Mann, Horace, "Census in Great Britain, 1851; Religious Worship in England and Wales, Abridged from the Official Report . . . to George Graham, Esq., Registrar-General." 1854.

———, "Census in Great Britain, 1851; Education in Great Britain . . . Being the Official Report . . . to George Graham, Esq., Registrar-General." 1854.

Marsh, Herbert, "An Inquiry into the Consequences of Neglecting to Give the Prayer Book with the Bible. . . ." 1812.

Martineau, Harriet, "Illustrations of Political Economy." 2 vols., 1834.

———, "The History of England During the Thirty Years Peace, 1816–1846." 2 vols., 1849–50.

Mathews, John, "Churchmen Dissuaded against the Bible Society." 1817.

Miall, Edward, "The Two Portraits, or Christianity and the Compulsory System Contrasted." 1838.

———, "The Nonconformist's Sketch-Book. . . ." 1845.

———, "The British Churches in Relation to the British People." 1845.

Morgan, Thomas, "A Lecture on the Views and Designs of the Birmingham Voluntary Church Society." 1836.
Newton, S., "Reply to an Affectionate Address. . . ." 1820.
Noel, Baptist W., "The Catholic Claims." 1843.
———, "The Early Fathers No Safe Guides." 1839.
———, "Essay on Union of Church and State." 1848.
"Notes on Lord John Russell's Marriage Bill." 1834.
Nugent, Lord, "The Ballot Discussed; in a Letter to the Earl of Durham." 1837.
Oastler, Richard, "Slavery in Yorkshire." Bradford, 1835.
———, "More Work for the Leeds New Thief-Catchers." Huddersfield, 1836.
———, "The Fleet Papers." 4 vols., 1841–44.
O'Connell, Daniel, "To the Ministers and Office Bearers of the Wesleyan Methodist Societies of Manchester." 1839.
Orme, William, "The Repeal of the Sacramental Test." 1828.
Owen, John, "The History of the Origin and First Ten Years of the British and Foreign Bible Society." 2 vols., 1816.
"Plain Directions for the Establishment of Schools on the Plan and Principles of the British and Foreign School Society." 1844.
Prentice, Archibald, "Historical Sketches and Personal Recollections of Manchester, 1792–1832." 1853.
———, "History of the Anti-Corn Law League." 2 vols., 1853.
———, "Organic Changes Necessary to Complete the System of Representation Partially Amended by the Reform Bill." 1839.
———, "The Pitt-Peel Income Tax and the Necessity of Complete Suffrage." Manchester, 1842.
Price, Richard, "Discourse on the Love of Our Country." 1790.
Price, Thomas, "The History of Protestant Nonconformity." 2 vols., 1836–38.
Priestley, Joseph, "Works." Edited by J. T. Rutt, 25 vols., 1817–32.
"Protestant Dissenters' Catechism." 17th ed., 1823.
"Protestant Dissenters' Manual." 1817.
Reed, Andrew, "Factories Education Bill.. . . ." 1843.
"Remarks on Religious Liberty and the Duty of Nonconformity to Human Prescription in Religion." 1828.
"Report on the State of Education in Manchester." Manchester Statistical Society. 1834.
"Report of Speeches Delivered at Manchester . . . for the Purpose of Petitioning Parliament for Redress of Dissenters' Grievances." Manchester, 1834.

Roebuck, John Arthur, "History of the Whig Ministry of 1830, to the Passing of the Reform Bill." 2 vols., 1852.
———, "Pamphlets for the People." 2 vols., 1835.
Sadler, Michael Thomas, "Ireland; Its Evils and Their Remedies." 1829.
———, "On the Catholic Question." 1829.
———, "The Law of Population; a Treatise . . . in Disproof of the Superfecundity of Human Beings, and Developing the Real Principle of Their Increase." 1830.
———, "Protest against the Secret Proceedings of the Factory Commission in Leeds Published at the Request of the Short Time Committee." Leeds, 1833.
———, "Factory Statistics. The Official Tables Appended to the Report of the Select Committee on the Ten Hours Factory Bill Vindicated in a Series of Letters." 1836.
Sandwith, H., "An Apology for the System of Wesleyan Methodism." 1825.
———, "A Reply to Lord John Russell's Animadversions." 1830.
Saunders, Samuel, "The Principles of Dissent." 1833.
———, "Lectures on Nonconformity." 1836.
"The School in Its Relations to the State, the Church, and Congregation." Committee of Council on Education, 1847.
Sedgwick, A., "Admission of Dissenters to Academical Degrees." 1834.
Sewell, William, "Thoughts on the Admission of Dissenters to the University of Oxford." 1834.
———, "A Letter to a Dissenter on the Opposition of the University of Oxford to the Charter of London College." Oxford, 1834.
———, "Christian Politics." 1844.
Senior, Nassau, "Letters on the Corn Laws." 1839.
———, "Letters on the Factory Act as It Affects Cotton Manufacture." 1837.
"Sketch of the History of and Proceedings of the Deputies Appointed to Protect the Civil Rights of the Protestant Dissenters." 1813.
Smith, Thomas Southwood, "Illustrations of Divine Government." 1816.
Solly, Rev. Henry, "What Says Christianity to the Present Distress?" 1841.
Spencer, Thomas, "The Prayer Book Opposed to the Corn Laws; or, Who Are the Nonconformists?" 1840.

Stephens, Sir George, "Anti-Slavery Recollections." 1854.

Stovel, Charles, "A Letter to Lord Henley on Church Reform." 1833.

———, "The Voluntary System." 1835.

"Strictures on the Corporation and Test Acts. . . ." 1819.

Sturge, Joseph, and Thomas Harvey, "The West Indies in 1837. . . ." 1838.

Thompson, Adam, "The Claims of the Dissenters on the Government." 1836.

Thompson, Thomas Perronet, "A Catechism on the Corn Laws with a List of Fallacies and the Answers." 1828.

———, "Adjustment of the House of Lords." 1829.

Toulmin, Joshua, "An Historical View of the State of Protestant Dissenters in England." 1814.

Trimmer, Sarah K., "A Comparative View of the New Plan of Education. . . ." 1805.

Ure, Andrew, "The Philosophy of Manufactures; or an Exposition of the Scientific and Commercial Economy of the Factory System of Great Britain." 1835.

Vaughan, Robert, "Thoughts on the Past and Present State of Religious Parties in England." 1838.

———, "Protestant Nonconformity in Its Relation to Learning and Duty." 1843.

Wade, John, "The Extraordinary Black Book, an Exposition of Abuses in Church and State." 1831.

Wilberforce, William, "A Practical View of the Prevailing Religious System of Professed Christians in the Higher and Middle Classes in This Country, Contrasted with Real Christianity." 1797.

———, "Appeal . . . in Behalf of Negro Slaves in the West Indies." 1823.

Wing, Charles, "Evils of the Factory System Demonstrated by Parliamentary Evidence." 1837.

Winter, Robert, "Pastoral Letters on Nonconformity." 1817.

———, "The United Committee's Statement on Test and Corporation Acts." 1827.

*Modern Authorities*

Adams, Francis, "History of the Elementary School Contest in England." 1882.

Adamson, John William, "English Education, 1789–1902." Cambridge, 1930.

Aspinall, Arthur, "Lord Brougham and the Whig Party." Manchester, 1927.

Balleine, G. R., "A History of the Evangelical Party in the Church of England." 1909.

Barnard, H. C., "A Short History of English Education from 1760 to 1944." 1947.

Barnes, Donald Grove, "A History of the English Corn Laws from 1660 to 1846." 1930.

Bedd, E. D., "Nonconformity and Social and Economic Life, 1660–1800." 1935.

Binns, Henry Bryan, "A Century of Education; Being the Centenary History of the British and Foreign School Society 1808–1908." 1908.

Blease, Walter Lyon, "A Short History of English Liberalism." New York, 1913.

Brock, William, "Lord Liverpool and Liberal Toryism, 1820–1827." Cambridge, England, 1941.

Bryant, Arthur, "The Age of Elegance 1812–1822." New York, 1950.

Butler, F. R. M., "The Passing of the Great Reform Bill." 1914.

Carlile, John C., "The Story of the English Baptists." 1905.

Christie, Octavius F., "The Transition from Aristocracy, 1832–1867." New York, 1928.

Church, Richard W., "The Oxford Movement." 1922.

Clapham, John H., "Economic History of Modern Britain." 3 vols., Cambridge, 1927.

Clark, George Kitson, "Sir Robert Peel and the Conservative Party 1832–1841." 1929.

———, "The English Inheritance." 1950.

Clark, Henry W., "History of Nonconformity: From the Restoration to the Close of the Nineteenth Century." 2 vols., 1913.

Colligan, F. H., "The Arian Movement in England." Manchester, 1913.

Cornish, Francis W., "The English Church in the Nineteenth Century." 2 parts, 1910.

Croft, W. R., "History of the Factory Movement; or Oastler and His Times." Huddersfield, 1888.

Dale, Robert William, "History of English Congregationalism." New York, 1907.

Davis, Charles H. W., "The Age of Grey and Peel." Oxford, 1929.

Dicey, Albert Venn, "Lectures on the Relation of Law and Public Opinion in England During the Nineteenth Century." New York, 1905.
Driver, Cecil, "Tory Radical, the Life of Richard Oastler." New York, 1946.
Drysdale, A. H., "History of Presbyterianism in England." 1889.
Elliott-Binns, L. E., "Religion in the Victorian Era." 2nd edition, 1946.
Faulkner, Harold Underwood, "Chartism and the Churches: A Study in Democracy." New York, 1916.
Fay, Charles R., "The Corn Laws and Social England." Cambridge, 1932.
———, "Great Britain from Adam Smith to the Present Day." 1933.
———, "Huskisson and His Age." New York, 1951.
Feiling, Keith G., "The Second Tory Party 1714–1832." 1938.
Fyfe, Henry Hamilton, "The British Liberal Party." 1928.
Gash, Norman, "Politics in the Age of Peel." 1953.
Gill, Conrad, "History of Birmingham." 2 vols., 1952.
Halévy, Elie, "The Growth of Philosophical Radicalism." 1928.
———, "A History of the English People in the Nineteenth Century." 4 vols., New York, 1949–51.
Hammond, John L. and Barbara, "The Town Labourer 1760–1832." 1917.
———, "The Skilled Labourer 1760–1832." 1919.
———, "Lord Shaftesbury." 1923.
———, "The Age of the Chartists 1832–1854." 1930.
Holt, Anne, "Walking Together, A Study in Liverpool Nonconformity." 1936.
Holt, Raymond V., "The Unitarian Contribution to Social Progress in England." 1938.
Hovell, Mark, "The Chartist Movement." Manchester, 1918.
Howse, Ernest Marshall, "Saints in Politics, the Clapham Sect and the Growth of Freedom." Toronto, 1952.
Hunt, John, "Religious Thought in England in the Nineteenth Century." 1896.
Hutchins, Beatrice L., and Amy Harrison, "A History of Factory Legislation." 1903.
Jones, Rufus M., "The Later Periods of Quakerism." 2 vols., 1921.
Klingberg, Frank J., "The Anti-Slavery Movement in England." New Haven, 1926.

Laprade, William Thomas, "England and the French Revolution." Baltimore, 1909.

Lincoln, Anthony, "Some Political and Social Ideas of English Dissent 1703–1800." Cambridge, 1938.

Lovett, Richard, "The History of the London Missionary Society 1795–1895." 2 vols., 1899.

Maccoby, S., "English Radicalism 1832–1852." 1935.

McLachlan, Herbert, "The Methodist Unitarian Movement." Manchester, 1919.

———, "English Education Under the Test Acts 1662–1820." Manchester, 1932.

Manning, Bernard Lord, "The Protestant Dissenting Deputies." Edited by Ormerod Greenwood, Cambridge, 1952.

Masheder, Richard, "Dissent and Democracy: Their United Relations and Common Objects." 1864.

Mathieson, William Law, "England in Transition 1789–1832." 1920.

———, "English Church Reform 1815–1840." 1923.

———, "British Slavery and Its Abolition." 1926.

May, Sir Thomas Erskine, "The Constitutional History of England Since the Accession of George III." 2 vols., 1886.

Overton, John D., "The English Church in the Nineteenth Century 1800–1833." 1894.

Park, Joseph Hendershot, "British Prime Ministers of the 19th Century; Policies and Speeches." New York, 1950.

Peel, Albert, "These Hundred Years, a History of Congregational Union of England and Wales, 1831–1931." 1931.

Quinlan, Maurice J., "Victorian Prelude, a History of English Manners 1700–1830." New York, 1941.

Redford, Arthur, and Ina Strafford Russell, "The History of Local Government in Manchester." 2 vols., 1939.

Reynolds, J. S., "The Evangelicals at Oxford 1735–1871." Oxford, 1953.

Robson, Adam Henry, "The Education of Children Engaged in Industry in England, 1833–1876." 1931.

Rosenblatt, Frank F., "The Chartist Movement." New York, 1916.

Seymour, "Electoral Reforms in England and Wales." New Haven, 1915.

Skeats, Herbert S., and Charles S. Miall, "History of Free Churches of England." 1894.

Slosson, Preston William, "The Decline of the Chartist Movement." New York, 1916.

Taylor, E. R., "Methodism and Politics 1791–1851." Cambridge, 1935.

Veitch, G. S., "The Genesis of Parliamentary Reform." 1913.

Waddington, John, "Congregational History 1800–1850." 1878.

Walpole, Spencer, "A History of England from the Conclusion of the Great War." 6 vols., 1902–05.

Warner, William F., "The Wesleyan Movement in the Industrial Revolution." 1930.

Watson, William Henry, "The First Fifty Years of the Sunday School." 1868.

Wearmouth, Robert F., "Methodism and the Working-Class Movement of England 1800–1850." 1937.

———, "Methodism and the Common People of the 18th Century." 1945.

Webb, Sidney and Beatrice, "English Local Government from the Revolution to the Municipal Act." 4 vols., 1906–22.

West, Julius, "A History of the Chartist Movement." 1920.

Whitley, William T., "A History of British Baptists." 1932.

Wilbur, Earl Morse, "Our Unitarian Heritage." Boston, 1925.

Williams, David, "John Frost, a Study in Chartism." Cardiff, 1939.

Woodward, E. L., "The Age of Reform 1815–1870." Oxford, 1938.

*Periodicals*

The Annual Register

Anti-Bread-Tax Almanack

The Anti-Corn Law Circular

Anti-Slavery Monthly Reporter

Baptist Magazine

The British Critic and Quarterly Theological Review

British and Foreign Evangelical Review

The British and Foreign Temperance Intelligencer

British Quarterly Review

Cambridge Intelligencer

Chartist Circular

Christian Observer

Christian Reformer or Unitarian Magazine and Review

Congregational Magazine

Eclectic Review

Edinburgh Review

The English Chartist Circular and Temperance Record for England and Wales

Evangelical Magazine
General Baptist Magazine
The Inquirer
The League
Leeds Mercury
Manchester Guardian
The Monthly Repository
Morning Chronicle
Nonconformist
The Northern Star
The Patriot
The Quarterly Journal of Education
The Quarterly Review
The Record
School Guardian
The Standard
The Times (London)
The Voluntary Church Magazine
Wesleyan Methodist Magazine
Westminster Review

# Index